ADDICTION LOGIC

TREATING THE CAUSE, NOT THE SYMPTOM

RICK BREITWEISER

DEDICATED TO:

Mom and Dad ... we are only a short time away.

ACKNOWLEDGEMENTS

Chris & Lisa, Mary B., Tommy & Sue, Ralph, Paul F., Lanie J., Jimmy P., Sean B., Melissa S., Kostis P., Arun K., Denae M., Caitlin L., Bre S., Janice P., Dan N., Edward S., Alex D., Derek R., Lloyd O., Barbara S., Sandy R., Jeff R., Larissa M., LADAC, Peter M., Renata R., Kurien M., Stu K., Courtney R., Malaika J., Daniel C.

CONTENTS

SECTION 2: ADDICTION MANIFESTATION

SECTION 3: GETTING HELP

SECTION 4: FIXING YOURSELF

SECTION 5: SPIRITUAL BY NATURE

SECTION 6: A LIFE WORTH LIVING

PREFACE

In March of 2018 I showed up at a recovery campus in Atlanta for addiction. By this time, I was already clean and sober for six months and had a previous stretch of sixteen years of abstinence from all substances that began when I was thirty. There we attended psychology classes, peer and process groups, and seminars. Every night we were required to go to a twelve-step addiction meeting off campus. I had never experienced such meetings, so this was all entirely new to me.

What the twelve-step meeting's program revealed to me was that mere abstinence from mood and mind-altering substances, including alcohol, did not equate to a rehabilitated life. I listened attentively, becoming a dedicated student of alcoholism and recovery from substance abuse. My fascination with addiction led me to earn a degree from the Georgia Council on Substance Abuse, and I pursued further education to become an addiction counselor. Unfortunately, the outbreak of COVID-19 disrupted my efforts towards completing my CAC certification (Certified Addiction Counselor).

In 2020–21 I penned my first book, *I Didn't Ask to Be Me*, which drew extensively from the wisdom I gleaned from AA (Alcoholics Anonymous) and beyond. After learning the AA way, I discovered and have consistently asserted, "I didn't come to AA to become a better alcoholic, but a better person." I was resolute about not surrendering my life entirely to AA but rather integrating what I found useful into my own existence. *"I Didn't Ask to Be Me"* simplifies much of the dated writings from the early 20th century when alcoholism and substances first gained prominence. While I firmly believe my initial book provides a highly viable and simplified understanding of the AA and NA (Narcotics Anonymous) methods, my goal today is to deliver a new thought-provoking book with a fresh perspective for those seeking an alternative approach to achieving freedom from a variety of addictions, overcoming habits, and obsessions. Expect to embark on a journey guided by logic, common sense, rational thinking, introspection, human nature, lived experiences, street smarts, and fundamental psychology.

This book is not intended to be a medical or clinical journal; rather, it is based on the author's studies and research, personal experiences, and a variety of trustworthy sources. The stories are derived from one-on-one interviews relevant to the topics covered throughout the book.

I am a self-proclaimed rebel when it comes to "my" recovery approach. I call myself a "good" rebel though, because I have no intention of causing harm or disparaging the ways of others or the programs that came before me. Over these recent years, I've found myself in disagreement with some of the writings and sayings in certain recovery circles. In all my books, I share my experiences and perspectives. Everyone has their own, and their interpretations may differ. I examine things, analyze them, and determine their validity in the world, according to Rick. I invite you to consider the value in my thinking and to dismiss anything that does not align with your own perspective.

"Two brains are better than mine, and the whole world can't be right or wrong."

Rick Breitweiser

INTRODUCTION

I can't say I know anyone who hasn't experienced some sort of habit, obsession, or addiction. While smoking may seem worse than collecting Pez dispensers, it's still not as dangerous as abusing drugs or alcohol. Inevitably, only addiction unequivocally emerges as problematic, with its patterns spiraling into excessiveness beyond manageability. However, we may develop physical dependencies for things like caffeine, the necessity for cell phones, or an overwhelming desire or monstrous craving for dark chocolate.

There is a cause for every inclination that drives us, and it goes much deeper than a bad habit, strong compulsion, or addiction to distinguish the full gamut of these behaviors. This book is here to put all levels in perspective, take you through understanding, and provide logical solutions for all their causes. The terms discussed encompass a wide range of behaviors and activities, each falling into different categories based on psychological, habitual, recreational, or organizational aspects. For example, habits and compulsions, especially OCD, are behavioral, whereas routines, regimens, and hobbies are activities. But should you infuse overindulgence into any, they will ascend to the level of being troublesome or problematic.

It is pivotal to distinguish between having an obsession and having a passion. An obsession dictates a "must-have at all costs" mentality, while a passion implies a desire after putting in the work. Shifting from the negative connotations of "habit", or bad habits to the neutral "routine" or "regimen", as in healthy routines or regimens, opens a new perspective. This reframing enables us to discuss "good routines" or "healthy regimens." With this outlook, the book explores the challenges of bad habits, unhealthy obsessions, and addiction, all of which are inherently harmful. Its purpose is to help you recognize and comprehend the underlying causes of your condition, providing a logical approach for coping and ultimately overcoming these challenges.

As conditions intensify, so do the proposed treatment options. Although individuals are familiar with conventional remedies such as social workers, counselors, psychologists, medical professionals, treatment centers, and support groups, they also possess inherent resources including logic, common sense, street smarts, lived experience, insight, and intuition. Rational problem-solving often commences by identifying the root cause. Consider the example of someone who was prescribed Lexapro for anxiety and is now struggling with weight gain. The pills themselves contribute negligibly to the weight, whereas an increased appetite is the true culprit, leading to excessive eating.

In my research, I've observed a distinction in terminology between the recovery community and mental health organizations: "character assets" and "defects" versus "assets" and "liabilities." Rejecting the term "character defects," I propose viewing ourselves as flawed yet fixable through repetition, akin to the concept behind the 1975 "Lemon Law (Magnuson-Moss Warranty Act)." These hindrances, inhibiting our pursuit of contentment and peace of mind, should be acknowledged. This book aims to assist you in identifying and comprehending the causes of your condition, providing a logical approach to cope with and eventually overcome it. It undoubtedly offers valuable insights into understanding addiction, obsessions, OCDs, and troubling habits. A deeper exploration of your personal history and character makeup, including traits, behaviors, and distinctive qualities, facilitates connecting the threads of your life, leading to wellness and peace of mind.

SECTION 1
ADDICTION AND OBSESSIONS

UNDERSTANDING ADDICTION

Anything you willfully engage in repeatedly without moderation or control, but with occasional guilt, is addiction.

Addiction, in its essence, is the act of repeatedly engaging in something without restraint or control[1]. As if being on autopilot with a broken control system. It is a treatable, chronic medical disease[2]. Research indicates addiction to drugs and alcohol, as well as gambling, is 50–70% hereditary (genetic), like hair loss[3]. However, credible sources also highlight the contributions of trauma and mental illnesses such as anxiety and depression to the cause of addiction[4]. That said, in my judgement, it would make sense that these minority contributors to addiction could likely be the cause of all other non-substance addictions. This includes environment, peer influence, and even prescribed medications to the development of addiction[5].

In broad terms, addiction entails an inability to cease using a substance (ranging from tobacco to illicit drugs) or engaging in a behavior (from shopping to extreme sports, and even sports gambling) despite adverse consequences. This phenomenon is underpinned by the brain's reward center, which releases dopamine in response to pleasurable experiences, anticipation of reward, or heightened arousal[6]. As individuals repeat these behaviors, more dopamine is released, intensifying their compulsion to revisit them.

Consider the case of Gene Simmons from the band Kiss, who claims never to have consumed alcohol or drugs in his life[7]. Certain religions also view illicit substances and alcohol as taboo. Notably, substances do not exhibit addictive symptoms until they enter the bloodstream. Once introduced, the mind and body of an individual with an addiction become consumed by cravings and obsessions[8], not just for immediate consumption but also for the near future. Tolerance develops as more of the substance is needed to imitate the initial effects.

Today, addiction is often referred to as a substance use disorder (SUD), encompassing the continued use of substances despite severe health and social repercussions. Alcoholism (alcohol use disorder) and (SUD) are not only addictions but diseases as well. Addiction is either mental, physical, or both[9]. I am not a medical professional, but I don't see the need to change the terms. In fact, since licit drugs (mostly prescription medications) are included, I think the analogy of abusing legal drugs makes more sense than having a "using disorder." That is my logic on display. With sex, there is the physical act along with mental stimulation. And it's easy to understand why gambling and video gaming are mental addictions that release adrenaline into the body as stimulation. With drugs and alcohol, it has been repeated, "we drink because we like the way it makes us feel" or "makes us forget", or for the effect. With that said, drugs also apply. And if you consume drugs or alcohol just to numb the pain or escape a bad situation, you are again trying to change the way you feel. Alcohol is a depressant, but not to depress. It turns things down to numb.

Alcohol is a depressant, but not to clinically depress. It is frequently labeled as a "depressant" due to its ability to reduce brain activity and slow down various bodily functions. While it initially produces feelings of euphoria or relaxation and may temporarily alleviate feelings of stress or sadness due to its effects on neurotransmitters like dopamine and serotonin, excessive alcohol consumption can disrupt the balance of these neurotransmitters in the brain. The depressant effects of alcohol may then contribute to feelings of sadness or low mood, particularly when consumed in exorbitant amounts or over a prolonged period[10]. The use of alcohol is not an effective or healthy long-term solution for managing depression. In fact, excessive alcohol consumption can worsen symptoms of depression and increase the risk of developing a substance use disorder.

Addictions are relentless, compulsive actions that inflict harm on individuals and those around them, leaving them powerless to moderate or govern their actions. People grappling with addiction find themselves trapped in compulsive behaviors, persisting even when these actions yield detrimental consequences[11]. Consider obsessive-compulsive disorder (OCD), which affects 1% of the global population. While considered a disorder, OCD's exploration is relevant here due to its connection with obsessions and habits. A disease, in contrast, is a distinct and quantifiable condition, whereas a disorder suggests the possibility of a specific disease without sufficient clinical evidence for a definitive diagnosis. Chapter 13 provides comprehensive coverage of OCD.

Behavioral or mental addiction might include shopping, gambling, tanning, cosmetic surgery, etc. There is no physical pleasure, but there is still satisfaction, and a reward is felt in the brain[12]. Dual addiction comes from something both mentally and physically rewarding, not a dual addiction like being addicted to drugs and alcohol. Examples include tattoos or sex where, mentally, you are compelled to want more, often accompanied by physical sensations that may even involve a little "sweet pain" like bondage or S&M.

In a world of 8,045,311,447 people, only 8 ½% (or 107M) of the world has been diagnosed with Alcohol Abuse Disorder (AUD). The male population accounts for 70%, while the female population accounts for 30%[13]. Of course, the general population would be reduced considerably due to religions that are alcohol-free in their beliefs, and the younger ages that wouldn't have been exposed to alcohol yet. The number might be relatively high as a disease; I believe that there are factors that cause people into having drinking problems. The biggest are genetic predisposition (embedded genetic flaw from birth) or heredity. Not everyone in a family with the same parents gets the gene. I come from a family where I was the only one who got it. Unfortunately, it never goes away, but it can be managed without any further consequences.

Chapter's Logical Take-Away: This chapter explores addiction, emphasizing its complexity with factors such as genetics, environment, and behavior. It acknowledges addiction's diverse forms, ranging from substance use disorders to behavioral addictions, and underscores the role of the brain's reward system in driving addictive behaviors. Addiction, a chronic condition, entails compulsive engagement despite harm, influenced by genetics, trauma, and mental illness. Substance use disorders activate the brain's reward system, while behavioral addictions release dopamine. Alcohol's initial euphoria can exacerbate depression, and dual addiction involves both mental and physical rewards.

<u>How did I get my Addiction(s) of substances (dwg.)</u>

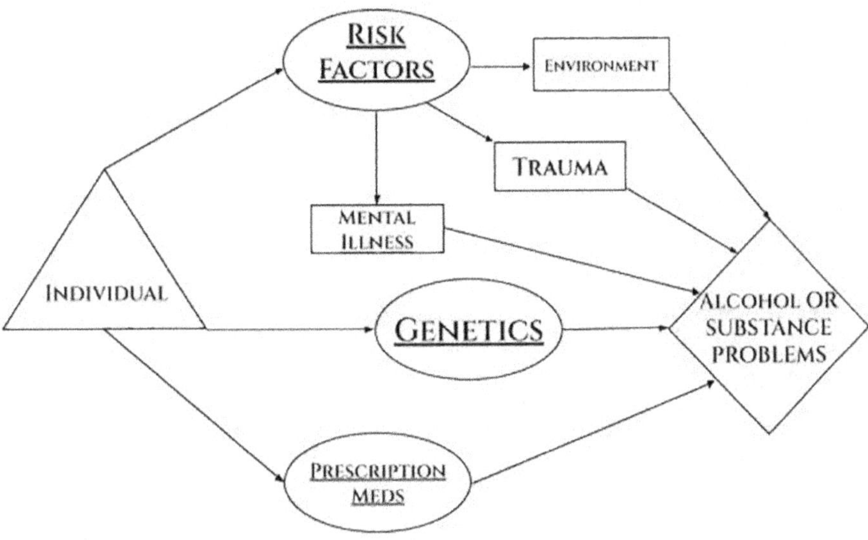

Fig.1

ADDICTION TYPES

*Not everyone is handed balance and
moderation, it is a gift for some.*

The path to solving problems often begins with identifying them and tracing back their origins, and this holds true for addictions.[14] It's essential to distinguish between pleasurable activities and addictive behaviors. So, how can you discern the transition from an enjoyable pastime to a dependency? There are several common signs of addiction[15] to look out for, including:

- Priority Shift: Are other aspects of your life, such as work, school, or social interactions, diminishing in importance compared to your drug use, alcohol consumption, excessive spending, pornography use, credit card use, or gaming?[16,17]
- Lack of Control: Do you find yourself returning to the same behavior even when you acknowledge it as a problem?[18] Are you able to detect the trigger (e.g., environmental cues)?

- Increased Tolerance[19]: Do you need larger amounts of a substance or more of a particular activity to achieve the same pleasurable feeling you once had? Whether it's drugs, alcohol, shopping, gambling, eating, or gaming, is there an escalating need? Are you always looking for novelty?
- Increased Risk-Taking[20]: Are you becoming less concerned about the risks and consequences involved in pursuit of that pleasurable feeling? Often, addicts jeopardize their health, safety, relationships, and financial security to sustain their addiction.
- Withdrawal[21]: Do you experience unpleasant physical or psychological symptoms when you're unable to engage in your substance or activity of choice?

It's important to note that comparing the severity of different addictions is challenging. Each addiction is unique, but they often share commonalities.

Addictions ultimately stem from your brain's response. Unless you are physically coerced into consuming a substance, your brain plays a pivotal role. In cases where addiction is present, the individual may have a genetic predisposition[22]—a flawed gene, so to speak—that renders them unable to control their addiction despite how tough of a fight their PFC (prefrontal cortex, the decision-making part of a brain) puts up[23]. While this genetic disposition cannot be repaired, the symptoms of this addiction can be managed with assistance.

Consider fever blisters (cold sores)—a form of herpes simplex that remains in your body once contracted[24]. Symptoms manifest only when triggered by specific factors like certain foods, vitamin deficiencies, and stress. Managing these triggers can keep fever blisters at bay.

Regarding alcohol consumption, it's worth pondering why a non-alcoholic would choose to drink alcohol when non-alcoholic beverages are available. While some may appreciate the taste of wine or beer, it's essential to recognize that normal drinkers and alcoholics both enjoy the effects of alcohol. The key distinction lies in moderation: normal drinkers can regulate their consumption and avoid crossing the line that alcoholics often transgress[25].

Addictions can be categorized into three primary types:

- Behavioral Addiction[26]: Addiction isn't limited to substances like drugs or alcohol; it can also manifest as an addiction to specific behaviors. Common addictive behaviors include shopping, sex, gambling, and video gaming. Engaging in these compulsive behaviors can provide a rush or high similar to substance addiction.

- Substance Addiction[27]: Substance addiction involves a physical dependence on a specific chemical. This can encompass prescription medications (e.g., opioids) or illicit drugs (e.g., crystal meth, heroin, cocaine). Alcoholism is also considered a form of substance addiction.

- Impulse Addiction[28]: Impulse control disorders may lead to impulse addiction. Individuals with these disorders struggle to manage their emotions and actions, often feeling at the mercy of their compulsions, potentially leading to theft, emotional outbursts, or destructive behavior. Such behaviors can become addictive, and impulse addiction may coexist with other mental health issues, including substance abuse.

Chapter's Logical Take-Away: To effectively address addiction, it is crucial to recognize and comprehend it. To mitigate the impact of addiction on one's physical and mental health, relationships, and overall well-being, it is essential to identify the warning signs before they get severe and seek assistance on time.

A BOUNDLESS WORLD OF OBSESSIONS AND ADDICTIONS

There are no limits to what might qualify as an addiction or obsession—think of anything!

Obsessions and addictions have no boundaries. Anything you can imagine can develop into an obsession or addiction. On the other hand, if the flow of addiction becomes constant, people often find themselves seeking higher stimulation. Beyond the scope of substance dependence, which includes illegal drugs and alcohol, there exists a multitude of other compulsions and cravings that plague our lives today. Among them, prescription drug abuse stands out—a practice where prescription medications are used in ways not prescribed by medical professionals[29]. This misuse encompasses everything from taking a friend's prescription painkiller for your own discomfort to snorting or injecting crushed-up pills to chase a high.

Likewise, addiction and abuse of legal and prescription drugs are rampant. These drugs include nicotine, opioids, benzodiazepines, ADHD medications, Ambien, and prescription cough syrup[30]. Other seemingly harmless items, such as smartphones, caffeine, chocolate, sweets, tanning, exercise, smoking, and tattoos, also find their way into the addictive territory, posing moderately similar harm to that of alcohol and drugs. It is important to have a clear understanding that the word "abuse" is negative; it means the misuse or improper use of something. Therefore, anything you abuse is, in some way, harmful. When you are abusing or misusing a legal substance, or overindulging, overusing, or abusing any type of activity, be it doom-scrolling, binge-watching, overspending, etc., you are, at the same time, harming yourself, both physically and mentally.

However, I gather that there needs to be a distinction between what qualifies as an addiction and what can be deemed compulsions. While they all might reach a certain level of being "addictive," that level must be determined by the individual to be truly classified as an addiction. As a way of distinguishing between what might be an addiction and something less severe, such as desires or cravings, I created another way to classify and understand the group. So, here are what I call "Classes of cravings": A, O, H, N

- A (Addiction): Anything I can't control and causes me to seek more to satisfy a mental or physical part of my ordinary living style. Prioritizing indulgence over responsibilities is one qualification. An inability to stop (or fight) the addiction is a defining characteristic.
- O (Obsession): These are mind-driven desires reinforced through repetition in neural pathways, marked by an intense magnetism that one finds hard to resist. They can be controlled to some extent, but doing so is a struggle and is often met with resistance.

- H (Habit): Habits entail a desire for repetitive actions, often undertaken without awareness of their frequency and with little conscious effort. Stopping these habits becomes a challenge. It is important to note that bad habits are to be broken and good ones are to be embraced.

- N (Necessity): This one is tricky because something that we are reliant upon for everyday function, like a cell phone for communications or food for nourishment, can become problematic in the form of overindulgence, as in social media, and in the form of gluttony (especially in the overconsumption of fast food). This could be understood as "in moderation" or "in control".

Examining various addictions and classifications in depth reveals that there are no absolute, definitive ways to distinguish them. Many determinations are subjective in nature.

In my other self-help works, I explore how "fear" can be linked to almost anything, similar to the "six degrees of Kevin Bacon" separation game; if you haven't heard of it, look it up—it's entertaining. Likewise, you can manipulate Google to provide answers that align with your curiosity. Given that all obsessions and addictions involve some degree of mental behavior, almost anything has the potential to be classified as either.

> **Chapter's Logical Take-Away:** The world of obsessions and addictions is vast and ever-expanding. There is substantial evidence of a connection between addiction and mental health conditions. In the right circumstances, almost anything can become a compulsion or addiction.

3a: Top Addictions, Habits, and Obsessions:

"Classes of cravings":

    (a)- Addiction
    (o)- Obsession
    (h)- Habit
    (n)- Necessity

(a) Nicotine – Tobacco smoking, chewing (dipping), vaping

(a) Alcoholism

(a) Illicit (illegal) Drugs or misused legal and prescription substances

(a) Gambling, Masochism, and Tattoos – The addiction or obsession is satisfied mentally and/or physically with an adrenaline rush.

(a) Sex

(o, a) Pornography

(o, a) Video gaming

(o) Smartphones – FOMO (fear of missing out)

(o, n) Internet

(o, n) Cell Phones

Ranking of the Most Common Substance Addictions in the US

1) Nicotine (found in cigarettes, e-cigarettes, and other tobacco products)

2) Alcohol

3) Marijuana

4) Opioids (such as prescription painkillers like OxyContin and fentanyl and illegal drugs like heroin)

5) Cocaine

6) Heroin

7) Benzodiazepines/" Benzos" (such as Valium and Xanax)

8) Stimulants (such as cocaine, methamphetamine, and prescription drugs like Adderall and Ritalin)

9) Hallucinogens (such as LSD and PCP)

10) Inhalants (such as paint fumes, glue, and aerosol sprays)

11) Barbiturates/Sedatives (such as phenobarbital and secobarbital)

12) Methadone

13) ADHD Meds

14) Ambien

15) Anabolic steroids

3b: Nicotine & Tobacco:

Nicotine & Tobacco use includes smoking, vaping ("e" or electronic cig-arettes), and dipping. Nicotine is a highly addictive chemical found in tobacco products. Nicotine dependency (also known as tobacco addiction) is a complicated medical disorder characterized by physical and psycholog-ical elements that make it difficult to quit smoking, even if the individual wishes to do so[31].

Nicotine Fixed

I have a friend who began smoking when she was around fourteen years old. She used to smoke a pack a day, and this habit persisted for thirty-seven years. She admitted that she found smoking enjoyable, especially in social atmospheres while drinking. Every day began and ended with a cigarette. She would sit outside on the porch in the morn-ing, but only to have a cigarette, and in the middle of the night if she couldn't sleep. In between meetings and breaks at work afforded her time for another cigarette.

Despite wanting to quit for many years, the realization of the detri-mental impact on her health finally prompted her decision to quit. Additionally, this would rid her of having clothes that reeked of tobacco smoke. Studies have shown that seven out of every ten smokers would like to quit smoking altogether[32]. She had short stints of abstinence lasting four to six months; the longest period she ever stayed away from cigarettes was two years. Despite the arduous journey of quitting, she succeeded in gradually diminishing her nicotine intake by transitioning from cigarettes to e-cigarettes, which only lasted a few months. Then she turned to nicotine gums, and finally, she used a nicotine patch for very short periods. A couple of years after achieving nicotine-free sta-tus, she experienced a notable improvement in both her mental and physical well-being.

Since embarking on the compilation of this book and conducting interviews to ascertain firsthand experiences with obsessions and addictions, my research has unveiled updates in some short stories. Some individuals among the tobacco users interviewed have slightly deviated from complete abstinence. In particular, my acquaintance who smokes cigarettes, potentially compounded by her alcoholism, succumbed to a relapse in drinking, subsequently leading to smoking again. Fortunately, this relapse was a brief episode lasting only a week.

Over the preceding two to three months, she had been dealing with relationship, occupational, family, and medical issues, which finally led her to succumb to drinking and smoking, both of which followed in immediate succession. But as of this writing in December of 2023, she is abstinent once again and is resolutely focused on her recovery from both addictions and all the underlying issues that triggered her relapse.

Arresting the Addiction to Tobacco Dipping

I cannot say that I have ever seen a woman with a pinch of chewing tobacco bulging from her lower front lip, spitting tightly into a disposable cup or an empty Mountain Dew bottle. However, I have observed numerous guys and adolescent boys engaging in this behavior, often with the impression of a tobacco tin in their pocket. When you notice all these signs, it becomes apparent that it's not a round disc of mint candies at all.

The "dipper", or smokeless tobacco user whom I know, has successfully refrained from dipping tobacco for five years. Approved and evidence-based methods, such as behavioral therapy, counseling, and pharmacotherapy (nicotine replacement therapy, prescription medications), are commonly recommended by healthcare professionals[33]. However, he told me about a new and unproven method called cold laser therapy, also known as low-level laser therapy (LLLT) or photo biomodulation[34], which involves using low-intensity lasers or light-emitting diodes on specific points on the body.

True believers of cold laser treatment for smoking cessation claim that it can help reduce cravings, withdrawal symptoms, and the desire to smoke by stimulating certain acupoints or altering cellular function[35]. Nevertheless, after one year of complete absence from nicotine, he has felt the necessity to replace his source of nicotine with oral pouches. For him, it doesn't represent an optimal strategy of complete abstinence but rather a preferable alternative to chewing tobacco, which poses health risks, including mouth cancers. This substitution can be likened to the use of methadone as a substitute for heroin.

Make Sure to Spit out the Juice

I was introduced to James, a member of a twelve-step program for alcoholism. On this day, James was open to sharing his experience with "dipping," or smokeless tobacco, a habit not uncommon among individuals susceptible to dual or multiple addictions.

James was first introduced to chewing tobacco (dip) at the age of 18 when he enlisted in the military. A buddy of his received a sleeve of Copenhagen brand dipping tobacco, which they then shared. After getting past the initial discomfort caused by the nicotine's effects, James quickly developed an addiction to dipping. He consistently had a pinch between his cheek and gum morning, noon, and night.

For thirty years, James was going through a half a tin of "dip" each day. Although he never smoked, he was addicted to nicotine, where smokeless tobacco contains more nicotine than cigarettes. Furthermore, nicotine from dipping is absorbed into the bloodstream and lingers longer, making it as addictive as cocaine and heroin.

Despite numerous attempts to quit, James, like with his alcohol addiction, could only quit when he was truly ready. The longest period of abstinence he achieved was one year. Fortunately, he never experienced the mouth-related issues (teeth and gum problems) commonly associated with dipping.

Today, at the age of sixty, James boasts twelve years of abstinence from dipping and four years without a drink. Surprisingly, he attests that quitting dipping was ten times more challenging than achieving sobriety from alcohol. James attributes his success in overcoming nicotine addiction to prayer, a common thread in many addiction recovery stories. On a related note, I know someone who turned to hypnotism to conquer his dipping addiction, and the obsession was lifted after just one session; he has been dip-free for five years.

3c: Gambling (including track betting, casino games, poker, lottery, etc.):

Gambling is marked by compulsive behavior similar to that of alcohol or drug addiction[36]. Gambling disorder is currently the only "non-substance-related disorder" in the category of "Substance-related and Addictive Disorders." It is a progressive mental health condition classified as, but not limited to, a behavioral addiction[37]. A gambling addiction can have profound and far-reaching effects on an individual's personal life. It is essential to understand that gambling addiction is a serious mental health condition, and its impact can vary from person to person.

Here are some common personal effects experienced by individuals struggling with a gambling addiction:

<u>Financial Consequences[38]:</u>

- Debt Accumulation: Excessive betting often results in substantial debts as individuals attempt to recoup losses.
- Bankruptcy: In severe cases, bankruptcy may be the outcome of an inescapable debt-spiral[39].
- Loss of Savings and Assets: People may deplete their savings, sell valuable possessions, or resort to theft to fuel their gambling habit.

<u>Emotional and Mental Health Effects:</u>

- Anxiety and Depression: Money-related stress due to current financial instability can lead to anxiety and sadness[40].
- Suicidal Thoughts: In extreme cases, hopeless individuals may contemplate or act on suicidal thoughts as a last resort[41].

Relationship Issues:

- Strained Relationships[42]: Lies, infidelity, and financial troubles strain relationships with family, friends, and partners.
- Social Isolation: Gambling can isolate individuals from their loved ones[43].
- Divorce or Breakups: Relationship problems may culminate in divorce or the end of long-term partnerships[44].

Physical Health Decline:

- Sleep Disturbances: Gambling addiction can cause anxiety and stress, disrupting sleep patterns, leading to a vicious cycle[45,46].
- Neglect of Self-Care: Addicts may neglect proper nutrition and exercise, leading to long-term health problems in most cases that could shorten their lifespan[47].

Legal Consequences:

- Criminal Behaviors: Some resort to theft or dishonesty to support their habit, resulting in arrests and legal issues[48].
- Court-Imposed Fines and Penalties: Breaking the law can lead to fines, probation, or imprisonment[49].

Employment Impact:

- Reduced Job Performance: Obsession with gambling, absenteeism, and decreased productivity harm job performance[50].
- Job Loss: Frequent job changes or job loss may occur, leading to career instability[51].

<u>**Self-Esteem Issues:**</u>

- Feelings of Inadequacy: Repeated financial losses and debt accumulation can erode self-esteem and self-worth[52].

<u>**Health Problems:**</u>

- Stress-Related Health Conditions: Long-term stress can contribute to heart disease, obesity, sleep disorders, high blood pressure, and gastrointestinal issues[53].

Have you experienced any of the following problems related to gambling? These questions aim to assess the impact of gambling on various aspects of your life and well-being:

1. Have you ever missed work or school/college due to gambling?
2. Did you ever gamble to make money to pay off a debt?
3. After losing money while gambling, did you ever feel the urge to quickly try to recoup your losses by gambling again?
4. After a winning streak, did you ever have a strong desire to continue gambling for more gains?
5. Did you frequently gamble until you had exhausted all your available funds?
6. Have you ever borrowed money to fund your gambling activities?
7. Have you resorted to selling possessions to finance your gambling habit?
8. Were you ever hesitant to use your gambling winnings for regular expenses?
9. Have you ever been careless about your own well-being or that of your family due to your gambling habits?
10. Have you ever contemplated or engaged in illegal activities (e.g., selling drugs, selling pirated games/movies, etc.) to obtain money for gambling purposes?

11. Has gambling ever disrupted your circadian rhythm?

12. Do you experience the urge to celebrate excessively after a gambling win? Or suffered deeply after a crushing loss of money?

13. Has your gambling behavior ever reached a point where it led to self-destructive tendencies or thoughts of suicide?

It's important to note that individuals struggling with gambling addiction can seek help and recovery. Seeking professional treatment through therapy, support groups, or counseling is a crucial initiative. The support of family and friends can also play a significant role in encouraging treatment and offering emotional support.

On a Roll Again

It all started in Billy's case in the early '70s on the streets of Boston when the notorious "Whitey" Bulger took some of the younger neighborhood kids under his wing of racketeering. Whitey controlled a significant share of Boston's drug deals, illegal gambling, and arms dealing, while the kids ran the "numbers" (the lottery before it was legal) for the Irish mob boss. He treated them well with sporting equipment and a little spending money. This was Billy's initial exposure to the world of gambling.

In his twenties, Billy was now old enough to bet in casinos. Whether it was cards, slots, or roulette, it didn't matter; he loved the adrenaline rush from gambling. He was bitten by the gambling bug. He would even fly from Boston to Vegas three times a month to indulge his compulsion to play. Additionally, he would wager on sports games and place bets at the track, all of which proved lucrative during a ten-year stretch. At his peak, he won as much as $300K in a single day. Keep in mind what Isaac Newton said: "What goes up must come down." This book is strongly rooted in "logic." The overhead to operate a casino or a horse racetrack is exorbitant. The losers foot the bills, benefiting only the fortunate few, the winners and owners of these venues.

Eventually, this proved to be the case. Billy's winning streaks were evidenced only as spurts, as his reserves had all but run dry. But Billy was always "good for it," so he was able to borrow from friends to win it all back. However, this didn't happen for Billy, as with most people who get addicted to gambling. This is a familiar path: you lose everything that you started with, next the payouts, and then the money you borrowed. One day you're well off, and the next you want to "off yourself."

The term "paradox" is a recurring theme in this book, illustrating how something negative often precedes a positive outcome[54]. You see, Billy already had an addiction to pain pills from an accident on the job, similar to Gunther's story, which reached a critical juncture. After three failed suicide attempts, he finally entered a treatment program to "kick" his opioid addiction. The time spent in treatment facilities also kept Billy away from all forms of gambling, allowing him the space and time needed to overcome his gambling addiction as well.

Today, Billy is a manager at a sober living facility, leading a life of freedom and contentment, having successfully overcome both his substance addiction and the mental addiction to gambling.

3d: Opiate Use (natural, illegal):

Opiates are powerful analgesics derived from the opium poppy plant[55]. Opiates are different from opioids with a simple distinction: they are natural. These include natural opium-base drugs like heroin, morphine, codeine, and opium[56].

Imagine yourself being in the New York City or Las Vegas nightclub scene during the '80s when cocaine was the king, and you were the king if you were in possession of it. For me it was so hard to break away from my addiction when everything was so easy for me back then. Nevertheless, I was very fortunate to get out when I did because crack cocaine suddenly became popular, overshadowing powdered "eight balls" that were losing their appeal.

Not everyone was able to resist the allure of crack, and unfortunately, my friend couldn't escape its grasp when it became widespread among junkies. Soon, regular coke use became a thing of the past for him. The bright, kaleidoscopic city lights didn't make his escape any easier, as it seemed like everyone else was now abusing crack.

However, after enduring more than a decade of debilitating addiction, the mental anguish finally pushed him to seek change. Thankfully, his thirteen-year struggle eventually came to an end. With the support of a twelve-step program, he now has over twenty-five years of sobriety and a life that's "1000 times better."

3e: Opioid Abuse (natural and synthetic, or combination thereof):

Again, opioids are strong painkillers primarily made of synthetic substances rather than naturally occurring plant material. The majority of opioids are manufactured in laboratories or synthesized to mimic their effects. While they can effectively relieve pain, they pose serious risks[57].

These substances interact with opioid receptors in the brain and spinal cord, altering the perception of pain and inducing feelings of euphoria. Prescription opioids such as oxycodone and hydrocodone are effective pain relievers, but they carry a risk of dependence and addiction. Prolonged use may lead to physical dependence, addiction, hypoventilation, and overdose[58]. The opioid crisis today has resulted in a widespread epidemic affecting communities and individuals worldwide[59].

In Chapter 20, titled "A Costly Prescription," I address the issue of addiction to pain pills. For those who have suffered an injury or have undergone surgery, the use of highly addictive prescription medicines becomes a double-edged sword. These medications are initially administered to cope with the pain or discomfort associated with recovery and sleeping. However, when the prescribed amounts and dosages have served their purpose and are no longer necessary, many individuals find themselves both mentally and physically addicted.

3f: Stimulant Abuse:

Stimulants are considered to be highly addictive and include both licit and illicit drugs. One of the most widely used substances to treat ADHD is stimulant-based medication, including Adderall, Ritalin, and Vyvanse, as well as weight loss medications that usually contain phentermine or ephedrine, which means there are medicinal benefits; however, they are highly addictive. Methamphetamine, cocaine, and crack cocaine are the most commonly known illicit forms of stimulants abused today[60]. Methamphetamine is a man-made synthetic stimulant, and the dangers just from making this drug due to the chemicals used are toxic fumes that can poison those around and pose a risk of explosion or fire[61]. Cocaine is created from the coca plant, making it a naturally occurring stimulant like nicotine[62]. Crack is made from cocaine by mixing it with baking powder or baking soda[63]. Remember the story about cocaine and crack in the New York City and Las Vegas night club scene in Section 3d of this chapter.

So, a stimulant is any drug that increases activity in the central nervous system, which is comprised of the spinal cord and the brain. By increasing this activity, you are also changing the way the reward network in your brain works, thereby causing long-term effects on the ability to find joy in things and function normally without a stimulant of some sort activating your reward system and central nervous system[64]. Withdrawal from stimulants is both physical and psychological in nature, but we do see a higher prevalence of psychological symptoms, which is why it is one of the harder classes of drugs to stop using. Apathy, irritability, anxiety, and fatigue are reported as some of the most difficult symptoms to deal with when withdrawing from stimulants[65].

MDMA/ecstasy is both a hallucinogenic and a stimulant drug. It makes users experience a rush of good feelings (a high) and makes feelings much more intense, whether they're good or bad[66]. The drug's effects usually last up to 6 hours. MDMA is widely used as a "cut-in" for methamphetamine. The intended purpose of stimulants is to give you that rush, euphoria, and overall feeling of being on top of the world, as if you can do anything. There is a burst of energy that comes with initial use, and after long-term use, your body and mind essentially become dependent on that rush or stimulation to function at a normal level, meaning you are no longer seeking a high but rather seeking to function. The problem with this is that when abused in any form, permanent psychological damage can be done, as well as damage to the liver, kidneys, brain, and lungs[67]. Inherently, the idea of overdosing on stimulants is hard to fathom for some individuals, but in fact, overdose is common among those who abuse stimulants. Because of the false narrative that you can't really overdose on stimulants, we do see a large number of young people trying and eventually becoming addicted to meth, coke, and crack, especially in the party scene. Long-term effects that cause irreversible damage to blood vessels in the brain and permanent damage to the heart increase an individual's risk of heart attack and stroke exponentially. Crack cocaine is specifically said to be almost instantly addictive[68], and one use of crack or cocaine can cause a fatal heart attack[69].

While caffeine and nicotine are also stimulants, they were discussed separately in 3b. and 3f. of this chapter.

3g: Caffeine/Coffee:

Caffeine addiction, also known as caffeine use disorder or caffeine dependence, is a physical and psychological dependence on caffeine. Caffeine is a stimulant found in coffee, tea, energy drinks, soft drinks, and a variety of other foods and beverages[70]. Renowned for its ability to heighten alertness and energy levels, it is crucial to emphasize that while moderate caffeine consumption is generally considered safe, excessive intake can result in adverse health effects[71]. Moreover, individual tolerance to caffeine varies, and susceptibility to addiction or heightened withdrawal symptoms can differ[72]. Therefore, it is advisable to consume caffeine in moderation, mindful of its potential impact on health.

In the 1990s, I was engaged to a girl who accompanied the chairman of Thompson Medical on his private jet. One of their products, Dexatrim, boasted the best-selling non-prescription diet pill on the market, with caffeine as its primary ingredient. Understanding how people can develop addiction, especially when caffeine is employed to suppress appetite in diet pills, becomes apparent.

Individuals can develop addiction to coffee, tea, or caffeine for various reasons, often tied to the stimulating effects of caffeine on the central nervous system[73]. Key factors contributing to caffeine addiction include its stimulant properties. Caffeine, a natural stimulant found in coffee, tea, and other beverages, stimulates neurotransmitters like dopamine and norepinephrine, resulting in heightened alertness and improved mood. The temporary energy boost creates a desire for repeated consumption. For instance, some individuals opt for a Coke or Pepsi every morning instead of a cup of coffee to kickstart their day.

- Regular caffeine consumption can lead to physical dependence as the body adapts its chemistry to the presence of caffeine. Abrupt stopping may result in withdrawal symptoms such as headaches, fatigue, irritability, and difficulty concentrating[74]. To avoid these symptoms, individuals may continue consuming caffeine. I have personally witnessed withdrawal symptoms, like headaches, when abstaining from caffeinated coffee. Similar experiences are commonly shared by others who abstain from caffeine during periods like Lent.

- The ritualistic nature of preparing and consuming coffee or tea can become a daily habit, creating an association between specific activities and the craving for caffeine[75]. In my book, *I Didn't Ask to Be Me*, I shared a story about my morning coffee routine at the gas station, getting $10 worth of gas daily to accompany my medium coffee in a paper cup with whole milk—a routine bordering on OCD behavior.

- Coffee and tea's integration into social and cultural practices contributes to habitual consumption during social gatherings, work meetings, or as part of cultural traditions, making it more challenging to break the habit[76,77,78].

- Many individuals believe that caffeine enhances cognitive function, concentration, and overall performance, driving continued consumption for perceived benefits[79].

I recall hearing that tea had more caffeine than coffee when I was young. I played baseball and was quite fast, I was a base stealer. I had never drunk coffee until I was an adult, but I heard caffeine might make me quicker on the base paths. I remember one day before a big game; I steeped a half dozen tea bags in a cup and even squeezed out all the juice. I downed it before the game that day. I don't recall running any faster on the bases. This experiment was a one-time occurrence which I never repeated.

- The widespread availability and marketing of caffeinated products, facilitated by coffee shops, cafes, and convenience stores, contributes to consumption patterns, further reinforcing the caffeine habit[80].

3h: Sugar:

Sweets addiction, also known as "sugar addiction", is a complicated phenomenon involving physiological, psychological, and environmental factors[81].

Craving a "sugar high" refers to the desire[82] for the temporary burst of energy and mood enhancement that can come from consuming sugary foods or drinks. There are several reasons why people may experience this craving:

- Instant Energy Boost: Sugars, especially simple carbohydrates like glucose, can be quickly absorbed into the bloodstream, providing a rapid increase in blood sugar levels[83]. This surge in energy can lead to a feeling of alertness and a temporary boost in mood.
- Brain Reward System: Consuming sugar activates the brain's reward system, releasing dopamine, a neurotransmitter associated with pleasure and reward. This reinforcement mechanism can create a desire to repeat the behavior, leading to cravings for sugary foods.
- Throughout human evolution, sweet foods were often associated with energy-rich sources, such as ripe fruits[84]. The preference for sweetness may have evolved as a survival mechanism to encourage the consumption of high-calorie foods for energy.
- Stress and Emotional Eating: Some people may turn to sugary foods as a way to cope with stress or emotional challenges[85,86]. The temporary mood elevation caused by sugar consumption may provide a brief escape from negative emotions.
- Habit: Over time, individuals may develop habits and conditioned responses to certain cues (such as stress, boredom, or specific environments) that trigger cravings for sugary foods[87]. This can lead to a cycle of repeated behavior. This can be evidenced with

all stress-related eating, not just sugary foods. I know people who look to eat when they are stressed out.

While occasional consumption of foods heavy in sugar may not appear to be harmful, excessive intake can have negative health effects, including weight gain, an increased risk of metabolic disorders, and dental issues[88]. It's important to maintain a balanced diet and be mindful of overall sugar intake to support long-term health and well-being.

Pour Some Sugar

When Barbara was young, she was deprived of the sweets that most of the other kids were allowed to have. Her mother wasn't punishing her; she just didn't think cookies and candy were suitable for her as a child. It reminds me of the twelve silver fillings I earned in just one visit to the dentist chair. It was probably November when I buzzed through all the Mounds, Reese's, Butterfinger, and Nestle Crunch bars, and my Batman costume was packed away for next year.

One of Barbara's earliest and fondest memories that comes to mind was when she was given lunch money for school every day; it always included a single jumbo chocolate chip cookie as dessert. It was a satisfying way to finish up lunch before having to go back for afternoon classes.

After resenting her mother for such rules as a child, Barbara came to the age of independence and busted out crying for sugar. Now, no one could tell her that Corn Pops, Sugar Smacks, or oatmeal heaping with brown sugar and overflowing with maple syrup was no way to start her day! I remember sitting down with Cap'n Crunch many mornings myself. When all the "crunch" was gone, and the floating soggy cereal was skimmed off the milk; you want to talk about sweet milk!

Barbara recalls not having bread around much. But like many people I know, all you need is a spoon when you have peanut butter, "Fluff" (marshmallow spread), or Cool Whip right from the tub or folded into yogurt to masquerade the appearance of something healthy-looking. These were some of her "go-to" and staple indulgences when it came to sweets.

The obsessive nature of her craving for sugar included soda, preferably Dr. Pepper. No wonder she developed an addiction to liquor that was high in sugar content. She describes a ritual on how she would make plans to enjoy her beverage. Methodically, she would set an ice-filled glass in front of her before lighting a cigarette. Next came the unmistakable snapping sound of an aluminum can ring being unlocked so she could transfer the pop into a chilled-ready soda glass. This daily routine provided her with the means to get a liquid sugar fix in a glass.

But one day, like most days for Barbara, something changed. While looking for a late-night soda in her refrigerator, none showed themselves. It was already a quarter till 10(pm), and she would have just fifteen minutes to dash to the corner store to get a DP (Dr. Pepper) and arrive ahead of the "CLOSED" sign on the glass door. That night Barbara was the victor, in more ways than one. The mood was right now, and the ritual was about to commence. But a strange thing happened between the soda glass and her mouth. She took 2 short sips and laid the glass back down in front of her. There was probably nothing wrong with the soda or the glass, but at that moment, she had lost her appetite for it anymore. That was an awakening she still has no explanation for.

Today Barbara has curtailed her obsession for sugary products. If she feels like having a donut, she has "A" donut. Moderation and balance are the keys to a successful, content-filled life!

Consuming chocolate increases the natural brain chemical enkephalin[89]. Enkephalin (endorphin-like substances acting as natural painkillers) stimulates opioid receptors in the same way that heroin and morphine do[90]. This chemical causes the brain to crave more chocolate after the initial consumption, which can lead to addiction[91]. Chocolate is irresistibly delicious, and it can be addictive for some people. However, it is not considered an addiction. Chocolate addiction is not a recognized medical condition. Even so, it is possible to have chocolate cravings and eat more than you should.

The widespread love for chocolate can be attributed to a combination of sensory, psychological, and cultural factors[92,93]. Here are some reasons[94] why people tend to enjoy chocolate so much:

- Taste and texture: Chocolate has a rich, complex flavor profile that combines sweetness, bitterness, and often creaminess. The smooth texture of well-made chocolate can be very pleasing to the palate[95].

- Sugar and Fat Content: Chocolate often contains sugar and fat, which can activate the brain's pleasure centers[96]. The combination of these ingredients can create a satisfying and indulgent experience.

- Release of Endorphins: Chocolate has been associated with the release of endorphins, which are neurotransmitters that contribute to feelings of pleasure and well-being. This chemical reaction in the brain can create a positive association with chocolate consumption[97].

- Cultural, Social Factors, and Emotional Connections: Chocolate is often associated with celebrations, rewards, and comfort. Many cultures use chocolate in rituals, ceremonies, and gift-giving, reinforcing its positive connotations. This may appear to be very one-sided, but hearts, sweethearts, and chocolates in heart-shaped boxes are given to those sweethearts on Valentine's Day[98]. And let's not forget chocolate bunnies on Easter or all the chocolate candy bars on Halloween.

- Chemical Composition: Chocolate contains substances such as theobromine, caffeine, and phenylethylamine, which can have mood-enhancing effects and contribute to the overall appeal of chocolate[99,100]. All types of chocolate contain caffeine, except white chocolate[101].

- Marketing and Advertising: The chocolate industry invests heavily in marketing and advertising, associating chocolate with pleasure, romance, and luxury. This can influence people's perceptions and preferences[102].

- Versatility: Chocolate is a versatile ingredient[103] that can be incorporated into various forms and recipes, from candies and desserts to beverages and savory dishes. This versatility allows for a wide range of culinary experiences with chocolate[104].

From Alcoholic to Chocoholic

I met Sandy not knowing how much she once loved chocolate. I mean, she bakes a cake every week for a group we're in together, whose main ingredient always includes some form of chocolate: frosting, filling, or the cake, yet she's in great shape for a woman in her mid-forties. She must only get to lick the mixer.

During her childhood, she and her brother would pool the little bit of money they had together and paddle the family rowboat across the lake to Hoffman's tackle and variety store after school, all in pursuit of sweet treasures. Now Sandy loved colorful candies like Mike and Ike, Skittles, and Sour Patch Kids, which they got to mix and pay for by weight like a salad bar, as well as Hostess Zingers and SnoBalls, but the big jackpot was to have enough for a 100 Grand Bar, with chocolate, caramel, and crisped rice (Rice Krispies). Today she admits Reese's are right up atop her list of favorites, but the 100 Grand candy bar gets the gold for her.

I mentioned a group Sandy and I go to once a week. This is a recovery group for alcoholism. When people stop drinking, they frequently seek alternatives for the absent sugar. Notably, wine contains sugar, while most harder liquors like vodka, gin, rum, or tequila do not on their own. The added sugar and calories often come from mixers in cocktails. So, it's no coincidence that there are bowls of Halloween candy on every table, and a bake-sale table array of cookies and cakes at some of the twelve-step meetings I attend. This is where Sandy found the choco-late candy bars that got her through in early recovery, and where I got hooked on oversized chocolate chip cookies.

This presents another problem for someone who has given up alcohol, they often "trade addictions" by substituting one with another. I have witnessed many individuals turn to smoking, but it's hard to conceal the weight gain resulting from the chocolate and sweets they embrace as their saviors. Sandy recalls secretly stashing her favorite baked cookies in the refrigerator, insisting they were for her son. It's awkwardly pur-chasing something and claiming, "they're for a friend." As she would go on and eat them all, only to have to replace them in case her son is ever in the mood for them.

There is nothing wrong with craving German chocolate cake, or double-stuffed Oreo cookies, but there is a prob-lem eating the whole row of them at one sitting.

Sandy had a fondness for chocolate to the extent that she made it a requirement for all the guys in her past relationships to not only re-member to show up with a box of chocolates on Valentine's Day and her birthday, but also every half-birthday. Personally, I struggle to recall anyone's whole birthday!

However, there came a day when Sandy needed surgery, marking a turning point for her health. All the ice cream infused with chocolate candy bar chunks, brownie bites, fudgy treats, and the chocolate cheesecakes she brought home weekly from Olive Garden, where she worked, came to a halt. Her recovery from surgery led her to the gym, and insights from her alcoholism recovery program helped her overcome her obsession with anything chocolate.

Today, Sandy adheres to at least two healthy programs to live by. As for me, I simply steer clear of oversized chocolate chip cookies.

3j: Eating Disorders:

People who have eating disorders have a variety of serious psychological and physical health problems that are related to their eating habits and body image[105]. Getting to the root of the problem. Why do we overeat? Taste? Boredom? Depression? Eating disorders are complex mental health conditions marked by irregular eating habits and intense anxiety about body weight, shape, and food. They have the potential to affect people of all ages, genders, and backgrounds. While the precise causes of eating disorders are unknown, they are thought to result from a combination of genetic, psychological, environmental, and social factors[106].

Suppose you are a person who is preoccupied with your physical appearance all the time; wouldn't that constitute being troubled? On the other hand, individuals who are obsessed with their physical appearance all the time go to any lengths to maintain it. The immediate thought of a solution might be to assess the changes needed to solve this problem. Unfortunately, that is not the problem. The issue is that you are you, and you can improve your appearance only so much physically to please yourself. But going beyond the boundaries will be to put on a fake façade for others to perceive. Optimally, learning how to appreciate who you are is the fix! But if you, like me, suffer from a touch of vanity and lack the self-worth we all deserve, there are things you can do to enhance your appearance in healthy ways in order to feel better about yourself and regain your confidence.

If you're not happy with your appearance, there are steps you can take to improve it. Start by maintaining a healthy diet and exercising regularly to manage your weight and tone your body. If your teeth are dingy, you can use a whitening toothpaste to correct that. Consider changing your hairstyle if you think it will make you feel better. Practice good hygiene, including well-kept nails and adequate hydration; it's essential for a polished appearance. However, it's important to remember that these external changes can only boost your confidence and well-being to a certain extent. I'm living proof and a firm believer that real transformation comes from not just addressing the inner aspects but challenging them, just like if you're going to restore a car, it's the mechanical parts on the inside that get you down the road.

The Skinny on a Happy Ending

I know—let's say a lean woman—who has an eating disorder. She suffers from Bulimia Nervosa[107], or commonly, Bulimia. This is a life-threatening eating disorder that is characterized by regular, often secretive bouts of overeating (bingeing), followed by self-induced vomiting or purging, strict dieting or fasting, misuse of laxatives, and extreme exercise, all associated with persistent and excessive concern with body shape, not weight. You may remember Karen Carpenter, who died from this disease on February 4th, 1983.

It would appear that the rewards would be quite worthwhile: eating without gaining weight and having boys and adults complimenting her appearance. Even when it came to sports, (soccer/basketball/track and field/tennis) she was faster and stronger. So, why would anyone abandon something that seemed to be working so well if everyone started complimenting her on how fantastic she looked without knowing what it took to maintain that "look"? Though for her, it became her "dirty little secret." For twenty-four years straight, she had been binge eating and purging her food up to 10+ times per day. All her troubles disappeared like magic, and the voices in her head subsided. She experienced a general numbness. She loved the taste of food and then when she purged it was like this rush. Eventually, it would become automatic, and habitual. It was merely an ordinary experience that developed into an intense obsession. It was all she could think about—day and night. "I was dreadfully afraid of putting on weight," she said. "I would come apart if I gained even a couple of pounds, and I would binge and purge until I found relief. I felt so amazing for a very long time, thanks to the attention from men and comments about how slim I was. But during the past three to four years, I formed a hatred with all the compliments pouring in. It was getting to me, making me question my actions, because I knew what I was doing was behind closed doors." This eventually led her into a deep depression where she became suicidal. She couldn't see ever overcoming her bulimia because the situation appeared to be so dire and out of control. She stopped binging and purging only because it was the worst place anyone could possibly be in. "I was terrified to live and terrified to die," she exclaimed. She didn't know which one was worse. It was such a traumatic time for her, as she so desperately wanted to love herself and be accepted. "I just didn't have the faintest idea as to how I was going to change," she said. "I reached out to my parents for help. My dad was the first person I ever told after twenty-four years."

"I finally got help when I went to a treatment center for ED (eating disorders). I am an active member of Eating Disorders Anonymous and attend meetings daily. I am no longer active in my eating disorder, but still struggle with body dysmorphia (more about BD in section 3K). My abstinence date is 1/10/22. There are times when I have thoughts about binging and purging, but I catch myself. I follow a meal plan that the dietician helped me come up with during the treatment. I don't follow it exactly, having gotten to a different point with my program, but it is an integral part of my everyday living."

"Surprisingly, I only have one physical health concern or consequence. My teeth were in bad health as a result of the years' worth of acidic vomit. I would argue that depression and body dysmorphia are the main reasons I take medication and visit a therapist. But fortunately, I've come a long way since then. Even if some days are harder than others, I respect myself today, and accept myself. I think of my body as a structure and focus more on who I am as a person—my principles, ethics, values, and integrity—than on myself as a physical specimen to be examined for my appearance."

"Today, my life is unrecognizable compared to almost two years ago. I have friends who I hang out with. I am a part of something bigger than me. I am more comfortable in my skin. I have a healthy relationship with my parents. I have a job that I enjoy, and I volunteer on the side. Today, whenever I smile, I think of those years I went without hardly ever smiling. Most importantly, I am developing a healthy relationship with myself."

3k: Self-Harm (Non-suicidal Self-Injury Disorder):

Non-suicidal self-injury, often simply called self-injury, is the act of harming your own body on purpose, such as by cutting or burning yourself. It's usually not meant as a suicide attempt[108]. This type of self-injury is a harmful way to cope with emotional pain, sadness, anger, and stress[109].

While self-injury may bring a brief sense of calm and a release of physical and emotional tension, it's usually followed by guilt, shame, the pain of wounds, and the return of painful emotions[108]. Life-threatening injuries are usually not intended, but it's possible that more serious and even fatal self-harm could happen.

Common areas for self-harm are the arms, legs, chest, and abdomen[110]. Self-harm behaviors are most likely to start between ages twelve and fourteen[111]. But it can start earlier. Becoming upset can trigger urges to self-injure. Many people self-injure only a few times and then stop. But for others, self-injury can become a longer-term, repeated behavior[112].

Self-harm has several causes, but anxiety, sadness, and borderline personality disorder (e.g., impulsivity, mood swings, and distorted self-image) are typically connected. Trauma, abuse, neglect, gender identity, sexual orientation, and social isolation can also lead to self-harm[113]. Self-harm may temporarily relieve tension, but guilt and humiliation return the painful emotions. People do not do this to cope with emotional pain, sadness, anger, or stress.

<u>People engage in self-harm for various reasons[114]:</u>

- To cope with their emotions.
- As a form of self-punishment.
- To express their distress.

<u>**Signs of self-harm include[115]:**</u>

- Patterned scars.
- Discussing helplessness, hopelessness, or worthlessness.
- Cut, scratch, or stab using sharp objects.
- Match or cigarette burning.
- Carving skin with text or symbols.
- Headbanging, striking, biting, or hitting.
- Wearing long sleeves or long pants to hide self-injury, even in hot weather.

Cut to the Chase

I ran into someone from an alcohol recovery program who revealed her vulnerabilities by telling me about two of her other struggles: bulimia and self-harming. For the purpose of this book, I asked her if she would be willing to share some of her insights on both subjects as there is a connection between the two. Earlier in the chapter, I had already shared a story from another woman who had battled bulimia, so the primary emphasis here would be mainly about self-harming.

Probing deeper into their experiences revealed a common thread, a profound dissatisfaction with their own bodies, and their appearances. It became evident that the solution did not lie in inducing vomiting but rather in understanding the root causes behind their negative self-images. This is the message I have consistently been pounding throughout this entire book. What's the deepest and most "logical" cause for your troubles? If happiness begins with a seed, and the goal is to end up with a flower or fruit, then we need to travel up the vine to see at what point we went wrong or where we were flawed (where the metaphorical "galls" on the leaves started to grow) to determine where we first encountered feelings of inadequacy or self-doubt.

This particular woman already had a history of emotional challenges. Her mother had battled anorexia and had an intense repulsion of being overweight, which left a deep impression on her. Her own struggles began at the age of nine, as she would resort to self-punishment by hitting herself with a brush. It wasn't until she was in her thirties that she first experimented with "cutting," a behavior that continued to trouble her even as an adult. While self-harm is commonly associated with individuals between the ages of twelve and fourteen, and sometimes among college students, her experience highlighted that the impact of these emotional struggles can persist well beyond those age brackets.

This pattern of behavior has persisted for nearly a year. You may recall that I had previously known this individual through an alcohol recovery program. She has a history of alcohol abuse, so relapse has been a part of her story. As a form of self-punishment, the shame of relapse prompted the cutting. The cutting can be relatively short, sometimes lasting only a few days, during which the number of self-inflicted cuts can range from a few to more than a dozen in a single session. From our conversation, it became clear that this is a form of self-punishment, not intended to inflict severe harm or result in suicide, but rather as an emotionally driven release.

She has made attempts to seek therapy and explore support groups for this condition, but it hasn't quite taken hold for her yet. She carries a sense of shame about her condition and confines this behavior to the bathroom, where she can avoid confronting herself. There is, however, a significant ray of hope for my friend. Her self-harming behavior follows a cyclic pattern (bingeing), with periods of cutting lasting a few days followed by substantial abstinence periods, sometimes as long as five months. These breaks provide her with opportunities for self-reflection, learning, and improvement between episodes.

In my perspective, it's evident that "cutting" is not the root issue; instead, it serves as her coping mechanism or, as I like to put it, her escape.

31: Body Dysmorphic Disorder, or Body Dysmorphia:

Today, more than ever, we are witnessing a growing interest in diverse body enhancements and alterations. This begs the question: What fuels this sudden fascination? This book is about "treating the cause," and not the symptom; the answer is quite clear … people are not happy with the way they look. About 40% of people with BDD are men, and about 60% are women116. Now the causes for these feelings may run deep and are more than likely linked to their mental well-being. While professional counseling or prescribed medication would appear to be the optimal solution to address these concerns, the pursuit of swift results has given rise to a surge in both permanent and temporary procedures. These procedures provide a rapid solution for individuals in search of a fresh makeover, offering a quick boost to their self-esteem. The majority of these people, to some extent, suffer from BDD. "Body dysmorphic disorder is a mental health condition in which you can't stop thinking about one or more perceived flaws in your appearance—a flaw that appears minor or is invisible to others117. However, you may avoid many social situations because you are embarrassed, ashamed, or anxious. When you have body dysmorphic disorder, you obsess over your appearance and body image, checking the mirror, grooming, or seeking reassurance repeatedly throughout the day, sometimes for many hours118. Your perceived flaws and repetitive behaviors cause you significant distress and interfere with your ability to function in daily life.

The most popular body enhancements include[119]:

- Tanning: A healthy tan or glow is probably the easiest and most affordable to accomplish on the list. Our sun is the most natural provider to achieve results, but possibly the most dangerous for our skin when exposed for long periods and over time. Tanning beds, booths, and lamps may provide a quicker and safer tan, but again, only in moderation[120]. I have been careful to use substantial sunscreen my entire life when everyone was getting "bronze." Today, I found a great, safe tan in a bottle.

- Tattoos and Body Piercings: These have been long-standing forms of body modification and self-expression[121,122].

- Cosmetic Surgery: Procedures like breast augmentation, liposuction, rhinoplasty, and Botox injections have been widely popular for enhancing physical appearance[123,124].

- Dermal Fillers: Injectable fillers[125] like hyaluronic acid have gained popularity for enhancing facial features and reducing the appearance of wrinkles.

- Hair Transplants: Restoring hair growth through transplantation has been a common procedure for individuals experiencing hair loss[126].

- Hair Colors: More on hair transformations; it's essential to discuss the long-standing practice of hair coloring[127]. With a wide range of available colors today, and they're everywhere, the options are extensive. There are products designed to cover gray and others that create wavy styles, offering diverse choices. Additionally, for individuals facing persistent graying in their facial hair, there are a variety of beard dyes available in your color, providing a vibrant solution.

- Laser Hair Removal: Permanent hair reduction through laser treatments has been in demand for those seeking a long-term solution to unwanted hair[128].

- Body Contouring: Non-surgical treatments for body contouring, such as CoolSculpting and laser treatments, have become popular for reducing fat and achieving a more sculpted appearance[129].

- Teeth Whitening and Cosmetic Dentistry: Procedures like teeth whitening, veneers, and dental implants have been popular for enhancing smiles[130].

- Cosmetic Tattoos and Microblading: These techniques involve tattooing or semi-permanent makeup application for features like eyebrows and lips[131].
- Augmented Reality (AR) Filters: While not physical enhancements, the use of AR filters on social media platforms allows users to alter their appearance in photos and videos[132]. There is not a day that goes by that I don't see this technique utilized on social media. Scary!

It's important to note that societal trends and preferences do change, and new technologies and procedures have probably emerged since the writing of this book. Always consult with qualified professionals before undergoing any body enhancement procedures.

3m: Muscle Building:

Muscle Building are included in this category more frequently than you might think. Working out and bodybuilding obsession refers to an extreme and often all-consuming emphasis on physical fitness and muscle development. Individuals who are obsessed with getting in shape generally engage in rigorous training regimens, strict diets, and might take supplements or even performance-enhancing medications (e.g., anabolic steroids) to acquire their desired physique[133]. This level of involvement can result in beneficial outcomes, such as better health and self-confidence, but may also cause physical injuries, body image issues, and strained relationships[134]. To avoid the harmful impacts of this fixation, it is critical to balance a commitment to a realistic fitness program with your general well-being. As a nation, we have become so out of shape and obese. Surprisingly, more than 70 percent of Americans are classified as overweight or obese[135]. While it's true that being overweight is a risk factor for developing type 2 diabetes[136], it's important to remember that other factors, including family history, age, and race, also contribute to this risk.

One common misconception is the belief that a pound of muscle weighs the same as a pound of fat[137], which is scientifically true, but there's a crucial difference: a pound of fat takes up about three times as much space in the body as a pound of muscle[138]. It's worth mentioning that muscle mass tends to decrease as people enter their thirties. However, it's never too late to take steps to improve your health and increase muscle mass. A well-rounded fitness and nutrition program involves adopting a sensible workout and exercise regimen, coupled with a balanced diet. This combination is key to achieving and maintaining good health.

Muscles Build Strength

Someone I'm acquainted with has successfully struck a balance in her life. She isn't obsessed with her workout routine, but she's definitely passionate about it. It's evident to me that she's not pursuing bodybuilding, but rather focused on building muscle. She dedicates half an hour to an hour each day to her gym routine. On certain days, she focuses on strength training with weights, while on others, she opts for a gentler walk to avoid overexertion. She's been following this regimen for half of her life and has turned it into a career as a fitness director for a Global 500 company. Already in her forties now, she has run a nutrition and fitness consulting business for the past twelve years. While she isn't obsessed with bodybuilding or weightlifting, she does participate in Hyrox races, which challenge her overall fitness. Though her current emphasis on fitness is geared towards maintaining good health as she ages, with a well-structured program in place.

Maintaining a healthy gym routine has proven to be effective in reducing stress and anxiety for her. According to my friend, it's the most natural way to manage emotions, surpassing any antidepressant available on the market. She notices signs of irritability if she deviates from her workout routine. For me personally, when I begin to skip days in my daily walking routine, I become disappointed in myself. There's a certain satisfaction, both mentally and physically, in the act of burning calories!

3n: Sex Addiction:

Sex addiction, also known as hypersexuality or compulsive sexual behavior, remains unacknowledged in the DSM-5 (The Diagnostic and Statistical Manual of Mental Disorders)[139], despite considerations for other non-substance or behavioral addictions such as exercise and shopping, which were ultimately excluded due to insufficient peer-reviewed evidence identifying them as mental health disorders at this time[140]. However, it is diagnosed or considered a symptom of disorders such as borderline personality disorder, bipolar disorder, schizoaffective disorder, PTSD, and OCD[141,142]. Individuals experiencing sex addiction struggle with intense and uncontrollable urges to engage in sexual activities despite potential negative consequences for themselves, their partners, or their relationships, disrupting personal, work, and social aspects of life[143].

Symptoms of hypersexuality include persistent and intense sexual interests, urges, fantasies, or behaviors related to atypical objects, activities, or situations[144], such as voyeurism, fetishism, masochism, and sadism, all of which align with manias recognized in the DSM[145].

When I hear "he or she's a 'sex addict'", I immediately think they are addicted to sex. I also can't help but associate nymphomania with that individual. Nymphomania[146] is an outdated and common term that historically described excessive or uncontrollable sexual desire in women. The term has fallen out of favor in professional circles due to its pejorative and stigmatizing nature. It is not a recognized medical or psychological diagnosis, although other forms of mania are.

Research suggests that millions of people, with an estimated 30 million in the US alone, are affected by sex addiction, despite its lack of recognition[147]. While there are medications purported to help reduce sexual impulses, support groups like Sex Addicts Anonymous and specialized therapists offer treatment options.

Not So Sexy

All but one person I ever met likes pizza, and only a few who don't care for chocolate; but who doesn't like sex? Then there is Shantaa too, who likes pizza and chocolate, but in her case, likes sex too much.

Did you ever think too much sex would ever be too much? Sounds unmanageable right! However, Shantaa learned the hard way. By the time she was fourteen her sexual desires got pretty intense. Due to the constant urge to view pornography and masturbation, she began seeking older males who engaged in light sex practices, and eventually resulted in pregnancy by the time she was sixteen.

Then along came the internet, and by the time she was twenty-two, sites like Myspace provided a forum for all the sex Shantaa would need. Random strangers, with no names, were now right there for the sex themselves. You can imagine the level of danger this could be for a female who went on one of these 'hook-ups.' She would even get a babysitter when her sexual compulsions drove her. Think of the health risks. Shantaa eventually contracted HPV[148], a virus that led to cervical cancer and necessitated a hysterectomy.

Shantaa's hypersexuality condition put her in precarious situations that led to dealings with issues of domestic violence. This, along with the shame of her lifestyle and love for her child, brought her to treatment. Because the solution for sex addiction is therapy-based involving counseling and support groups, only treatment is prescribed when medicines are administered. Shantaa attended therapy once a week, and then every other week for two years, and 6 months with a weekly support group.

With only one relapse that lasted a year, today Shantaa has five years of abstinence from hypersexuality or compulsive sexual behavior. She has 4 children and is in a healthy relationship and has a career helping others. I know this because she helped me with parts of this book.

3o: Pornography:

Unlike substance addictions such as drug or alcohol addiction, "porn addiction" is not a formally recognized medical or psychological diagnosis[149]. However, some people may struggle with compulsive and problematic pornographic consumption, which can have an impact on their overall well-being and quality of life[150].

Addiction to pornography, like any other form of addiction, can have various negative consequences for an individual's physical, mental, and social well-being. It's important to note that not everyone who consumes pornography will develop an addiction, and the impact can vary from person to person. However, for those who do experience addiction, some potential consequences include:

- Negative Impact on Relationships: Excessive consumption of pornography can lead to relationship problems, as it may contribute to unrealistic expectations, communication issues, and a decreased interest in intimate activities with a partner[151].
- Psychological Effects: Addiction to pornography can lead to psychological issues such as anxiety, depression, guilt, and shame. It may also contribute to low self-esteem and body-image issues[152].
- Impact on Sexual Functioning: Some individuals may experience difficulties in sexual functioning, such as erectile dysfunction or difficulty reaching orgasm, due to the desensitization that can occur with frequent exposure to explicit material[153].
- Time and Productivity Loss: Addiction to pornography can consume a significant amount of time, leading to decreased productivity in other areas of life, such as work or academics. This can contribute to neglect of responsibilities and strained personal or professional relationships[154].

- Social Isolation: Individuals with a pornography addiction may withdraw from social activities and relationships[155], preferring to spend time alone consuming explicit material.

- Financial Consequences: in some cases, addiction to pornography may lead to financial issues, if a person spends money on subscriptions, memberships, or other related expenses[156].

- Legal Consequences: In extreme cases, addiction to pornography might lead to legal problems if an individual engages in illegal activities[157], such as accessing or distributing explicit material involving minors.

3p: Adrenaline Addict:

(An addiction that is not mentally recognized)[158] An adrenaline junkie who enjoys the sensation of epinephrine release will sometimes chase this sensation. As a result, they frequently participate in thrilling or exciting activities such as extreme sports like snowboarding or skiing, downhill mountain biking, or motorcycle riding. Skydiving, whitewater rafting, bungee jumping, and going on rollercoasters are all thrilling activities[159,160]. Shark diving and storm chasing are two examples of exciting hobbies.

> *"When skydiving, you don't need a parachute*
> *unless you wanna go twice."*

Epinephrine, or adrenaline, is a hormone and neurotransmitter that triggers the "fight or flight" response[161]. The adrenal glands on top of each kidney create it. Adrenaline is released during stress or threat. It raises heart rate, dilates airways, and diverts blood to vital organs and muscles to prepare the body for action. In harmful situations, these physiological changes help the body react quickly. As part of the sympathetic nervous system reaction, adrenaline boosts alertness and physical readiness[162].

As I mention later in Chapter 53, I am afraid of heights, so I will undoubtedly experience an adrenaline flow when I am up high or even watching someone else who is. Come to think about it, I am not a fan of high speeds either. In that case too, my body prepares myself for danger with a release of adrenaline.

These activities are not for everyone, as they often involve inherent risks and require a certain level of skill, training, and safety precautions. Adrenaline junkies are drawn to the intense sensations and the challenge of conquering their fears and pushing boundaries. Adrenaline junkies seek intense and thrilling experiences that provide a rush of adrenaline. Several factors contribute to satisfying the cravings of adrenaline junkies:

- Risk and Danger: Adrenaline junkies are often drawn to activities that involve an element of risk or danger. This can include extreme sports such as skydiving, base jumping, rock climbing, or white-water rafting.
- Speed: Activities that involve high speeds, such as racing sports (car racing, motorcycle racing), downhill skiing, or zip-lining[163], can provide a significant adrenaline rush.
- Height and Depth: Activities at great heights or depths, like bungee jumping, paragliding, or deep-sea diving, can trigger a strong adrenaline response due to the perceived risk and exposure[164].
- Novelty and Variety: Adrenaline junkies often seek new and novel experiences[165]. Trying different activities and pushing personal limits can keep the thrill alive.
- Physical Challenge: Engaging in physically demanding activities, such as extreme endurance races, obstacle courses, or free climbing[166], can provide a sense of accomplishment and an adrenaline rush.
- Unpredictability: Activities with an element of unpredictability or lack of control, like big wave surfing or off-road racing, can heighten the adrenaline response[167].
- Competition: Competitive sports[168], especially those with high stakes and intense rivalry, can satisfy the adrenaline cravings of individuals who thrive on the challenge of competing against others[169].
- Natural Elements: Being in natural and challenging environments, such as steep mountain slopes, raging rivers, or deep forests, can enhance the overall experience for adrenaline seekers.

- Peer Influence: The social aspect of participating in these activities with like-minded individuals can contribute to the enjoyment and satisfaction of adrenaline junkies.

- Personal Mastery: Overcoming fear and mastering a skill or activity can be powerful motivators for adrenaline junkies[170]. The sense of achievement and conquering challenges can be highly rewarding.

A behavioral addiction characterized by excessive and compulsive playing of video games[171], especially role-playing ones, often to the detriment of other aspects of a person's life, is known as gaming disorder[172]. It's important to note that not everyone who plays video games is addicted, but when gaming starts interfering with daily responsibilities, relationships, professional obligations, and overall well-being, it could be a sign of addiction[173]. I had no idea that playing video games could lead to such a strong addiction or obsession.

Shoot to Win

Someone I know was telling me about his passion for gaming. He loves "shooters" (characters with weapons, firearms, and long-distance artillery), but his favorite is Spiderman. He can't wait for the next edition to come out; like me as a 16-year-old waiting for the newest Kiss album to hit the stores. He plays after work for a couple hours to get his fix, but that's it for the day, it doesn't interfere with his job. He does have to play seven days/week, and if he's not near his PlayStation, he goes to his phone. And although he tells me that he has been playing video games in some form for about forty years now, I would probably say that he is obsessed and not addicted because it doesn't interfere with his daily life.

Playing the Game

Like a gambler who's on a winning streak, it's hard to walk away. Nick, an avid video gamer, found it almost impossible to set aside his PS5 wireless controller when all the villains were falling just as he had planned.

Now thirty-one, Nick began playing video games from the time he could barely walk. He claims to play for five to six hours every day, which could be considered excessive or obsessive. However, he insists that he can walk away when something important demands his attention. Despite this, gaming has occasionally made him late for appointments or led to calling out from work.

Nick has a brother who is also a gamer, and they play against each other from time to time. However, Nick's gaming preferences lean towards RPGs, or "role-playing games," where he engages with the virtual world rather than competing directly with others.

Similar to a reader who can't decide what to read from their stack on any given day, Nick has a library of games for every mood.

Occasionally, he and his brother decide to split the cost of a new game to get more value for the $60–$70 expense. Purchasing a new game on his own every other month can become costly. And like the Apple phone enthusiasts, Nick has waited for the rollout of a highly anticipated new game to be one of the early ones to experience it.

Nick has confided in me that he acknowledges having a problem with alcohol, leading him to join a support group. As he grapples with this challenge, he finds himself dedicating less time to gaming. As of now, neither gaming nor alcohol has resulted in the ruin of his life. However, the objective is to effectively manage these compulsions to prevent them from doing so. His gaming hours have been reduced to a more manageable three to four hours per day, down from the previous five to six hours, as part of his commitment to overcoming his challenges with alcohol.

I have heard stories where gaming addiction has destroyed marriages. However, in Nick's case, he enjoys and looks forward to playing a few hours every day. I could surmise that video games could be therapeutic and provide a healthy, challenging exercise for the brain.

And finally, Nick shared this story with me over lunch. He admitted to contemplating how he's going to strategize a game in his mind during the interview. He also mentioned that when he is losing, he sometimes gets frustrated. Isn't that just life?

3r: Smartphone Addiction:

Excessive and compulsive use of smartphones that interferes with daily life, relationships, work, and other important activities is referred to as "smartphone addiction," also known as problematic smartphone use or "smartphone overuse[174]." It can have a variety of negative effects on a person's well-being and ability to function. Due to blue light, it can contribute to sleep patterns being disrupted[175,176]. Eye strain is due to too-small fonts[177]. And bad posture might lead to neck pain[178].

Addicted to or obsessed with smartphones (as all cellular phones are considered "smartphones" today) is only a valid statement when it is associated with social media[179]. However, on the other hand, social media doesn't necessarily have to be accessed through a cellphone. In this scenario, the computer existed before the smartphone. With the capabilities of Wi-Fi and Bluetooth, both devices can be employed for similar functions; nevertheless, people typically don't develop addictions or obsessions related to making phone calls. Although messaging on a phone, with its mobility feature, can become an obsession for many[180].

While sitting in a lecture one day, I casually placed my cell phone on the empty seat beside me for easy reach. Throughout the hour-long session, I found myself frequently pressing the screen illumination button without much thought, whether to check the time or for messages. I am certain I also picked it up as many times, sometimes never looking at it. When I mentioned this to a friend, he compared it to a security blanket for so many.

The next time you are in a room full of people, take a look around and notice the number of people looking at their phones at the same time. On one occasion, I took notice of everyone in attendance immersed in their phones, and even a guy playing Candy Crush a few seats away. How did we let ourselves become so dependent on these devices?

When individuals consistently engage with their phones, typing and scrolling anytime, anywhere, they are inevitably satisfying their obsession with social media using their smartphone as the conduit. Smartphones are equipped with incredible features that simplify life[181]; they are a necessity for many, but they also come with numerous dangers. Several books cover the myriad ways cellular phones can impact your life[182]. However, it is crucial to emphasize that using your smartphone while driving or when strict attention is required is when it becomes most hazardous.

3s: Social Media Addiction:

Compulsively using Facebook, Instagram, Twitter (now called "X"), Reddit, and TikTok. This behavior entails continually monitoring, posting, or engaging with content on digital platforms, sacrificing real-life activities and well-being[183,184]. As people seek affirmation, validation, and comparison online, it can diminish productivity, strain relationships, cause mental health concerns, and distort self-worth[185,186]. Getting notifications on these apps' releases dopamine[187]. Avoiding social media addiction requires managing use (limiting the engagement, turning off notifications, etc.) and balancing offline life[188].

Social media outlets are not exclusively for the younger generation; they serve as dynamic marketing and advertising tools within the realm of goods and services, exhibiting an unparalleled impact in today's marketplaces[189]. The challenge does not lie in their utility for users; rather, it surfaces when individuals invest excessive time in unproductive and entertaining activities on these sites.

While these platforms offer a means for people to connect, they are often reduced to glorified gossip forums. This trend has become increasingly apparent, especially since the inception of the first true social media sites roughly twenty years ago, starting with Friendster[190], followed by Myspace, and eventually culminating in Facebook[191].

3t: FOMO Obsession:

The term FOMO, or "fear of missing out", first emerged as recently as 2004[192]. It has been extensively used since 2010 when it was linked to social media. This is viewed as a negative behavior disorder, hence the word "fear". People turn to social media to find out what they might not have been part of, "what they missed[193]." Missing something memorable is difficult to process for people with this disorder. CBT (Cognitive Behavior Therapy) is one treatment option[194].

FOMO, or the fear of missing out, is characterized by an intense desire to stay connected and involved in what others are doing, often driven by a fear of being left out or missing rewarding experiences. CBT (Cognitive Behavioral Therapy) helps individuals identify and challenge the negative thoughts and beliefs that contribute to FOMO[195,196]. This may involve recognizing irrational or unfounded beliefs such as "I must always be included," or "If I miss out, I'm a failure." Rather than conditioning yourself to believe that there are no consequences if you miss out on certain situations or events, it's important to acknowledge the potential outcomes realistically. Challenging yourself by gradually exposing yourself to FOMO triggers can help assess your reactions. While FOMO can indeed cause anxiety and insecurity for many, not everyone experiences it in the same way. There are various strategies discussed throughout this book for coping with anxiety and overcoming insecurity. FOMO is a personal experience, emphasizing the importance of focusing on your own feelings and not allowing others to dictate your expectations. CBT can also aid in improving social skills and assertiveness, fostering confidence in social situations, and reducing the constant need for validation or approval from others.

That Ship has Sailed

I remember the day well, as if it were yesterday, yet I wasn't even present. A good friend of mine was celebrating his sixtieth birthday, along with his wedding anniversary on the same ship he and his wife got married on thirty-one years ago. My friend likes to "go big," so what a gala event it was, but one I would have to miss.

You might remember, in May of 2018 I was at a treatment center in Atlanta for addiction. I had only been there for sixty days when I received my invitation. There were going to be almost 200 people on the boat, many I knew, and probably expecting to see me. There was no way I could miss this one; it was a once-in-a-lifetime event. But my counselors at the campus thought it would be unwise for me to go so early in recovery and advised me not to. A significant part of recovery from addiction is to "do what they say."

In my opinion, FOMO is unfounded and fabricated anxiety.

With FOMO (fear of missing out), I am not fearful or afraid of missing out; my "addiction logic" thinking is really saying, "I just want to be a part of the moment." I don't know exactly what the party will be like, nor will it ever be a memory for me, but so what? I always say in situations like this: "You won't miss what you missed." I have written before… if I fall asleep before the ball drops, it will be the start of a new year when I wake up.

From what I was told, everyone who attended my friend and his wife's celebration had a great time. Someday, my ship may come in, but today, I don't fear that I will miss any boat!

3u: Workaholic:

A "workaholic" is someone who is addicted to work, often spending excessive hours on it and neglecting other aspects of life like family, social activities, and personal well-being[197]. Workaholics are intensely dedicated to their work, finding it hard to disconnect even during leisure time. While dedication to work is generally positive, workaholism can result in burnout, strained relationships, health problems, reduced creativity, and an imbalance between work and personal life[198]. Striking a healthy balance is crucial for overall well-being.

In my years in business and with the people I've been around who might be considered workaholics, I've found they have two primary motivations for their actions: financial gain or ego boosts. Further in this book, I mention that ego is not a bad thing; however, as stated in this section regarding manias, an egomaniac is one with excessive ego[199]. Put otherwise, don't allow your diligence to take you to that level.

Both hard workers and workaholics alike strive to afford nice things. The concept of hard work and rewards is often associated with the capitalist model, the "American Way[200]." I've also noticed that not everyone who becomes a "workaholic" remains one forever. Sometimes people adopt the ways of a workaholic to reach material and psychological objectives. Once they have attained that degree of fulfillment, they are then able to slow things down.

Like the gamers who shared their stories for this book, there are individuals who simply enjoy what they do. In fact, they are not obsessed but rather satisfied by the work they perform or the games they play, much like an athlete who dedicates themselves to being the best for the love of the game!

I say many times throughout this book, "everyone's different." For the reasons listed above, I suppose I used to be a workaholic, but I live with a constant thirst for achievement now. I carry the constant need for accomplishment every day. It's just my way. When I don't get anything done or am not productive, I feel like I may have squandered a nice day. That must be what motivates me.

3v: Shopaholic:

A "shopaholic" is someone who has a compulsive and excessive desire to shop, often leading to extravagant spending and accumulating a large number of items, sometimes beyond their actual needs[201]. While these terms are commonly used and understood, it's essential to note that being a shopaholic can have negative consequences on one's health, relationships, finances, and overall well-being[202]. Achieving a balance between work, leisure, and spending habits is generally considered healthier for a person's overall lifestyle.

Before there was the internet, people would shop in person at retail stores for necessities and non-essential luxury items like jewelry, fashion, and home goods. But eventually, shopping by television broke through, where advertising drove the development of an entirely new industry[203]. Shop-from-home programming like HSN (Home Shopping Network) or QVC (Quality Value Convenience) was convenient and exciting, especially for housewives who could not work. They would see it on TV and dial the number on the screen to have it delivered, right from the comfort of their couch. Most times, it was impulse buying where no assessment was made to see if they even needed the product[204].

Does money burn a hole in your pocket that "stuff" fills?

This had become more than an obsession for some, to the point of sickness or addiction. Boxes would arrive by mail and begin to pile up, sometimes never being opened. They remained unopened because, on the day they were delivered, these patrons would already be in their place in front of the TV, as it was a new day and a new session to shop for more. This exercise provided everyday gratification by stimulating their brain's reward circuit. I compare it to the pursuit of something. I wonder how many items bought were eventually returned.

An even more inventive and practical method of making purchases emerged with the advent of the internet. Envision all the necessities arranged in a single location for easy comparison shopping: cost, accessibility, and helpful unbiased reviews to assist you in selecting the ideal goods, like having a copy of Consumer's Reports for everything[205]. It's exactly what we need—another lazy approach to accomplishing tasks. Today I've fallen into that trap by having things I can get online delivered the next day or so instead of accumulating a weekly list.

3w: Lying and Stealing:

People lie and steal for various reasons, and it's important to note that individual motivations can differ. Compulsive and pathological lying is frequently the result of an underlying mental health disorder. Individuals diagnosed with antisocial personality disorder are prone to manipulating or harming others without remorse, as well as committing dishonest acts of theft and deception[206]. The fundamental differentiation between compulsive and pathological lying pertains to the intrinsic motivation driving the former. Compulsive liars frequently do so out of anxiety or fear, sometimes attributed to low self-esteem or narcissism. On the other hand, pathological liars may lie with the intent of manipulating or deceiving others[207]. It is my conviction that individuals who engage in pathological lying for the sole purpose of personal gain are also inclined to steal for the same motive.

Certain individuals have difficulty managing impulsivity or impulse control. Individuals with disorders struggle to maintain control over their behavior. This deficiency in self-control may result in hasty, impulsive deception or theft. Illnesses characterized by challenges in impulse control, such as kleptomania or intermittent explosive disorder, may incorporate deceitful actions into their impulsive behaviors. People who are afflicted with addiction or compulsive behaviors may resort to deceit or theft as a means of financing their addiction. This is especially prevalent in instances involving substance abuse[208].

In certain circumstances, people may deceive or steal because they observe others engaging in such conduct and find it socially acceptable; they may also be influenced by peer pressure.

We Weren't Brought up This Way

Two brothers got together to catch up. It had been a while since they were reminded of their upbringing under the same roof. Honor and integrity were ingrained in everything they were taught to be. Lying, cheating, and stealing represented the most unacceptable behaviors. Yet today, the people running the world want you to believe it's alright to behave this way.

Compulsive liars can't help themselves; it is out of habit and driven by anxiety or insecurity that they lie. They find themselves unable to resist the urge to fabricate stories. In contrast, pathological liars exhibit a deliberate intent, lacking remorse, and often lie with a specific goal in mind. These individuals not only weave a web of deceit but also engage in thievery, reaping the benefits of other's hard work to enrich their own lifestyles. For pathological liars, dishonesty becomes a pervasive and convenient way of life. The prospect of telling the truth is overshadowed by the pain it brings, making evasion and manipulation their way of being. Accepting reality becomes an unbearable challenge for those who have succumbed to the compulsive nature of their lying. This behavior is indicative of a personality disorder, something acquired over time.

Unlike the addict who is born with the disease of addiction, I am able to be empathetic, so they may fix a problem they didn't ask for. However, when it comes to pathological liars and crooks making headlines, sympathy can only be withheld. Their affliction is self-inflicted, born out of a toxic blend of greed and selfishness, driven by an insatiable desire to exert control over all people.

In society, these individuals are afforded little leniency, as they willingly cultivate their own sicknesses at the expense of others. The distinction between those struggling with inherent challenges and those who purposefully manipulate and deceive underscores the need for accountability and consequences. As we navigate the complex landscape of human behavior, it becomes essential to differentiate between those who seek help for involuntary disorders and those who, through their actions, perpetuate a cycle of deceit and exploitation.

DEALING WITH THE DEPTHS OF DESIRE

*Managing the level of what interests us
is a testament to our restraint.*

Drawing upon the Introduction of this book and the opening text of the previous chapter (Chapter 3), much has been discussed about obsessions and addiction. On page 129, Fig. 2 illustrates how something that catches one's interest may escalate to the level of great addiction. Comparable to a graduated cylinder, each incremental level propels us nearer to despair.

In Chapter 3, I introduced a code to denote "classes of cravings", assigning a letter for each class or level of craving: 'A' for addiction, 'O' for obsession, 'H' for habit, and 'N' for necessity. Cravings represent what the body feels as it desires what drives an individual. If we contemplate this short list of identifiers, we could extend it to encompass anything that captures one's attention and holds interest.

Clinically speaking, psychology and addiction studies refer to the progression that leads to addiction as the "cycle of addiction" or the "stages of addiction." This cycle progresses from initiation, experimentation, regular use, dangerous use, dependence, and addiction. to progressively compulsive and destructive substance use or activity behaviors[209]. Not everyone passes through all levels, and the rate varies substantially.

During an interview with one of the gamers on page 84 ('Shoot to Win'), I learned a valuable insight into the progressions leading to addiction. People don't necessarily have to be addicted to something to enjoy it. The gamer in the story plays for hours after work; the key words being after work, as in not interfering with his job. I asked him, what happens if you are called to leave while playing a video game after work? He simply replied, "I put down the controller and go". Therefore, his gaming habits do not impede other responsibilities, whether preplanned or unexpected. We might conclude that he has a hobby, routine, or possibly a habit that compels him to play extensively. He insists, he just loves to play, prompting the question: what if his PlayStation were taken away? Would he experience withdrawal symptoms? Might he become angry enough to lead to an outburst? Considering his favorite games involve digital warfare, it raises pertinent concerns.

With addiction, the aim is often to eliminate addictive behavior to regain sanity and health. One method is by removing the elements of the addiction. This approach represents a positive step towards overcoming addiction or obsession. However, it also entails taking away the pleasure that keeps individuals satisfied.

Like the first gamer in Chapter 3, whose journey likely began with interests, desires, routines, and habits but halted there, individuals with addiction progress further, traversing a spectrum from compulsion to addiction.

What then is a compulsion?[210,211] It is a powerful, irresistible urge or impulse to engage in a specific action, often despite the awareness that it may be unnecessary or harmful. Compulsions play a significant role in the addiction process. As addiction advances, individuals often experience a compelling need to consume addictive substances like alcohol or heroin or engage in addictive behaviors such as gambling or sex.

You may recall from the preface that I am a member of an alcohol recovery program. You also know that the subtitle of this book is: "Treating the Cause, Not the Symptom." So when I hear one of the many juvenile statements made on a daily basis from other members, I wonder why it's even necessary to repeat them. For instance, the statement "I drink because I am an alcoholic" has become thought-provoking, especially for someone like me, who might say in this case, "am I missing something?"

After mining below the surface to gain a better understanding, I came up with the simple fact that consuming alcohol is how an alcoholic treats their alcohol dependency—by drinking alcohol. There's no other reason why an alcoholic would have a compulsion to drink. Now, the alcoholic may have their reasons depending on the circumstance, but alcohol is their only remedy when it comes to satisfying the physical cravings. Non-alcoholics don't drink out of dependency. This is almost so obvious that one might say "duh!"

Examining various addictions and classifications in depth reveals that there are no absolute, definitive ways to distinguish them. Many determinations are subjective in nature.

Chapter's Logical Take-Away: Only for some does the level of their interest in substances or activities top out as addiction. For others, the pure enjoyment they seek is all they desire. Knowing oneself and understanding our limitations are the keys to keeping oneself in check.

THE PERILS OF ILLICIT DRUGS

How could I possibly be an addict...?
I am very smart!

Substance Use Disorder (SUD), as it is now called (no longer substance abuse), should only refer to the abuse of legal substances[212]. Connecting the word "use" to any illegal drugs in this context makes no sense. "Illegal" means not legal or permissible, which overrides the term. While there is a substance involved and it is duly deemed a disorder, I don't believe it is inaccurate to classify legal drugs with illegal drugs or substances. Let's call it Illegal Substance Use Disorder (ISUD). This chapter details the addictive nature of the most well-known illegal drugs of this era.

<u>Controlled substances</u>: are drugs that are subject to high levels of regulation because of government decisions about ones that are especially addictive and harmful. There are five types, classes, or "Schedules" of controlled substances[213]:

- Schedule I (1)—Drugs with a high abuse risk. These drugs have NO safe, accepted medical use in the United States. Examples of Schedule I include heroin, lysergic acid diethylamide (LSD), marijuana (cannabis), 3,4-methylenedioxymethamphetamine (ecstasy), methaqualone, and peyote.

- Schedule II (2)—Drugs with a high abuse risk, but also have safe and accepted medical uses in the United States. Examples of Schedule II narcotics include hydromorphone (Dilaudid®), methadone (Dolophine®), meperidine (Demerol®), oxycodone (OxyContin®, Percocet®), and fentanyl (Sublimaze®, Duragesic®). Other Schedule II narcotics include morphine, opium, codeine, and hydrocodone.

- Schedule III (3))—Schedule III includes substances, drugs, pharmaceuticals, and chemicals that have a moderate to low potential to cause physical and psychological dependence. The potential for the abuse of these substances is higher than that of Schedule IV drugs but lower than that of Schedule I and Schedule II drugs. Examples of these might include anabolic steroids.

- Schedule IV (4))—Include drugs, substances, or chemicals are defined as drugs with a low potential for abuse and low risk of dependence. Examples of Schedule IV substances include alprazolam (Xanax®), carisoprodol (Soma®), clonazepam (Klonopin®), clorazepate (Tranxene®), diazepam (Valium®), lorazepam (Ativan®), midazolam (Versed®), temazepam (Restoril®), and triazolam (Halcion®).

- Schedule V (5)—Schedule V drugs, substances, or chemicals are defined as drugs with lower potential for abuse than Schedule IV containing limited quantities of certain narcotics. Schedule V drugs are generally used for antidiarrheal, antitussive, and analgesic purposes. Some examples of Schedule V drugs are: cough medicines with less than 200 milligrams of codeine or per 100 milliliters (Robitussin AC).

It is important to note that not all illicit drugs or substances, hereinafter referred to simply as "drugs," are inherently bad. Many were initially developed for medical purposes but became illegal due to misuse and abuse over the years. At the time of this publication, marijuana, and fentanyl, both of which have legitimate medical applications, are discussed as well-established illegal "street drugs" or "club drugs[214]."

While marijuana maintains legal status in 29 states and Washington, D.C[215]., on a state level, it remains prohibited under federal law and is widely employed for pain management, particularly among cancer patients. Fentanyl, on the other hand, is legally produced and distributed in the United States, but licit (legal) fentanyl pharmaceutical products are frequently diverted through theft, fraudulent prescriptions, and illicit distribution, involving patients, physicians, and pharmacists, according to the DEA (Drug Enforcement Administration)[216].

- Marijuana, one of the most widely misused illicit substances, owes its effects to THC (tetrahydrocannabinol), its principal psychoactive component, inducing temporary euphoria followed by drowsiness, lethargy, reduced reaction times, and heightened appetite[217]. The National Institute on Drug Abuse says marijuana can be addictive and is considered a "gateway drug" to using other drugs[218].
- Fentanyl, a potent opioid that is eighty times more potent than morphine, is used as a filler in illicit heroin. Due to this drug's extreme potency, even a minor dose adjustment can be fatal. Fentanyl, initially approved by the Food and Drug Administration for pain relief and anesthesia, is 100 times more potent than morphine and 50 times more potent than heroin as an analgesic[219].
- Cocaine is a powerful stimulant that is extracted from the leaves of the coca plant native to South America, typically found in the form of a fine powder. Crack cocaine, usually in solid blocks or crystals, is more effective than powder cocaine because it is smoked, allowing for faster absorption into the circulation. Cocaine is often

linked with illicit drug usage, however it is also utilized for medical purposes as a topical treatment in ear, nose, and throat (ENT) therapy[220]. This application aids in nasal surgeries, diagnostic procedures, and the management of nosebleeds.

- Ecstasy, embraced by numerous high-schoolers and young adults, serves as a quintessential party or rave drug[221], offering psycho-active experiences marked by heightened sensory perception and diminished inhibitions.

- PCP, mushrooms, and salvia exemplify the world of psychoactive substances, capable of altering the mind's perceptions[222]. LSD is included in this classification.

- LSD, lysergic acid diethylamide, is a psychedelic hallucinogenic drug derived from lysergic acid found in ergot fungus on grains. LSD is considered a semisynthetic drug. Hallucinogens change the way people sense the world around them[223]. It has no medical use and is considered a Schedule I drug.

I recall one of my elementary school science teachers in the early 70s saying something to the effect that one day LSD will be used in medicine due to its chemical make-up being the closest to the liquid in our nerve synapses.

- Heroin is an extremely addictive substance that is synthetically derived from the opium poppy plant. It comes in the form of white or brownish powder or as a black and sticky substance known as "black tar[224]."

- Inhalants encompass everyday household items, like spray paints, markers, and cleaning supplies, which are inhaled for their mind-altering effects[225]. This is commonly called "huffing."

- Ketamine ("special K"), originally intended for veterinary anes-thetic use, takes on a hallucinogenic guise when abused, provoking hallucinations, sedation, and confusion[226].

- Methamphetamine ("Meth") constitutes an extremely perilous stimulant with an instant addiction potential. Prolonged Meth use yields a litany of issues, including violent behavior[227], severe dental problems, cardiovascular complications, neurological damage, psychosis, and intense paranoia[228].

Chapter's Logical Take-Away: The susceptibility to addiction extends across a wide range of legal and illegal substances, suggesting that intelligence alone is insufficient to protect against the allure of addiction.

LEGAL DRUGS AND THEIR POTENTIAL FOR ABUSE

Legal drugs have legal limits.

In this chapter, much like the previous one, we explore the arena of medications, which this time includes both prescription and over-the-counter pharmaceuticals. When these substances are misused or abused, they can lead to a mood-altering or mind-altering state. For instance, when taken as prescribed, substances like Nyquil[229] should not lead to such effects. Manufacturers include disclaimers, warnings, and potential side effects to shield themselves in case of rare occurrences. For instance, doxylamine, an antihistamine in Nyquil, lends sedative effect.

These drugs earn their status as medicines by their capacity to treat various ailments. Nonetheless, their abuse, despite being lawful, can yield consequences similar to illegal substances. Certain components in common medicines are also present in illicit substances. It is difficult to manage abuse since over-the-counter (OTC) medicines do not require a doctor's prescription, making them convenient and appealing. With the ease and accessibility of the Internet today, and the ability to self-diagnose, people are treating the symptoms of their ailments and not the root causes without ever consulting a doctor. Some symptoms may overlap across multiple conditions. I have been saying for a while that you can get Google to give you any answer you are looking for. Self-medicating leads to ignoring underlying health issues. The common belief is that over-the-counter medications are risk-free because of their legal status and accessibility. However, long-term or repeated use might have detrimental consequences on vital organs.

Several years ago, I underwent lower back surgery. Upon waking up, I was prescribed Oxycodone and Percocet. I insisted that I wouldn't need them, and that a prescription wouldn't be necessary. The nurse advised me to have the prescription just in case. Knowing my high pain threshold, I reluctantly left with a few white squares of paper with illegible writing on them. Though I consider myself tough, who wouldn't be at least a little sore after being sliced open? I eventually caved, partly out of curiosity. In my upcoming book, *The Proof Is in the Pudding*, I discovered that one pill made me nauseous, and the other made me sleepy. This served as evidence that these pills were not suitable for me. Being the genius that I am (LOL), I researched both medicines and found that one (Percocet) contained Tylenol, which I already had at home. The amber prescription bottles just got bumped. I don't recall if I ever needed Tylenol, but I can certainly say that I never got hooked on opioids.

Chapter's Logical Take-Away: Legal drugs, both prescription and over the counter, can be abused when taken in ways that induce altered mental states like drowsiness. Ignorance, cost and accessibility, and peer pressure are some reasons for their abuse.

<u>**Popular Prescription Drugs Prone to Abuse**[230]</u>:

- Oxycodone (OxyContin)
- Codeine
- Fentanyl
- Meperidine (Demerol)
- Alprazolam (Xanax)
- Clonazepam (Klonopin) and diazepam (Valium)
- Amphetamine (Adderall)
- Methylphenidate (Ritalin)

THE LOGIC OF ADDICTION

Only you know if you have an addiction, sometimes you don't.

You can fake an orgasm, but you can't fake addiction. You can be less than addicted (on a healthy level), and overly drawn to anything that might really interest you, but this is not the same as full-blown addiction. Different classifications exist for varying levels of compulsion and the frequency of your desires.

If I am addicted to speed (adrenaline addiction), it's not the motorcycle, the car I'm driving, or the road I'm on; it's the rush I get from how fast I am going.

Similarly, if I am addicted to sex, the fixation doesn't revolve around a specific individual but rather centers on the act of sex, serving as the catalyst for heightened desires. The focus isn't necessarily on a particular person to satisfy my addiction but rather on the broader sexual experience, potentially involving different partners. It's crucial to note that emotions like love or infatuation for an individual don't inherently indicate sexual addiction. Nevertheless, within the realm of love, there exists the potential for fulfilling one's sexual needs.

Like the saying goes, "Too much of anything is not good for you." Certainly, this is the case with addiction, but seemingly good or bad, the proverb is without bias. If you are concerned with the frequency of a healthy activity or with anything that is good for you, that doesn't pose any danger. If you limit yourself, you will keep it in check from becoming obsessive and appreciate it more as a treat. I call it the "favorite song syndrome." I promise you that if you hear your favorite song every hour on the radio, it will soon fall off your charts. We get tired or bored with it after too much. That also happens with alcohol and drugs when our tolerance is elevated. We need an increased amount of stimulants to overcome the boredom of the same high.

The reason why it is so hard for the addict to stop drinking or doing drugs is because they know they can easily get high as soon as they have one drink or do a drug. This allows them to mentally escape from their feelings and quickly alter their mood. The active addict or alcoholic is already fixated on obtaining what they crave, almost salivating or experiencing a buzz (the anticipatory thrill) before even consuming the substance. These individuals are unwilling to invest a significant amount of time in naturally feeling good; their mindset revolves around seeking instant gratification. Moreover, the difficulty arises from the elusive nature of attaining the desired buzz or the ideal level of intoxication for the addict or alcoholic. What starts as a mere buzz eventually escalates to being thoroughly intoxicated, and very few aim to reach that extreme point. Furthermore, without any mood- or mind-altering chemical in my system, I am capable of accomplishing anything humanly possible. So, you can see the moral of the story.

Many people struggle with drug and alcohol abuse today. Complete abstinence from both substances is necessary for true sobriety. Drugs and alcohol—while they sometimes hit different neurotransmitters, they impact a brain's reward system—typically go hand-in-hand, making this difficult. To live drug- and alcohol-free, you must abstain from both.

There are people who are not alcoholics but still have reasons to stop drinking. They might be dealing with health conditions like diabetes or following a diet plan. Some could be athletes or have other medical concerns[231]. Additionally, as mentioned in Chapter 19, legal issues may necessitate abstaining from alcohol. Most importantly, alcohol is generally unhealthy for everyone.

We should also consider that there are people who participate in good, healthy activities to the point of excess and cannot stop despite hurting themselves both mentally and physically. I know a woman who is a passionate, dedicated street runner. She loves how it makes her feel mentally and what it is doing for her body, but the constant pounding of running on hard surfaces is damaging her joints and surrounding tissue. Yet, it's hard for her to walk away from her routine. Elliptical machines are a suitable option, but a TV can't replace the great outdoors.

Chapter's Logical Take-Away: Recognize the nature of addiction and the importance of acknowledging one's own addiction. Ideally, finding satisfaction without excess would be wonderful, but for addicts, this equilibrium can be elusive. It's a constant balancing act.

THE PERFECT BUZZ

*When a Porsche starts to slide out on a turn,
the only way not to lose control is to give it more gas.
That implementation is not easy to accomplish
when alcoholics start to lose their buzz.*

In my opinion, there can only be one type of person who truly chooses to get inebriated. Those who seek refuge from the harshness of overwhelming reality turn to forgetfulness. Some use alcohol to numb their feelings after experiencing a tragedy or traumatic occurrence; not everyone, but those who might not be mentally equipped to handle such situations take this easier way out[232]. Social drinkers and even those with an affinity for alcohol do not seek the state of being bombed and incoherent. Why would they? Where's the pleasure in a blackout?

We have been told that everyone drinks for the effect and that they like the euphoric or stress-reductive feeling they get from alcohol. I would go on to say that this holds true for anything that makes you feel good, be it drugs, gambling, or even sex, unless the experience turns unpleasant.

The problem for the person with addiction is that they can't control their appetite once they start. The social drinker might have two glasses of wine over a period and get a satisfying, relaxed feeling and be good with that. On the other hand, the problem drinker or alcoholic is unable to hold that line, succumbing to addiction. It becomes a balancing act for them; just add a little more when the good feeling begins to wane.

So, what's the allure of the buzz, anyway? Many wrestle with issues of insecurity, especially in matters of confidence and self-esteem, especially in the area of romance. Alcohol is a depressant that reduces anxiety, especially social anxiety around people. Its calming effect relieves stress, loosens us up, and reduces our inhibitions, which in turn takes away our fears. It can boost confidence, increasing people's willingness to participate in social or sexual activities[233].

There's nothing inherently wrong with enjoying a buzz from alcohol (provided you're not putting yourself or others in harm's way), but a buzzed alcoholic is only at the beginning of a path that inevitably leads to drunkenness.

After two swift Tanqueray and tonics, I'm already thinking I'm James Bond, clad in a tuxedo, and about to drive my Aston Martin. Alcohol became my voice and my ability to get the words out when I couldn't on my own. This is how alcohol got the nickname "liquid courage". But wouldn't it be great to be so comfortable with oneself and be able to do so without needing alcohol for courage altogether? I suppose the "perfect buzz" would be none at all.

You've all heard the phrase "take the edge off." Typically, this means to lessen the intensity, severity, or stress of something. For instance, people often say they need a drink to take the edge off after a stressful day, indicating that it helps them relax or alleviate some of the tension they're experiencing.

We are all part of the same species—homo sapiens—evolving for the last couple hundred thousand years, as we learned in school. Yet, no two individuals are identical, not even identical twins. This is why fingerprints and dental records serve as unique identifiers. We are distinct beings in countless ways, and our brains are no exception.

Our brain chemistry exhibits unique variations, influencing how we metabolize substances entering our circulatory system compared to others. Additionally, the reaction to these substances is influenced by our blood composition, including factors like food, minerals, or pre-existing chemicals. Consequently, I may metabolize alcohol differently than someone twice my weight, and my response to a foreign substance may vary, especially when the substance changes. The same goes for drugs. For instance, wine makes me tired quicker, gin makes me lively, and dark liquors make me ill.

As I mentioned earlier in this chapter, our inhibitions disappear the more we drink. Without fear, we are not in control. We tend to say things that are beyond bold and sometimes cause us more harm than good. Hence, a well-devised program for recovering from alcoholism becomes essential.

People's experiences with addiction are highly individual. You know the term "lightweight" when referring to someone who gets drunk quickly on a small amount of alcohol? Some physically larger individuals in stature have three drinks, and they lose it. They can't "hold their liquor.". And then there are men or women who are petite or skinny that can put them away and not seem affected by the large amounts of liquor they consume.

> **Chapter's Logical Take-Away:** The educated problem drinker or alcoholic knows that it's impossible to get drunk unless you take a drink. And so he also knows the "perfect buzz" is a thing of the past for them.

MAGIC WORDS OF ADDICTION

Not all words are created equal!

Nearly at the onset of my exposure to alcohol and substance abuse treatment, I was struck by the language used in the teachings. Ordinary words took on entirely new meanings within the context of "recovery." Over time, these words became what I affectionately referred to as "my magic words of addiction." They were just everyday words, now filled with a different message for those struggling with alcoholism and addiction. For example, with the word "boundaries;" in the conventional sense, we might envision walls, fences, or lines to separate spaces. In sports like football and basketball, boundaries define the playing field, and stepping out of bounds brings a halt to the action. Likewise, walls and fences typically separate properties. A boundary in a relationship is established to maintain a sense of personal and behavioral space. However, in the world of recovery, boundaries take on a different definition. Here, they often refer to mental barriers we fabricate in our minds, safeguarding us from venturing into areas where we remain vulnerable or spiritually unprepared (a topic I examine extensively in Chapter 67). If alcohol or drugs are our adversaries, then these boundaries dictate that we should avoid places where alcohol is served or where drug users may be present.

Throughout this book, I expound on their meanings within the specific context in which they appear. And if you're just curious, I have put together some charts of these words and their recovery meanings in the back section of this book.

Chapter's Logical Take-Away: Today, I don't profess to teach conventional lessons; rather, I offer memory aids like these to those willing to note, tools that I've devised for my own benefit and for those on the path to recovery. As I've always maintained, "If what I say is unrelatable, then it's useless information."

THE SUBSTANCE ADDICTION CYCLE – SIMPLIFIED.

*Remember when the funhouse
was fun, until you got lost.*

On the surface, most people might assume obsession and craving imply the same meaning. However, in the context of addiction, there exists a clear distinction between the two, which comes down to order.

Obsession, or obsessing over something, involves the intrusion of unwanted, fleeting thoughts, images, or impulses in the mind. The feeling of pull. The crucial point here is that they are "unwanted;" they simply pop into your head[234]. This marks the initial phase.

With craving, there is an intense desire for a specific object, substance, or experience. But before whatever it is that you crave, it has to be introduced to the body first. This agitates the allergy in the body of an addict, or, as some prefer to call them, a person with addiction.

This is where it becomes a balancing act. When the obsession develops, the brain relays, "having a beer is a good idea." Following the brain's decision, the person drinks the beer, resulting in a change in brain chemistry and a temporary sense of happiness caused by the alcohol in the beer. You may begin by saying you'll have just one drink, but after that initial one, a different version of you orders the second, the version exhibiting dominance over the rationality. With each subsequent drink, our state of mind becomes progressively altered. So, in the case of the alcoholic, if one beer feels good, then another must surely make him feel much better. I believe that if there was a formula that could bring all drinkers to that perfect level of intoxication and hold them there, alcoholics might not exist. Non-alcoholics find one drink satisfying.

We chase unsustainable happiness when we use liquor or substances to take us there. What we really should be after is contentment and peace of mind, which doesn't come in any bottle or package.

In a typical brain, alcohol is metabolized into simple sugars. This form doesn't trigger any desire for more alcohol. But for the alcoholic "brain," the alcohol is converted into acetone, a solvent similar to nail polish remover. Acetone persists in the brain for an extended period, altering neural pathways and provoking a strong urge for more alcohol.

They don't crave another, nor do they "future trip" or dream about drinking liquor. But everyone is different, so everyone metabolizes alcohol at a different pace. The issue arises when, while the body is processing the alcohol, cravings emerge in an attempt to sustain the pleasurable sensation by adding more alcohol before the "buzz" fades. This forms a three-part cycle: the obsession of the mind, the allergy of the body, and the craving of the mind; then it repeats[235]. As I've mentioned in the past, for alcoholics, this cycle only ends when the liquor supply runs out, they pass out, or, sadly, they die.

Sustained treatment and ongoing recovery efforts can play a pivotal role in effectively managing alcoholism and averting relapse in the long run[236]. While there might not be a straightforward "cure" for alcoholism, as addicts might still relapse chronically or due to genetic factors, the condition is treatable when addressed.

Chapter's Logical Take-Away: Often used interchangeably, obsession and craving are different in addiction. It really comes down to wants and needs. An easy way to see the difference is to plug in these words into something you desire. "I want" or "I would like to have." If anything you desire fits with this equation, it is an "obsession." For instance,

1. I would like a fit body.
2. I would like to be successful.
3. I want to be in a long-term relationship.
4. I would like to be liked more.
5. I would like more nice things.
6. I want to make the New York Times Best Sellers List someday.

Now with cravings, try the words "I need" or I must have" in the model.

1. I need a cigarette.
2. I have to have a drink.
3. I need to be loved.
4. I need a vacation.
5. I need money to pay my bills.
6. I have to get in shape.
7. I need to eat French fries.

DOPAMINE – "THE HAPPY HORMONE"

"Love Is the Drug" —Roxy Music

opamine is a neurotransmitter, or simply a chemical messenger. It is released in the brain to carry feel-good messages throughout the brain and body. People with obsessions and addictions experience that "good" feeling when the dopamine starts flowing. It flows when stimulated, which is at the anticipation of engagement of your addiction or obsession. There is a great deal of science behind brain chemistry and the neurotransmitters and the nervous system, but for our purposes here, the dopamine release is as direct result of the introduction of a DOC (drug of choice)[237]. And mind you that "drug" can metaphorically be any addiction, "… is my drug."

People dependent on substances such as nicotine, cocaine, and alcohol, as well as those addicted to activities such as video gaming, sex, eating, shopping, and exercise, all engage in these behaviors to stimulate the release of dopamine. The dopamine release, or flow, travels down the reward pathway in the brain to provide pleasure. Adrenaline addiction[238] (for thrill-seeking individuals) is another hormone that increases blood flow and heart rate and may also be present in the rewards process. The addicted or obsessed gambler's rewards are met even if they are losing. They experience the ever-popular "adrenaline rush," similar to the dopamine flow or release. Even in the near-misses, gambling addicts still feel the rush.

Everyone has these neurotransmitter hormones, which play an important role in many body functions in everyday life. Dopamine is one neurotransmitter whose role is crucial in various brain functions, including mood regulation, reward, and pleasure. Many drugs, including alcohol, can directly or indirectly impact dopamine levels in the brain. Prolonged addiction can diminish the brain's production of dopamine, and it needs to be balanced. People with ADHD often have low dopamine levels.

For the "non-addict," dopamine still plays an important role in the brain's reward system. Everyone needs dopamine to survive. It dates back to Homo sapiens, as they needed to repeat certain activities like finding food, shelter, and reproducing. All for survival. Its role might be to deliver positive emotions, from the pride of a job well done to the happiness of quality time spent with friends and family. Even in the absence of addictive behaviors, dopamine can encourage people to pursue objectives and engage in activities that enhance well-being and enjoyment.

> **Chapter's Logical Take-Away:** Dopamine is a neurotransmitter linked to pleasure and reward sensations in the brain. It is released during addictive or obsessive behaviors, like substance abuse, leading to feelings of fulfillment and often accompanied by an adrenaline rush. In non-addicts, dopamine enhances positive emotions and motivation, encouraging engagement in activities that enhance well-being and happiness.

OBSESSION VS. ADDICTION

*Obsession is a thought that overrules
(TRUMPS—had to say it!) all thoughts.*

Obsession can be described as a relentless fixation that takes precedence over all other thoughts. When we discuss obsession in relation to addiction, we find that obsessions are typically the conscious desires for a particular object or experience[239]. An obsession becomes an addiction when these abnormal feelings for something are acted upon in an unhealthy pattern or routine. Obsession is like a constant gnawing presence in your brain. However, if you manage to divert your thinking and free your mind, it still might remain excessive or persistent, yet not necessarily problematic. However, it can become a habit, which is something that we find hard not to think about. On the other hand, though, addiction takes it to the next level; it's the inability to function without fulfilling that need. It becomes the foremost thought in your mind, and redirecting your focus seems extremely difficult, if not impossible.

Obsession and addiction might exhibit similar behaviors and thought processes, but their roots are different. Take gambling, for instance. A person who gambles every week, spending roughly $10 on lottery tickets, can exhibit both obsessive and addictive tendencies. The obsessive aspect lies with the compulsive need to gamble at the same store, on the same day, with the same numbers—any deviation is seen as a hinderance to winning. Past wins don't matter; it's all about adhering to a specific routine. On the other hand, the addictive part revolves around daydreaming about how the winnings will be spent, what will be purchased, and who will benefit from the windfall. This maladaptive daydreaming is engaging, enticing, thrilling, and can consume an entire day with thoughts of possibilities. When you're addicted, you can become irritable when you can't physically satisfy the desire on your own terms. With addictions, you may experience both physical and mental withdrawal, whereas with obsessions, you might simply miss what you obsess over.

Consider your first drink—it's a conscious decision unless alcohol or drugs are already in your system, causing a physical craving. Otherwise, it starts as an obsession in your thoughts. If you experience symptoms like delirium tremens (DT's), characterized by shaky hands[240] due to withdrawal, this is an indication your body is desperately craving more. It's your body's response to adjusting to the absence of alcohol, and at this point, detox (or detoxification) might be necessary if you've chosen to break free from addiction. Alternatively, you might choose to drink more to satisfy the body's demand for alcohol and stop the shaking. The choice is yours to make.

Chapter's Logical Take-Away: Obsession is a persistent, overpowering thought or desire that typically involves ritualistic behavior. Addiction is an uncontrollable urge to continue a substance, activity, or behavior despite being aware of its negative effects.

CHAPTER 13

INTRODUCTION TO THE PROGRESSION OF ADDICTION

Just because it's appealing doesn't mean it's good for you.

Addiction, a compulsive propensity towards an activity or substance that provides pleasure and enjoyment, isn't limited to just alcohol or drugs, as discussed in Chapter 2.

Some individuals find themselves compulsively drawn to video gaming, shopping, or even sex. It's crucial to recognize that addiction is not merely a habit; it's a medical condition, similar to an illness or disease, necessitating proper treatment and therapy.

Just as addictions are not all the same, so too are the people who have them. One thing we do know is that addiction is a progressive disease. In most cases, addiction takes root gradually. As I've indicated in fig. 2, from my own personal experience, addiction may only begin as a "curiosity." This initial curiosity can evolve into a deeper interest, leading detrimentally to regular engagement and habitual behavior.

The next progression on this route is obsession. You see, there is a fine line that separates obsession from the addicted that is fear vs. pleasure. Obsessions are ritualistic routines generated by fear, as I interpret it, to alleviate anxiety.

With addictions, participation would be purely for pleasure and involve dopamine release in the brain. These compulsive actions are designed to provide pleasure by changing the way you feel.

Addiction is a chronic disease or long-term condition[241], in contrast to acute or short-term diseases like influenza or the common cold. The central term associated with addiction is "dependency.[242]" Just as a "curious" proposition can lead to addiction, once you find yourself at that juncture, seeking help becomes a very wise idea.

> **Chapter's Logical Take-Away:** Addiction includes everything from shopping to sex, video gaming, and pornography, as well as drugs and alcohol. It progresses from idle curiosity to sporadic consumption, deeper exploration, habit, obsession, and, ultimately, addiction if left untreated.

Addiction Disorder Progression
INTERESTED
CURIOUS
ADDICTION
OBSESSION
HABIT FORMING

Fig.2

THE FAR-REACHING IMPACT OF OBSESSION AND ADDICTION

Alcohol doesn't kill ... alcoholism does!

It is not necessary to possess a degree in medicine or psychology to know that abuse of alcohol or drugs, illicit or legal, or anything addictive is unhealthy and thus ultimately harmful. The effects of addictive and obsessive behaviors imply physical, psychological, and socially unfavorable outcomes, sometimes ending with death[243]. It is often said that my disease is trying to kill me. That's silly! Many have the potential to kill, but it's your brain and your body that keep asking for the lethal amount (or dose) that can kill.

Both alcohol and drugs have the potential to cause significant, irreversible harm to the human body, both through their physiological effects and the broader societal repercussions of their misuse[244]. Understanding the lethal and harmful consequences of substance abuse is crucial for individuals and communities.

Having an obsession or obsessing over something is an unhealthy, extreme interest in it, with a focus on one particular person, thing, or activity. This is not to be confused with having obsessive behavior.

In my case, I was consumed by an obsession with collecting vintage guitar amplifiers, which, in hindsight, bordered on passion and eventually transformed into an expensive hobby. The term "obsessive" is used to describe someone who is generally over-controlling, compulsive, fanatical, overzealous, extreme, neurotic, etc., or someone who focuses on particular things to an extreme level. For the person with OCD (obsessive compulsive disorder) perfectionism makes it difficult to reach satisfaction[245]. Take "neat freaks (cleanliness)", for example. And fear of not being satisfied affirms the disorder. I have OCD, so you could say that I am a "perfectionist". I can hang a large picture on the wall and spot a "tilt" of just half an inch from twenty feet away. OCD is a mental disorder, one that I've grown somewhat comfortable with. I believe there is a correlation between OCD and creativity. Additionally, those who are obsessed often exhibit a degree of superstition, relying on lucky items like hats or jewelry for peace of mind and comfort. Thank God I don't have that going for me. When it comes to addiction to substances, the consequences can carry a heftier price tag. The physiological effects can lead to impaired judgment, reflex response, increased risk of accidents, and falling injuries due to loss of coordination, which could all lead to an untimely death[246]. John Bonham, former drummer with Led Zeppelin, died from an overdose on a half-gallon of vodka. The cause of death was alcohol poisoning[247]. Notable musicians like Jimi Hendrix, Jim Morrison, Dennis Wilson (The Beach Boys), Keith Moon (The Who), Jerry Garcia, Amy Winehouse, and Janis Joplin are just a few of the countless numbers who met their demise due to addiction-related causes.

Prolonged substance abuse can result in severe organ damage. For instance, alcohol abuse can cause cirrhosis of the liver, a wet brain, and pancreatitis, while drug abuse can damage the heart, lungs, and kidneys[248]. A woman I know was slowly killing herself with excessive binge drinking. You might think that prolonged dying seems no worse than prolonged hair loss until it starts happening to you. The thing about being an addict or alcoholic is that they continue to use and drink despite knowing how much damage they are doing to themselves.

With all the symptoms and evidence at her feet, she unwillingly had to come to terms with the fact that she was a "real alcoholic." But the big wakeup call came when someone said, "you are going to develop a wet brain." This condition can lead to brain damage and possible death. In other words, you may suffer for the rest of your life due to your alcoholic drinking pattern—and no one likes to suffer from anything.

Since addiction is fundamentally a mental disorder, one of the most significant dangers of alcohol and drug consumption is the potential for addiction. We know substance abuse (drugs or alcohol) is a progressive disease. Continuous use can permanently rewire the brain's reward system, leading individuals to become dependent on these substances for a sense of normalcy. Substance abuse is also closely linked to mental health disorders such as anxiety, depression, and psychosis[249]. These conditions can worsen over time, negatively impacting an individual's overall well-being and, as a result, those around them. Both alcohol and drugs can impair decision-making and judgment. This can lead to risky behaviors, such as driving under the influence or engaging in unsafe sexual practices, increasing the likelihood of accidents and exposure to diseases. Substance abuse often strains relationships with family and friends, leading to isolation, which can exacerbate mental health issues and potentially lead to self-destructive behaviors.

And lastly, of all the bad decisions made while under the influence, or influenced by drugs and alcohol, if you will, the ones that haunt us most are the ones that result in legal consequences, including arrest, imprisonment, and a criminal record, and sometimes estrangement with our loved ones as well[250]. These consequences can significantly impact our livelihood, social status, and even how we navigate the world.

Chapter's Logical Take-Away: Obsession and addiction to substances or behaviors cause harm. They destroy relationships, families, and society through legal and psychological issues. The effects extend beyond drugs and alcohol, permeating all aspects of life.

SECTION 2
ADDICTION MANIFESTATION

CONTROVERSIES AND CRITICISMS – ADDICTION ALLERGY

Quite simply, raw nuts never got me high!

An allergy is an abnormal reaction to a foreign substance (also known as an allergen) in the body[251]. This includes both good reactions and bad reactions. A bad reaction would be a bee sting, poison ivy or oak, or food allergies like shellfish and nuts[252]. Allergies can also extend to medications like penicillin. But an allergy can have a good or favorable reaction (at first) like drugs or alcohol[253]. However, your brain's chemistry undergoes a transformation. Your tolerance or breaking point increases, and your brain craves higher doses for stimulation, leading to either a positive or negative reaction[254].

Over the years, science has disapproved of this theory. In 1952, Robinson and Dr. Walter L. Voegtlin published the definitive study on the allergy theory of alcoholism titled "Investigations of an Allergic Factor in Alcohol Addiction" in the *Quarterly Journal of Studies on Alcohol*[255]. Robinson and Voegtlin's experiments were definitive: alcohol addiction is not the result of an allergy or alcohol antibodies. In his book *The Disease Concept of Alcoholism*, published in 1960, E. M. Jellinek pronounced the allergy theory dead as a doornail[256]. Despite this, AA has continued to support the notion that alcoholism is "an allergy of the body and an obsession of the mind," despite the scientific evidence[47].

Simply put, allergies are one of the most common chronic diseases that involve a dysfunctional immune system. They occur when a person reacts to substances in the environment that are harmless to most people. Alcoholism and substance abuse are progressive diseases; however, allergies are not. It is possible to outgrow an allergy when the body builds up a tolerance for the allergen causing the allergy. The tolerance associated with alcohol and drugs is different. Think of those tolerances as thresholds. When the threshold level is met, the body basically raises the bar, needing more to be satisfied. That is the progression of the diseases of alcohol and substances.

I've always found it perplexing – if you're allergic to something, why would you repeatedly expose yourself to it? For example, I know that I am allergic to raw nuts. I also know what happens when I ingest them. My gums swell and my windpipe constricts, making it difficult to breathe, so I remember to never, ever eat them! The same logic applies to other foods that I know I am allergic to.

I once spoke to someone who was allergic to strawberries and couldn't understand why they didn't crave them like they did alcohol. My response was straightforward: "Strawberries don't get you drunk or high." You don't get that euphoric feeling from them like you do with drugs and alcohol, which release dopamine and serotonin.

While certain foods might tantalize my taste buds, my body's immune system rejects them due to my allergy. In contrast, drugs and alcohol trigger a contented feeling in my brain's reward pathway as the substances travel through my bloodstream. I suppose the reward or sensation I experience from drugs and alcohol can't easily be substituted or replicated. However, when it comes to raw nuts or shellfish, I have other choices.

> **Chapter's Logical Take-Away:** The theory that alcoholism is caused by an allergy is untrue. Alcoholism and substance abuse are progressive diseases with ever-increasing tolerance levels. These tolerances are not the same as allergies, as they require larger amounts of the substance to achieve satisfaction and push the threshold, representing the progression of the disease.

THE PROGRESSION OF OBSESSIONS AND ADDICTION

When that feeling you bargained for is no longer, it's beyond its level of usefulness.

If you have an addiction or obsession, whatever it is, you don't have to be in direct contact with it for the cycle of insanity to begin and consume you. When the thought of being satisfied enters your mind, your brain becomes stimulated, and dopamine is released[257]. Just as the thought of a delicious steak or the anticipation of intimacy can stimulate you, it's the dopamine release that's at play with substances like cocaine, nicotine, or alcohol. All this begins in your brain, the command center of your body. Every decision your body makes gets a green light from your brain. Despite the cravings, your throat never said, "let's get drunk," and your nose never said, "let's get high." Your brain is the ultimate decision-maker, the Chief

Operating Officer (COO) of your being. No action is taken without my brain's approval.

In twelve-step programs, they talk about admitting we were powerless over our addiction, and that our lives have become unmanageable[258]. That to this day is the greatest reminder of my addiction with my program of recovery, and it should be everyone's. But as important as that statement is, there is a catch. "Were" and "that" imply, from past experience, that I already know I am powerless and that my life is already unmanageable. Which means I am *not* powerless, nor is my life unmanageable unless I give way to my addiction. I didn't walk into recovery knowing I was powerless and not in control. That's just where a new life of sobriety would begin. Once I "poke the bear" it's already too late for me. So, like they also say in the program, "Just don't drink no matter what" (easier said than done, right?), or whatever your addiction is, and you won't have to reach unmanageability.

The first time you engage in anything that gives you pleasure in the form of a rush; the likelihood of a second round is great. We are creatures of habit, so be careful; too many revisits too often turn into addictive habits. I have said that habits are bad and that regimens are good. You know, "bad habit" and "healthy regimen." Don't let a new pleasure become an unhealthy habit, because the next progression is obsession or even addiction. When you obsess over anything, your mind becomes preoccupied with the object of your obsession, thus dividing your ability to focus and think clearly[259]. With substances that include alcohol, the pathway to addiction doesn't take on the role of an obsession but may include different levels of consumption, which may eventually lead to one being addicted. Obsessed or addicted (including alcoholic), you are not the most you can be. Even those who are said to be "functioning" addicts or alcoholics are not functioning at their best. I have often said, "If you have something in your system, or occupying your mind, you can do better without it."

Chapter's Logical Take-Away: Addiction begins with the excitement, rush, and thrill of remembering past pleasures, leading to obsession and eventually addiction. It's all about the brain releasing "happy" chemicals like serotonin, dopamine, and endorphins when frequently exposed to a rewarding stimulus.

UNCOVERING ROOT CAUSES

If you haven't a solution,
you haven't dug deep enough.

What exactly is going on in terms of your addiction or obsession? To begin treating any disorder, it is necessary to dig deep beneath the surface to truly understand the extent of the problem. To effectively address any disorder, you must confront its underlying, deep-seated origins, not just scratch the surface. This is the first step toward overcoming any fundamental problems that exist. While genetics or heredity can account for a significant portion (50–70%) of addiction cases, it is necessary to recognize the potential influences of childhood upbringing (including trauma, abuse, and neglect), environment, and peer pressure, as they too may have a role in the development and progression of your current disorder[260]. Regardless of the specific addiction one faces, excessive behavior indicates underlying issues such as boredom, loneliness, chronic depression, or self-esteem struggles.

For instance:

- Excessive tanning may stem from self-esteem issues. The same issues are faced by those who excessively filter their photos to present their idealized version to the world.
- Being a "gym rat" may also reflect self-esteem concerns.
- Shopping in excess often arises from boredom.
- Overindulging in electronic gaming may be a response to boredom.
- Eating disorders are frequently linked to depression.
- Alcoholism can be associated with depression, much like drug addiction.

These excessive behaviors, driven by the endless pursuit of dopamine release, are fixable. Therapy, counseling, support groups, learning through reading and writing, willpower, mindfulness practice, and the substitution of healthier habits (like regular exercise) can all help in correcting these unhealthy patterns[261]. Just as nicotine gum and patches aid in overcoming smoking addiction[262], methadone treatment serves as a substitute for heroin dependency[263]. Those with shopping or gambling addictions can find solace in new hobbies or activities that divert their focus. In order to solve any problem, you should first look at the most glaring symptom present. I always think of a symptom as an indicator or sign of what you can assess on your own. If you want to remove a brown spot from an apple, start by removing a small amount from the afflicted area (for example a bruise), and then gradually increase the amount removed until no more layers of overripened apple remain. You've sliced to the core of the matter without having to toss the entire apple. Similarly, if you have a persistently runny nose, a box of tissues won't stop it from running. The first step in this instance is to identify the root cause of the symptom (in this case, the stuffy nose, or other underlying symptoms) and treat that. When the root of the issue is determined, treatment can begin. If these don't work, an antibiotic may be prescribed in addition to bed rest, water, and vitamin C. Just as with tissues, cold medicine might be a "quick fix" if you need it.

Troubleshooting is a process rooted in logic. It involves eliminating potential issues systematically. When your car refuses to start, a mechanic begins with the battery, then checks the fuse, then the starter, then perhaps the regulator, and so forth. Each component is examined methodically, using appropriate tools to identify the problem. A battery tester, a voltmeter, and a visual inspection may simplify the process.

If there is a broken connection or loose wire on a PCB (printed circuit board), nothing will come out on the other end. We have to troubleshoot the whole operation.

When dealing with depression accompanied by signs of an eating disorder, the symptoms of your depression might be evidenced by an abnormal change in the shape of your body. Logically, here, you would work backwards from an obvious eating disorder to the depression that caused the eating problem, tracing the origin of the process to what brought on the depression. Unlike the car that wouldn't start as mentioned above, the elimination process would go in reverse order. The body shape has changed—what caused the eating disorder to arise in the first place? Because if you are depressed, what are you dealing with that makes you depressed? And so on … Ya know, a good mechanic might check the water level of the battery, but a better one knows that even a good battery doesn't crank enough when it's negative ten degrees Fahrenheit!

To get to the bottom of anything, it's best to go back to the earliest recollection of where and when it all began and work from there. That's what doctors and psychotherapists all do.

Chapter's Logical Take-Away: Addiction, obsession, and related disorders require treatment at their roots for effective resolution. Symptoms are merely indicators; addressing the underlying issue is crucial to solving any problem.

THE PURPOSES OF RECOVERY

*AA doesn't save you from alcoholism ...
it saves you from yourself.*

So, let's look at what caused such a mess. It wasn't the drugs or the alcohol. Nor the long streak of unfavorable odds at the casino or the bad luck at the racetrack. It wasn't even the insane credit card bills from shopping or all the cigarettes reduced to smoke. It was the actions or consequences that were caused by addiction or obsession. But no matter how you got to this place, you had a choice: to be here or not. The fallout from substance abuse might involve jail time, the loss of a driving license, having to find new employment elsewhere, or losing control of your family. In other areas, perhaps you're spending an inordinate amount of time at the gym or glued to a gaming controller most of the day. Maybe you're just girl- or guy-crazy and find yourself watching sex rather than playing an active part in a relationship you committed to. This is unhealthy behavior and should be addressed immediately.

Recovery programs, or "mental restoration" as I like to call it, sometimes land in the laps of those fortunate ones as a form of punishment for their misjudgments and misdemeanors. Treatment centers, support groups (Anonymous groups), and classes provide preventative rehabilitation. If you've been given a second opportunity and enrolled in a program to safeguard your job, family, or physical and mental well-being, neglecting it could result in losing the very things that hold the most significance to you. Your level of truly wanting to learn how to overcome your addiction or obsession comes from your mindset. If you're mandated by law and only in the program to fulfill that obligation, your outcome may reflect just that—an obligation fulfilled. But you may also be the type of person who is here for that very same reason, who just happens to be the studious type and is intrigued by what is being taught at those centers. In that case, these are the people who are often more open-minded and willing to learn what makes their addiction a ticking time bomb and are determined to find lasting solutions to their problems. I came into AA as a human being with a problem with addiction, and I am leaving as a human being better off. An improved person.

Chapter's Logical Take-Away: The decision to enter rehab (or rehabilitation) often represents a second chance at life. Individuals who approach it with an open mind and a desire to learn and fix their past mistakes are more likely to succeed. The focus of recovery is on mental healing, often met with physical resistance at the start, and regaining control over one's life.

BEHIND THE WHEEL

Maybe once you just got lucky?

have talked about that one-time-only DUI (driving under the influence)[264], or DWI (driving while intoxicated in my era)[265], offender who might not have a drinking problem but, in fact, perhaps unknowingly, made a mistake in poor judgement. I say unknowingly, because that's what happens when you drink more than your body can safely process. Consequently, you are unable to accurately calculate your mental state of mind and physical condition. The offense of driving under the influence carries a form of punishment, and rightly so. This type of blunder in action cannot be undone but can be learned from so as not to repeat it in the future.

It is not uncommon for those who drink to get tipsy (or just for the heck of it) on occasion. Listen, AA got it right when they said, "Men and women drink essentially because they like the effect produced by alcohol ...." However, even the sought-after tipsy state falls under the category of "buzzed driving is drunk driving," highlighting the impact alcohol can have on one's state of mind and providing a deluded sense of ability. This is what alcohol does to you. On the other hand, some individuals drink and drive frequently without ever getting caught, and perhaps that's too bad. It's better to get caught than to have it end in tragedy. One-time offenders often find themselves in situations like office parties, since we crave social interactions, Christmas celebrations, weddings, and similar events where alcohol is readily available. The temptation to join in the celebration is strong, but if you receive your first DUI, you'll be surprised by the significant financial costs involved. Moreover, this doesn't even account for the shame in society and its potential impact on your employment.

Even while treatment centers may serve a disciplinary purpose, their true intention is to provide rehabilitation for patients who are willing to give up excessive alcohol.

> **Chapter's Logical Take-Away:** First-time DUI/DWI offenders may not have a drinking problem but made a bad decision due to alcohol.

A COSTLY PRESCRIPTION

The agony proved unbearable,
yet when the pain stopped,
so should the pills.

Remember what was said earlier about drinking … "they like the effect produced by alcohol"?

This tale revolves around an unfortunate predicament involving pain medications. Similarly, those who misuse or abuse any substance, whether legal or illicit, do so with the intent to alter their emotional state. In the context of alcohol and substance recovery programs, this is often described as "mood and mind-altering[266]."

The objective is to shift your mood from being down to feeling up (gradually but not exponentially), or up to an even higher point. I used the term "misuse," but this was not always the initial intention, particularly in cases involving injuries. Painkillers block the pain and numbness in the brain as well.

Your brain feels the pain, your body doesn't. When you have a high tolerance (or threshold) for pain, it means your brain has a high tolerance for pain, similar to the concept of tolerance with addiction.

I have met many people in recovery who are hooked on pain meds that were prescribed after a physical injury or surgery. This is a sad and unfortunate happening for those who didn't bargain for an addiction post-accident.

20a: This Was Not the Plan at All

Almost everyone I have encountered who is addicted to opioids, commonly known as pain pills, developed this dependency while recovering from an injury or surgery. Take—we'll call him "Gunther"—for instance, an individual injured on the job. Gunther diligently followed his doctor's instructions, including a pain medication regimen. The prescription initially called for 120 pills per month of OxyContin at a dosage of 40mg per day, a routine that continued for four years due to the chronic nature of his back pain resulting from the injury.

However, the situation worsened. After only a few months, the prescribed 40mg per day of OxyContin was no longer effective for Gunther. He built up a tolerance for the medicine, and he now required a higher dosage to function. At this point, he had become addicted and had to obtain additional pills beyond his monthly prescription to satisfy his addiction. The medication was no longer merely a means to alleviate pain but had become a necessity to maintain the "high" it provided.

The disability money he received was now being used to sustain his "drug habit." Unable to afford the escalating costs of OxyContin on the street, Gunther turned to heroin, a more cost-effective alternative. Eventually, he found himself using both heroin and his prescribed OxyContin. The pursuit of the "high" became a daily compulsion, leading him to experiment with other drugs like methamphetamine ("meth") and crack. Gunther had descended into the life of a junkie, a stark contrast to the original intent of the doctor's prescription for pain relief.

However, the story takes a positive turn. After reaching the depths of despair and surviving several suicide attempts, Gunther decided to seek help and checked himself into a hospital. This decision led to various short stays at treatment centers, eventually finding the support he needed through 12-step meetings. Today, Gunther has his own place and has been free from all mood- and mind-altering substances for nearly two years. While his journey is lengthy, this outcome is not guaranteed for all who face similar challenges. Having encountered many "Gunthers" over the years, addict, or non-addict, he remains the decent person he was always meant to be. After hearing his story, I can confidently say that I am proud of him and grateful to know him today.

Several years ago, after undergoing lower back surgery, I awoke to find myself connected to a morphine drip. I instructed the nurse to disconnect the IV hose because I didn't like the feeling it spread throughout my body. The next morning, I left with a prescription for 60 Percocet and 60 Oxycodone. In a cavalier way, I had told the doctor they wouldn't be necessary, but he replied, "Just fill the prescription just in case the pain is too much." I relented, but only wound up taking 1 of each. One made me tired, the other made me nauseous. But I had another thing working in my favor. I have a very high threshold for pain, and besides, I know myself and I'm aware of the risks of getting hooked on these pills. Other people who get addicted to pain medicines might not have the same tolerance for pain or the awareness of knowing themselves as I do.

> **Chapter's Logical Take-Away:** This is tricky because pain hurts, and anything that removes the pain is worth trying. Unfortunately, "painkiller" medications, especially addictive ones like narcotics, tend to be misused when the pain is gone but a newly developed desire for effect increases.

HOW MUCH DO YOU DRINK?

*If your drinking causes you problems
and you still continue to drink,
then you have a drinking problem.*

Not everyone who drinks on a regular basis is an alcoholic. Alcoholism is a mental disease, and not everyone is diseased.

I remember a friend from my late teens who I would jam with on guitar virtually every night in his parent's basement. We would exchange greetings with his father before retreating to the basement to play. It always coincided with his father returning from work, pouring himself a dark alcoholic cocktail while awaiting dinner. This might sound like something out of a television show; phrases like "I need a drink" or "You could use a drink" never meant a Pepsi in his world. Perhaps, I pondered, a stressful day could be remedied with an alcoholic beverage. When our jam session concluded, we'd exit through the basement stairs, sometimes glimpsing his father still sipping or even pouring another drink in front of the television. He was the first adult I encountered who regularly enjoyed real alcoholic beverages. In contrast, I also wore a suit for much of my business life but never found comfort in unwinding with a drink; I preferred a nap.

But Bill Wilson, co-founder of Alcoholics Anonymous (AA) had it right when he wrote the Steps of Alcoholics Anonymous. Step 1: *"We admitted we were powerless over alcohol–that our lives had become unmanageable."* Many, including myself, see this step as the most important piece of the program.

It has been commonly analyzed as having two parts: powerlessness and unmanageability. I am here to tell you that it has only one part in the step. It doesn't say, "We admitted we were powerless over alcohol *and* that our lives have become unmanageable". There's a hyphen implying that, as a result of our powerlessness over alcohol, our lives are unmanageable.

Powerlessness is like playing a game with alcohol that an alcoholic cannot win. Some people claim to be "a day drinker." That probably means days, nights, and weekends. Powerless means we cannot control or moderate the amount when we start. We cannot stop how many we will have once we start. When it comes to controlling my drinking, I have a subway analogy. Can you stay on the train through all the stops? Or are you taking the train to make the rounds, checking out the bars until they close? It's like making the restaurant circuit, using the valet parking for my ego, and getting a greater buzz with each stop along the way.

Individuals who exhibit an inability to function most usefully affirm that they are likely to suffer from the disease of alcoholism. Unmanageability prompts the question, "Are we operating at our utmost potential as individuals?" Are we, as fathers, mothers, sons, daughters, decent spouses, parents, and siblings? Am I fulfilling my responsibilities and carrying my weight in our relationship? Am I performing at my highest level at work?

This includes missing work as well. Am I continuously juggling my responsibilities, just enough to make it through?

*I knew I was an alcoholic, because at a wine tasting at the bar,
non-alcoholics spit, alcoholics, swallow! This is in manifestation also!*

Chapter's Logical Take-Away: When it comes to alcohol abuse, the first step of Alcoholics Anonymous (Step 1: "We admitted we were powerless over alcohol, that our lives have become unmanageable") is, in my opinion, the greatest truth you will ever learn from any recovery program. You don't have to be an alcoholic; anyone with addiction can comprehend and internalize this.

THE REAL YOU COMES OUT

You have control of who you are,
don't let anything control you.

In this chapter, we tackle the common belief that "Alcohol brings out the real you." Yet, this is not completely accurate. Alcohol can indeed alter your behavior for a time and lower inhibitions due to its effects on the central nervous system, but it doesn't necessarily reveal your true self in the way that the phrase suggests. Under the influence of alcohol, individuals may exhibit behaviors they wouldn't engage in when sober. They might become more talkative, outgoing, or impulsive. However, this change in behavior is not necessarily a reflection of someone's 'true self.'

I cannot undo what I have already done.
I cannot unsay what I've already said.

Human behavior is complex and multifaceted, unique to every individual, and influenced by various factors such as personality, emotions, environment, upbringing, social context, and more[267]. Alcohol can magnify certain traits or behaviors that are already present, but it can also bring out behaviors that are entirely out of character for a person[268]. People want to talk when they are drunk or high, at all hours, and mostly nonsense and gibberish. That late-night call when they are most talkative.

Additionally, certain individuals may act differently under the influence of alcohol due to societal expectations, peer pressure, or the desire to fit in. The belief that alcohol reveals the true self oversimplifies the intricacies of human behavior and psychology. It's important to remember that alcohol impairs judgment and decision-making and slows reaction time; actions taken while intoxicated may not accurately reflect a person's values, integrity, intentions, or personality. If you're looking to truly understand someone's character, it's more appropriate to observe their behavior across different situations and states of mind rather than relying solely on how they act when under the influence of alcohol or during their hangover.

*For some, alcohol often serves as a convenient
excuse for their irresponsible behavior.*

Alcohol is believed to disrupt cognitive function, potentially leading to increased aggression in individuals who typically control their temper. Those predisposed to aggression may find their tendencies heightened under its influence. In other words, deep down, the so-called "angry drunk" was always an angry person[269]. Since excessive alcohol and drugs alter our brain chemistry, when alcohol is consumed, the already angry person becomes even more so. This applies to any character trait.

Additionally, alcohol's association with sex in our society can lead to risky behaviors, contributing to instances of drug-facilitated sexual assault. For those prone to anger, alcohol may escalate confrontations, while others may seek affection or fulfillment of desires, sometimes leading to inappropriate or dangerous behavior. This can range from mildly inappropriate actions to serious violence, with alcohol often implicated as a factor in date rape incidents. While most people experience increased sociability when drinking, a small percentage may find themselves overwhelmed with sadness instead. The reasons for alcohol's contradictory effects on stress relief are not fully understood, but it may exacerbate underlying issues or simply release pent-up emotions. Ultimately, the impact of alcohol varies greatly among individuals, with some experiencing heightened stress responses or mood swings after consumption.

Chapter's Logical Take-Away: Alcohol doesn't reveal the true self; it merely magnifies or distorts existing traits. Behavior under its influence is influenced by various factors, like personality and social context. Alcohol can exacerbate aggression, lead to risky behaviors, or evoke sadness. Its effects vary widely among individuals, highlighting the complexity of human behavior.

WHAT KIND OF DRINKER ARE YOU?

"I am smarter and have greater willpower than the person next to me, yet I'm the one alcohol affects more strongly."

What defines your drinking habits? What category of drinker do you fall into? The diverse spectrum of drinkers mirrors the varying levels of beverage consumption[270]. Those who partake in alcohol moderately typically exhibit a sense of personal discipline and self-awareness, managing their actions within reasonable bounds[271]. The exemplar we aim to emulate is one who indulges in moderation or socially drinks on occasion, making it improbable for them to be classified as alcoholics.

In line with the "Dietary Guidelines for America, 2020–2025" from the U.S. Department of Agriculture (USDA), moderation entails limiting alcohol intake to two drinks or fewer per day for men and one drink or fewer per day for women[272]. The National Institute on Alcohol Abuse and

Alcoholism (NIAAA) characterizes binge drinking as consuming five or more drinks for men and identifies heavy alcohol use as ingesting four or more drinks a day (or over fourteen a week) for men and more than three drinks a day (or over seven drinks a week) for women[273]. Excessive alcohol consumption may unknowingly lead to issues such as kidney, liver, and pancreas complications, high blood pressure, and cholesterol problems[274], necessitating consultation with a medical professional or seeking assistance from an alcohol treatment center.

In our current era, there appears to be a test for every conceivable circumstance. Various online questionnaire-style assessments cater to individuals suspecting they may have alcohol-related concerns. These tests, accurate in their scrutiny, offer valuable insights into the presence of a serious drinking problem. Taking such a test can be a pivotal starting point and serve as a wake-up call for those already harboring suspicions.

It is difficult to identify functional alcoholism since people may appear competent and sober on the outside[275]. I used to consider myself a "functioning alcoholic," capable of doing my work well despite frequent drinking. Though my actions did not clearly indicate the presence of alcohol, its smell on my breath or flowing from my pores was a giveaway. Tolerance had allowed my body to rapidly absorb alcohol, resulting in a deceptive appearance of normalcy.

The phrase "functioning alcoholic" is subjective; let us use reasoning to demonstrate why. What is happening here? Carrying out a task or doing it exactly as specified without making any unintentional mistakes. It is not about being a 'good' alcoholic in any way, but about being an able human being in every way. Sure, I can swing a baseball or write my name with or without alcohol in my system, but how far can I hit the ball or how neat will my signature be when my faculties are impaired by alcohol? Here is what a functioning alcohol perceives to be.

Alcoholics often lack discretion or control over their decision-making before their initial drink, relying on more than personal determination and self-awareness to overcome addiction[276]. I encountered difficulty both in discontinuing and initiating drinking, highlighting the struggle associated with alcoholism. Despite periods of abstinence fueled by determination and reflective understanding, once I commenced drinking, maintaining control became elusive.

"If there were two doors, one labeled 'drink' and the other 'NO drink,' the alcoholic would be searching for a middle door."

For those diagnosed with alcoholism or substance addiction, prevailing wisdom advises complete abstinence, recognizing the exacerbating impact of even a single drink[277]. The prevailing belief is that only the individual can truly discern if they're an addict or an alcoholic. An insightful home test involves attempting controlled drinking with the aim of consuming only one drink over an hour. Deviation from this goal, tapping into additional drinks, suggests a lack of control, indicative of potential alcoholism. Perhaps, in the spirit of Jeff Foxworthy's comedic approach, we might explore a similar perspective: "You may be an alcoholic if…."

Chapter's Logical Take-Away: Just knowing your drinking patterns will help you determine your limitations in terms of alcohol consumption or non-consumption moving forward.

I KNOW WHAT'S BEST FOR ME

"If it works for me, it can work for you."

When you are faced with a habit, you want to break it. When you have an obsession, you want to remove it. And when you have an addiction, you want to manage it. People like me strongly believed we had an addiction. I went to a treatment facility in Atlanta for individuals dealing with alcohol and substance abuse. It's worth noting that not everyone who attended had an addiction or was an alcoholic. Some may not have even been problem drinkers; they might have been fulfilling a legal obligation or responding to a family intervention that brought them there. Some treatment centers address mental illnesses and other addictions, such as gambling problems and eating disorders; this book talks about many of those.

As I mentioned, in my case, I was there to learn how to manage an addiction to substances. I use the term "manage" because substance abuse and alcoholism are diseases without cures. Ironically, there is no test to determine if you have the disease or not. These diseases are both mental and physical. If you have organ damage, such as pancreas, liver, kidney, or heart disease, that is a good indication of being an alcoholic or addict. You can also claim such a designation if you find that you can't control your drinking or stop once you start, or cope with life without drugs or alcohol, or, of course, with as much in your system.

In the case of the facility I attended for ninety days, we were brought to an alcohol-based twelve-step program meeting every day; it wasn't an option to skip any of the ninety meetings in ninety days. Despite my addiction being with substances, I had no choice in the matter; as my father used to say, "We're not running a restaurant here." Fortunately for me, it is the most successful program for alcoholics, and not surprisingly, it was effective for my problem with substances. All treatment facilities know that twelve-step programs work for all addictions[278]. The count at this writing is approximately 180 twelve-step programs for addiction and other disorders. They all follow the same format, but substitute words related to the disorder itself in place of alcohol-related terms.

After six years of introspection regarding whether I am an alcoholic, I have concluded that I am not; however, I do acknowledge that I have a substance use disorder (SUD) and am a "problem" drinker. I am motivated to stop drinking because, as a problem drinker, I find myself needing an alcohol buzz first to experience the desired effects of the substance that follows. Hence, alcohol is my "gateway" drug. This has become my protocol, or formula.

"I never got high before I got buzzed."

Twelve-step programs embrace autonomy, allowing for the modification of the common or standard meeting format, provided they adhere to the established "Traditions.[279]" Consequently, some meetings stipulate, "unless you identify as an alcoholic, we ask that you don't share and only listen." Advocates of the program argue for the importance of respecting the "singleness of purpose," which essentially means focusing discussions within meetings on the nature of sobriety and freedom from alcohol and limiting discussions to problems related to alcohol. This commitment to a specific purpose is a common thread in twelve-step programs across various subjects.

If you attend a thirty, sixty, or ninety-day program or more, you are technically finished with your education about your illness. Twelve-step support groups are in place to help people stay clean and sober by supporting each other. People who are observing (individuals without similar disorders) often ask, "How long do you have to go to these meetings?" The most popular and suggested answer is "forever." We are never cured; managing our illness becomes a lifelong endeavor. However, at the treatment center I attended six years ago, my guess is that 80% of the people returned to work or their families and might never attend a twelve-step program again. Individual needs vary, and everyone needs to know themselves. If you think ninety days were all you needed to live life sanely, then that's what it took for you. Some need support groups for much longer, and sometimes forever. So, follow what you believe in; there's no wrong answer!

The Georgia Counsel on Substance Abuse, where I got a degree in addictions, uses the term "long term sobriety" (LTR). They consider a person with two years of sobriety (abstinence of all mind and mood-altering substances) someone in long-term recovery.

Chapter's Logical Take-Away: The goal is to manage addiction, as there are no cures. Despite the twelve-step program's focus on alcohol, it is highly effective for most addiction disorders.

ONLY YOU KNOW IF YOU ARE AN ADDICT OR AN ALCOHOLIC

*The difference between a drunk and
an alcoholic is the alcoholic
has to go to meetings.*

An active alcoholic is under the influence or in a state of insanity, or somewhere in between. Their thinking is not clear or logical. There were times during my drinking days when I needed to take antibiotics for infection. Antibiotics and prescription medicines don't mix well with alcohol. So, I would forgo taking the Z-pak (Zithromax) because I was unable to allocate just a four-to-five day stretch of medication because it would not be effective if I drank. It's amazing that I even concerned myself with the possible dangers of drug interactions. Then, there's the cost of a doctor's visit to get the prescription. What it really came down to was that dealing with my illness would interfere with my ability to drink. This is craziness or insanity to put getting drunk ahead of getting over a debilitating illness. I recently heard that insanity is lacking soundness of mind.

The addict or alcoholic is always caught thinking, "It will be different this time," or "It's the last time I'm drinking," which coincides with Einstein's definition of insanity: doing the same thing over and over and expecting different results[280]. But because the abuser is delusional, they might as well be saying:

> *"My thinking is not insane at all; I know exactly*
> *what to expect when I start drinking".*

For the alcoholic or the addict, the allure is powerful. It has a certain magnetism. It does not let you know that you have a problem. I was able to stop when I was thirty for sixteen years on sheer willpower alone. Willpower is a great accompaniment to any program, which I never had or even knew of.

Only an alcoholic can recognize their irrepressible urge to drink. It does not matter how much or how often you drink, or even what kind of beverage you consume. It means not knowing what will happen or how you are going to stop once you start. An alcoholic says that when I drink, two things are going to happen. First, I know what is going to happen! And second, I do not know what is going to happen! Which might come across as paradoxical.

> *If I could drink like a normal person, I'd drink every day.*

Moderation is represented when Grandma is asked, "Do you want another glass of wine?" And she replies: "No, I better stop, I am feeling a little tipsy." This is a great example of the "casual drinker," regardless of whether they are at a bar or at home.

Once we accept that we are alcoholics, there is a chance that we can change. But we can't change what we refuse to accept, so denial makes change impossible[281]. Those who want to stop drinking on their own should try different liquors with less alcohol content or drink only on the weekends[282]. We make promises to valued people in our world in an attempt to get them back. In the chapters ahead, "living amends" discusses how to accomplish just that.

Chapter's Logical Take-Away: This chapter emphasizes the inability to manage drinking as a significant difference between casual drinking, drunkenness, and alcoholism. The irrational behavior of addicts, who prioritize alcohol over health, and how it can't be controlled.

NO RECOLLECTION OF BLACKOUTS

Don't adjust the lights,
it's your lights that went out.

But what exactly is a blackout, and what does it entail in our discussion? This is a book about addictions, but it should be noted that blackouts can occur, in simple terms, when there is a circulation problem in the body[283]. Low blood pressure, epilepsy, heart disease, illicit drugs, and low blood sugar—as it relates to alcohol consumption, a blackout is a temporary condition that affects your memory. Enter the blackout drinker. The blackout drinker usually succeeds in blacking out every time they drink[284]. They can pass out or be conscious, but, as I would like to say, their mind is somewhere else. It is characterized by a sense of lost time. A gap in memory. Blackouts occur when your body's alcohol levels are high. Alcohol impairs your ability to form new memories while intoxicated. We only remember events when our cognitive senses are functioning. It does not erase memories formed before intoxication, but a stretch in time when experiencing this condition. I guess you could call it a mental blackout.

I was a big snow skier in my younger years. I remember skiing Zermatt-Matterhorn in the Swiss Alps at an altitude of 5,000 ft. I suppose I could have blacked out due to lack of oxygen, but instead I experienced a "white out." That's when the clouds roll into your vision, and you can't see even your hands in front of you. Like suddenly driving through fog, you don't know where you are. It's a scary feeling, and as with an alcohol blackout, you might emerge unscathed if you're lucky. As you drink more alcohol and your blood alcohol level rises, the rate and length of memory loss will increase. The amount of memory loss varies between individuals. During this time, you may have trouble walking, talking, standing, impaired judgment and reaction time, and blurry vision.

There are two types of blackouts: partial and complete. If you experience a partial blackout, visual or verbal cues may help you probe forgotten events[232,285]. If you have a complete blackout, memory loss during that instance or period is permanent. Even with cues, you are unlikely to re-member what happened during this time. The nature of blackouts makes it difficult for researchers to examine the correlation between memory recall and the type of blackout. Nonmedical-related issues like blackouts are often associated with alcohol. For many people, drinking too much alcohol too quickly, or on an empty stomach, can cause a blackout[286].

We often drink in response to our emotions, in order to feel and explore different emotions. Good reasons, as in the excuse for drinking I have heard, include "I was celebrating," or "A friend of mine forced me to try it." But we also have every excuse not to stop drinking. Such is typical addictive behavior. Like joining a gym. We usually have a good reason to "want to" start, but always a reason why we have not started yet. It usually boils down to procrastination and laziness. We must retrain our brains to overcome our addictive behavior. It is all in your head, right?

Chapter's Logical Take-Away: Alcohol-induced blackouts, which cause brief memory loss, are the main emphasis. Frequent experiences of alcohol-induced blackouts are closely tied to heavy alcohol consumption and result in memory lapses and irretrievable memory loss.

ISOLATING

Solitude is a time to think,
with loneliness, something is missing.

Self-isolation is unhealthy. And sure, anything can be isolated or separated from another; however, in the context of this narrative, "isolating" qualifies as one of my "magic words of addiction," with a focus on human connection.

When individuals choose isolation, they effectively shield themselves from reality, too afraid to face it with both people and the natural world[287].

In contrast, this is different from needing time to be alone to think, meditate, unwind, or recharge our brains. This sort of time alone has a time frame, where isolation really has no time limits and could fester in self-harming tendencies due to substance or alcohol addiction.

In my view, the opposite of isolating is "socializing" (not to be mistaken with introversion vs extroversion). I explore the realm of socializing in my first two books. People need people, since we are social animals, and our creator made us that way to collaborate, create, and grow. But when we isolate ourselves from the rest of the world, we become stagnant and are incapable of growth and promoting societal progress.

When the progression of addiction spirals out of control, especially with SUB (substance abuse disorders), it is very common for it to lead to increased isolation, consequently forming a shell[288]. We become less interested in socializing with our friends and acquaintances. Some of these substances even cause paranoia (unjustified suspicion and mistrust) of other people or their actions) which supports the desire for less social interaction[289].

> *"Partying can be by yourself,*
> *but it takes two to have a party."*

Did you ever miss a big holiday dinner with the family? Or your niece's graduation? Mortgage, rent, or car payments. Did you exceed your yearly sick day allowance because you were stuck in isolation due to addiction?

Let's face it, addiction inevitably paves the path to loneliness. Because we are social by nature, isolation can be emotionally agonizing.

> **Chapter's Logical Take-Away:** Addiction can cause loneliness and emotional discomfort due to decreased social interaction. Human connections are an essential part of life, but it hasn't taken away our primal need to live in "clans" or tribes."

AVOIDANCE

Avoiding society leads to isolation.

Along your road to recovery, there will be some words you might perceive as negative. However, they can be remodeled into useful tools when outfitted with a positive perspective. One such word is "avoidance." At first glance, it gives a negative connotation. Nevertheless, when thought of differently, it can help you navigate your way through the recovery process.

Avoiding people, places, and things may tamper with your preset boundaries and progress, particularly in the initial stages of recovery, when you're striving to maintain sobriety. That doesn't just mean going to bars for the person struggling with alcohol, but the same goes for the gambler who probably shouldn't go to Vegas, even for dinner and a show.

Addiction is like a very powerful magnet that pulls on you when you're within range of your weakness. Your senses can detect its presence, regardless of the specific addiction. The symptoms you will experience in this situation include a spiked heart rate and sudden rush of adrenaline. However, as time passes while going through intensive treatments via active participation, your mind gradually helps you drastically lessen the yearning of this addiction.

The concept of avoidance isn't exclusive to substance abuse; it also manifests in relationships and all kinds of obligations. It is plain to see that human relationships are founded on engagement and healthy communication. So, avoiding the people in your life is not a good idea for someone battling addictions. Seeking help has never been seen as a weakness. This goes back to my point on the importance of character-fixing as a key component in recovery from any addiction.

Someone with an avoidant personality disorder typically exhibits the following traits[290]: These can go on their list of "things to work on".

- Difficulty expressing or experiencing emotions openly. Emotional suppression as a means to protect their feelings.
- Uneasiness with physical intimacy and close contact.
- Being accused of being too needy or too attached to their partner.
- Resistance and reluctance to accept help or emotional support from others.

Chapter's Logical Take-Away: Avoidance is a common phenomenon with addiction rehabilitation. However, note that avoiding society, especially in early addiction recovery, can lead to chronic isolation. Thus leading to an unwillingness to receive emotional support from family, friends, and even professionals.

HITTING BOTTOM

An unaddicted new way,
a little faith and desire—and you
can have anything you want!

Addiction drains every ounce of a man's dignity, leaving a harsh reality of complete despair in its wake. In that, it has an adverse effect on the physical and mental health, relationships, career and finances, and overall quality of life of a person. In your view, things can't get any worse, or there's no room for you to change. For some, it brings upon tears as they turn to higher powers, like God. In prayers, they cry for salvation: "God, please help me," helpless tears stream down their faces. Though their addiction may not be limited to their physical condition, it spreads its grasp like a chronic wound into the minds of individuals with gambling problems, video gaming addiction, and substance and alcohol abuse.

I hold a profound admiration for Step 1 in all Anonymous programs: "We admitted we were powerless over… food, gambling, nicotine, cocaine, etc., that our lives had become unmanageable." In the context of Narcotics

Anonymous (NA), Step 1 reads: "We admitted that we were powerless over *our addiction*, that our lives had become unmanageable[291]." The usage of "all addictions" aligns best with the theme of this book.

The reason I am such an advocate of Step 1 is because once I understood and became ever conscious and mindful of it, I realized that it is the simplest method to prevent relapse. For instance, if playing video games is my addiction (weakness), when I am tempted to turn on my Nintendo, PlayStation, or Xbox, I only need to recall Step 1 (the trigger) in simple terms, "I can't stop when I start, and it won't be long before that's all I want to do for the rest of the day (or night)." This thought highlights the unmanageability of the situation . At this point, if your addiction is video gaming, logic dictates that you shouldn't even own a gaming console, much less think about it.

People who have an alcohol consumption disorder, or addiction are unable to accurately assess their drinking or drug problems. They usually develop a form of denial and convince themselves saying, "I am not that bad compared to others." This holds true for someone with a gambling problem as well[292].

Unfortunately for the individual in their active addiction, in that moment, things appear grim and seem to never get better but instead progressively worse. They feel the urge to take these substances, knowing it's going to kill them, but are ready to ignore these thoughts anyways and take the risk. It is at this point that some alcoholics come to the realization that maybe abstaining from alcohol is the right way going forward. Hence, this reckoning can be referred to as the turning point. This level is often referred to as "your bottom," or "rock bottom."

Everyone has been given unique traits by our creator, so everyone's bottom is not the same. Some can't help but lose everything, their homes, cars, job, family, their health etc., until they realize their mistakes and what they have done. Because their addiction seems so powerful that they can't help but keep "giving away" their most coveted possessions until there's nothing left to give away.

The reason we say "give away" or "gave away" is because most of those things still exist but are no longer yours. Your house never left the property, and someone else is probably driving your car. Family members have turned their backs on you, or possibly moved on, after giving up on you. Lastly, your job slot has already been filled, replaced by someone more competent. This is how you know that you've hit the lowest point in your life, and its high time for you to seek outside help. This fits the saying that pain is an impetus to both mental and physical change.

But do seek help ASAP, because there is a saying that, every bottom has a trap door leading to the abyss of an even greater hardship. This suggests that finally reaching your lowest point may lead to a way out or become a potential progression to make things worse.

Chapter's Logical Take-Away: When we refer to 'hitting bottom," we are inferring lowest point in a person's life. It's when you have nothing tangible, or intangible left to lose. When you say to yourself that the next thing I'm about to lose is more important than feeding my addiction. At this point, you can confidently say that addiction has finally taken a back seat in your life.

SECTION 3
GETTING HELP

SURRENDER TO TAKE HOLD

It's OK to have an addictive disorder, but once you are aware, it's not OK to let it perpetuate.

One of the most common words on my "magic words of recovery" list is the word "surrender." There's not a week of meetings that go by that I don't hear "surrender to win" or "surrender to this way of life" or "surrender to my fate."

The hidden message behind these phrases tells a lot about an individual. The word "surrender" is meant to be understood paradoxically, or opposite of its common usage. So, in this case, in the context of recovery, it's not surrendering to lose, but surrendering to win (which, by definition, is an oxymoron) in the long run.

With alcohol abuse as a foe, it's actually acceptable to be beaten by it. It simply indicates that you must admit that you are powerless in the face of your addiction and can't beat it. This is the first step to understanding how your addiction has absolute control over you. You've reached the point where you acknowledge that you're "broken (but fixable)," much like most individuals dealing with addiction.

At this point, you are somewhat willing to find ways to fix this condition once and for all. I have always said, "Once you identify any problem you are halfway there to fixing it."

A glimmer of hope begins to emerge as you make an initial commitment, the starting point of change. While you proceed on the path to recovery, you will likely experience a pull in the other direction, challenging your resolve, especially during the early stages. Even if you never look back physically, you will subconsciously be tempted to give your addiction a seemingly harmless try in the name of casual indulgence. I say "try," because your only intention is just one more drink, dose, or bet away from ending up back where you started. If we want to win at this game of life, we get no more "tries"!

You might remember that this happened to me after accumulating sixteen years of abstinence from my DOC (drug of choice). But since you are defenseless, the casual try takes you right back to where you were when you decided to call it quits not very long ago. For some individuals, this becomes a life-long cycle of inescapable defeat. I absolutely believe a psychic change (discussed in Chapter 55) must take place to win the addiction battle.

Chapter's Logical Take-Away: No one likes to be considered a loser. We, by default, think highly of ourselves and get defensive when challenged in ways we aren't prepared for. However, regarding addiction, the only losers are those who keep ruining their chances of getting better by going back on their resolutions over and over again. Remember Einstein's quote I mentioned earlier about insanity? Always remember that with conscious and intentional efforts, coupled with determination, comes great reward in the long run.

BREAKING THE SILENCE

"I can be the person you see,
and the one I guard."

Everyone knows someone who is addicted to something. A family member, a relative, a friend, a co-worker, or perhaps you, the reader. You don't have to think long to come up with a name. But that wasn't always a slam-dunk question. People kept that talk quiet. Addiction has always been an unpleasant reality, but today it's more openly discussed and accepted. We never wanted our name to come up in any of those conversations. It cannot be viewed as positive. Besides the obvious health issues addictions create, it's embarrassing and something to be ashamed of. It makes us appear weak. But the truth is, addiction is a disease—one we didn't ask for. Of course, visually, some are uglier than others, but an addiction is still an addiction where attention is needed. Oddly, drawing attention to our illness is the last thing we would want, but tending to it is what we really need to get well.

A major breakthrough occurred in 1956, when the AMA (American Medical Association) recognized alcoholism as a disease[293]. And in 1987, on a broader scale, addiction was also classified as a disease. The stigmatism of alcoholism and substance abuse took a big hit in a very positive way[294]. People became more open with themselves in order to get treatment for their "disease." Suddenly, outsiders became more empathetic to those who were cursed with a disease, rather than thinking they were just pathetic[295]. Winos, junkies, and addicts have been replaced with alcoholics and people with substance abuse issues[296].

We've come a long way. Once you acknowledge and admit your addiction, or even obsession, you're closer to personal freedom. Free from the ridicule and bias that were once shunned by society. In the past, the stigma attached to people with these disorders was unforgiving. But today, those people are more understanding.

Nowadays, almost every large corporation recognizes the importance of well-being for their employees, offering a wide range of assistance programs for addiction[297]. In smaller businesses, as mentioned at the beginning of this chapter, "everyone knows someone who is addicted to something," and the person in charge of these businesses may also be in recovery or have a family member who currently is. As they say, it takes one to know one, and you might just catch a break.

But there's a good cause for this awareness in the workplace. As I have been saying so far, people with any type of illness, mental or physical, are people first. And people change under the right circumstances. In most cases, they are just as intelligent and skilled as people without these types of disorders. They are just incapable of using their skills in the right direction. That's where professional help comes in.

But we've learned to accept the diseased and help them work through their issues with good care. We don't discard talented individuals who are fixable. We fix them. And everyone is fixable if they are willing to put in the effort and accept help as needed. Everything in this world comes at a cost, and recovery is no exception. Successful airlines don't dismiss good talent. They are among their greatest assets. You can't just buy flight hours or experience. Training is costly, so they rehabilitate them. The same can be applied where people are needed. They are given proper treatment under the right conditions.

I attend a twelve-step meeting, and I sometimes hear people introduce themselves as "I'm an addict or alcoholic, and my name is …." To me, that is so backward. I am a person before I am a person with the disease of addiction. I don't introduce myself that way when I meet someone for the first time in public. It should go like this: "I am Rick," and "I am an alcoholic," not the other way around. We are people first.

Eventually, you are going to be faced with questions about your new outlook as an unapologetic person with addiction. One way to handle this is by having a script to explain why you don't drink. In the beginning, I would simply say: "I decided to get healthy, so I eliminated the alcohol." There's nothing untruthful about that. Several years later, when I moved to Florida, people would ask me, "What brings you to Florida?" after noticing my Georgia plates. My answer was, "Well, I am originally from Jersey, but I came to Georgia four years ago to get professional help for a substance abuse problem. I stayed close to the program and never left until I got tired of the traffic in Atlanta, so here I am, closer to the beach."

After becoming clean and sober, it is up to you to decide whether to keep your sobriety private or not. No one has to know unless you are comfortable sharing that part about yourself; one's individual anonymity is highly personal. I have heard that you must earn the privilege before I tell you.

> *"All my life I wanted to be famous,*
> *yet here I am, anonymous."*

In my case, I didn't make a big announcement, but I have inferred enough innuendo for everyone to figure out. The next time you see a movie where "higher power," or "make amends" is mentioned, it's not crazy to wonder if the writer or screenwriter is in recovery.

Chapter's Logical Take-Away: Today, addiction is recognized as an inherent disease. People struggling with it are met with understanding rather than shame and embarrassment.

DETOXIFICATION AND WITHDRAWAL – RECLAIMING YOUR HEALTH

Out with the bad, and in with the good.

Detoxification, often simply referred to as "detox" or "detoxing," involves carefully and gradually tapering the body from the harmful side effects of substance withdrawal. This includes abstinence from alcohol in a controlled environment and close monitoring of vital signs and any withdrawal symptoms, all under the watchful eye of a professional[298]. You need to recycle your body's chemical makeup of your currently poisoned blood into clean, healthy, and uncontaminated blood. After all, this is the bloodstream that fuels the body and gets accurate messages to and from the brain. To do this, you need to flush out your system safely. Your body may not be equipped physically to handle the shock of going "cold turkey" on your own.

There are at least a dozen methods of detoxification available for drugs and alcohol. It is important to consult with healthcare professionals to determine the most appropriate detox method based on the individual's substance abuse history, health status, and other factors.

Here are some of the ways to detox from drugs and alcohol:

- Medical detoxification[299]:
  - Conducted in a supervised medical setting with professionals.
  - Medications may be given to manage withdrawal symptoms.
  - Goal: Ensure safety and comfort during detox.
- Inpatient detox[93]:
  - It involves staying in a facility 24/7.
  - Provides a controlled, supportive environment.
  - Minimizes external triggers.
- Outpatient detox [300]:
  - Treatment at home for those with mild symptoms and strong support.
  - Allows flexibility in overall routine while receiving care.
- Rapid Detox[301]:
  - Accelerated detox under anesthesia.
  - Quickly clears opioid receptors, shortening withdrawal.
- Holistic Detox[302]:
  - Includes acupuncture, yoga, meditation, and nutrition.
  - Addresses physical, mental, and emotional aspects.
- Social Detox[303]:
  - Relies on support from family, friends, or a sober environment involving those who have already gone through the process.
  - Limited medical supervision; focuses on a strong social network.
- Methadone Maintenance Treatment (MMT)[304]:
  - Uses methadone for opioid detox.
  - Reduces withdrawal symptoms and cravings.

- Buprenorphine Detox[305]:
  - Medication for opioid addiction gradually tapered off.
- Tapering[306]:
  - Gradual reduction of substance intake under medical supervision.
  - Manages withdrawal symptoms, prevents severe discomfort.
- Therapeutic Communities[307]:
  - Residential programs with detox and local community support.
  - Emphasizes peer support and care.
- Counseling and therapy[308]:
  - Cognitive-behavioral therapy (CBT), motivational enhancement therapy (MET), and other counseling approaches.
  - Addresses psychological aspects during detox.
- Self-Detox at Home[309]:
  - Not recommended for severe cases.
  - Requires a support system, strict discipline, and awareness of potential risks.

Because alcoholism and substance abuse are diseases where the mind obsesses over getting the substance by all means necessary and the body (the bloodstream, specifically) craves it until it receives it, the goal here is to remove the substance from the body safely altogether. This hunger is often referred to as alcohol or substance dependence, or "physical dependence." For the addict or alcoholic, it just means they depend on getting it to be satisfied. Alcohol dependence is one of the most common psychiatric disorders, second only to major depression[310]. And more often than not, both go hand in hand.

The approach to detoxification depends on various factors, including the type and quantity of the substance consumed as well as the gap between doses. Every individual is unique, and these differences influence the detox process and its specifics. Only a qualified medical professional can determine the best detox plan for you. Attempting to detox on your own is risky and should be avoided as much as possible. It falls in the same category of diagnosing yourself with the help of Google. It is essential to seek treatment in a facility equipped to handle detoxification and the processes involved. While there are diets tailored for alcohol detoxification, these should complement, not altogether replace, medical supervision.

Severe withdrawal symptoms can occur when heavy drinkers abruptly reduce or cease alcohol consumption, resulting in alcohol withdrawal (AW). Symptoms range from mild to severe, typically emerging a few hours after the last drink. Common AW symptoms include mild to moderate tremors, irritability, anxiety, and agitation. The most severe manifestations include delirium tremens, hallucinations, and seizures[311].

There are psychological withdrawal symptoms associated with detoxifying from drugs and alcohol too quickly. These include depression, anxiety, reduced motivation, difficulties experiencing pleasure, apathy, insomnia, and even more serious symptoms, such as the development of hallucinations and delusions[312].

At last, once you have a clean bloodstream, it is now time to begin and put in a continued effort if you're going to leave your dark past, its consequences, and everything else it entails behind. I call this the "educational" or mental aspect of recovery when nothing makes any sense yet. And for me, as a person in long-term recovery, this is merely a deep discovery of the "real you." Strengths, weaknesses, abilities, and limitations. Everything that constitutes to make you, you. "Know thyself," a self-discovery of finding out who you really are. Aristotle said that:

"Knowing ourselves is the beginning of all wisdom."

I believe self-awareness is the most important element to a successful and happy life recovery. The aim of this book is to outline comprehensive methods for fulfilling these emotions, whether addiction is a factor in your life or not.

> **Chapter's Logical Take-Away:** Overall, detox and withdrawal are essential to rehabilitation and recovery, treating the physical and emotional elements of addiction.

JUST DON'T ...
NO MATTER WHAT

It's hard to resist Magnum Ice Cream when you dream about it, but we must exercise discipline!

If a life of sobriety, or free of any addiction for that matter, is what you seek, there is one cardinal rule that you can never forget: "Just don't, no matter what." Just don't drink, drug, smoke, gamble, eat cake … no matter what! It's easier said than done, I know, but it is uncontestably logical. I have been in a twelve-step program for five and a half years at the time of this writing and have probably heard it over 500 times. And, like all the catchphrases and acronyms you hear in recovery, which all sound corny to me, they all become important when you deeply think about them and match them up with what they were supposed to mean.

If you ever enroll in a program for any addiction, you will most definitely hear "One day at a time" or "Just for today." If you ponder it for a bit and fit your understanding of that phrase into your recovery process, you will wind up with something like this: "I'm here, right now—today, fighting the urge to drink or indulge in sweets, and it's far from easy. But all I have to do is make it through the rest of today, or better yet, until bedtime. When I wake up, the prospect of a full day seems long, but bedtime is only sixteen hours away, and half of the day will be over after lunch." By looking at whole days in blocks and dividing them into bite-size hours, it goes quickly, and you make it through another day, and then another, and another. I used to do that when I worked at a job I didn't like. I said it's almost lunch, and I only have half a day, and it will be all behind me. It's mental reassurance, a way to trick your mind into thinking that the road ahead is not as long as you think it is.

The reason why "a day at a time" works is because one day is manageable, especially if you look at it as I just outlined it. But if you start saying, I made it through a week, now your mind is already preparing you to think that next week is going to be a long week to manage my addiction. It's way too much to put on yourself as it'll feel like climbing a mountain. You should celebrate the months, but still use the daily formula, perhaps until you feel more in control and have a better understanding of how your addiction needs tending to.

Sometimes, I find myself disagreeing with certain statements I hear in twelve-step meeting rooms. People often become so attached to phrases that they mindlessly repeat them without examining their accuracy; hence, their meaning ends up being lost. One widely circulated saying is, "The person who wakes up earliest has the most sobriety today." In this context, "today" is the only word with any real relevance here; sobriety should be seen as a means of living a clean and sober life, not just staying clean and sober.

Recently, I heard an older woman say she was looking for someone to help her with her recovery program. A much younger woman came forward and offered to help. The older woman asked the younger woman, "How much time (experience) do you have in the program?" The young woman then asked, "What time did you wake up today?" The older woman replied, "I got up at 8 am." The younger woman said, "Well, I got up at 5:30 am, so I have more sobriety than you do today." Such reasoning seems totally irrational and quite absurd. If you have one year of continuous sobriety, it doesn't matter what time you get up in the morning; you still have accrued one year of sobriety! What counts are the days spent without consuming alcohol, not the fact that you're an early bird or a night owl. Similarly, if you have ten years of continuous sobriety, you have amassed ten years of sobriety! It's simple math. Ten years of knowledgeable sobriety are worth far more than the person with one year of a life of uninformed sobriety. Of course, it's not about what you hear during your time in sobriety; it's about what you learn, internalize, and how you implement it that truly matters. In this illustration, the bottom line is all about what you have to give.

Another phrase frequently recited at every twelve-step meeting is "Progress, not perfection." What this means is that the process of recovery won't always be smooth sailing. As with any aspect of life, setbacks will occur from time to time. Rather than being discouraged by the mistakes we make, intentionally or unintentionally, and the things we don't do so perfectly, individuals are encouraged to recognize and celebrate the progress they have made so far, emphasizing personal growth over an unattainable level of perfection, that, let's face it, is never achieved by anyone. It encourages individuals to learn from their experiences, stay committed to their recovery, and continue moving forward with the "one day at a time" motto.

I heard someone say it, "Just don't drink, no matter what," with the right inflection and with conviction. Only then did I ponder over it and say to myself after five years as mere words, "If I do nothing right today, and don't drink no matter what happens, I will keep my consecutive sober streak intact, and I can remain a proud winner." I believe we all need to hear things in life a certain way that just seems so profound and convincing. I'm not only referring to addiction, but in any circumstances of life in general. In my book *Sales and Selling Yourself,* I share a story about my professor in a marketing class I was in. His definition of marketing was "getting the right product, to the right market, at the right time, with the right price, and the right profit." Hearing "just don't drink, no matter what" came at the "right" time for me that day.

> **Chapter's Logical Take-Away:** You will progress and feel more accomplished by breaking recovery into daily—or better yet, hourly—portions. Celebrating longer milestones is great, but focusing on a daily goal eases mental overload and increases your chance of success.

WILLPOWER

If you get stung by a bee, you can't use willpower for it not to swell up if you are allergic to bees. If you drink, you can't use your willpower to stop either.

For the problem drinker[313], it's so easy to have a drink, but it can be difficult not to have one. It becomes a struggle to resist. Similarly, it's easy to indulge in chocolate chip cookies, but hard to resist when they're in front of you. It takes a certain amount of effort to avoid doing things we shouldn't. This dilemma might require the help of willpower. Willpower, also known as self-control or self-regulation, is the ability to resist short-term temptations, impulses, or instant gratifications in order to achieve long-term goals[314]. The key is to delay gratifications. Understanding the psychology of willpower can help explain how individuals manage their thoughts, emotions, and, as a result, their actions.

I believe willpower and motivation (sustained by constant discipline) play a big part in our sobriety.

But with addiction, willpower gets a bad rep when it comes to fending off the inconceivable pull of addiction or obsession. They say you can't rely solely on willpower, which I must agree with. So, I concur that the magnetism of my addiction is stronger than my willpower alone. Hence, the balance will tip toward addiction.

I have always prided myself on my incredible willpower, which I say with a smirk that I got from the creator. I guess you can also say … I was given the disease of addiction, a twelve-step program to help me deal with it, and a large dose of willpower to lessen my struggles too. I believe willpower is part of every equation, and if God is in yours, faith and willpower are parcel to every outcome. However, with or without God, we all have willpower.

Motivation and the topic of willpower have captivated me from an early age. I have been the "motivated type" since I can recall from my youngest days of recollection, which makes sense since that's when we first become aware of psychological states (e.g., motivation), and are impacted by them. I am also very goal-oriented and draw motivation from my ambitions.

However, practicing what is being discussed here involves the utilization of mindfulness and can also be proactive by nature. You'll find these practices to be either circumstantial or instinctual when exercised properly. It's challenging to practice patience when there's no apparent cause for it since we can't not do things, but we can learn to be more patient as we go. The Milgram experiment is the best example of this, in which people are locked in a room with nothing to do except use a button that'll induce a mild electric shock[315]. Most often, people choose the electric shock over sitting still for an extended period. The same principle applies when we practice self-control, impulsivity, and self-restraint. I might spot something that is visually appealing to me, but after running it past the boss (my brain), I realize that I don't need it, as my senses might tell me otherwise.

Chapter's Logical Take-Away: Willpower at any level isn't enough when it comes to managing addiction. That, along with education, experience, and a little faith (in oneself and in God) is a formidable assembly for recovery.

MOTIVATION AND INTENTIONS

*Why am I drinking vanilla extract from
the bottle and not giving any to the cake?*

Everything in "your" world is driven by motive and intention. What's in it for me, and is my intention fair and righteous? Is my intention misplaced? What do I stand to lose financially? Conscious or subconscious, planned out more so, but our makeup with spontaneity are scenarios that lead to this determination. I held the door for an older woman without intent. It was only natural to be aware of what it had to be. I said, "No running," as she couldn't, but to make her laugh and with that intention. All that was done made me feel good, but there was only one thing I was aware of. She said thank you when she entered the elevator, and I said, "what floor?" Thank you probably came naturally with no intent.

What are your true intentions with addictions? If you accidentally take a sip of a drink that you didn't know had liquor in it, you get a pass because your intention was not to drink liquor to get a buzz or to get drunk. The same goes for a medicine or product that has an ingredient that is not good for your recovery, or the ingredients contribute to your inherent allergies. The only catch here, and it's a big one … you must be responsible with your choices. It takes conscious effort and thoroughness not to let this happen. If someone hands you a drink, it is your duty to ask if there's any liquor in it. And with medicines or even OTC products, you are expected to read the label and ingredients.

I drink Kombucha occasionally because it is good for digestion. It is a fermented beverage, so it has a small trace of alcohol. If I drink it every day because it changes my mood (for the feel-good or rush) or brain function, drinking for the effect is all wrong for me. INTENTIONS! And consider that if you are being drug tested, you may fail if you consume anything remotely related to substance, even with traces of alcohol in your bloodstream. Similarly, it is unwise to eat poppy-seed or everything bagels because the poppy seeds may register as opiates.

You've likely heard the expression: "Balance is the key to life." It's so profound that it could be considered a proclamation. Another statement that holds high esteem is, "If your intentions are good, then it's good enough." If we believe our motives are honest, there is nothing to worry about!

Chapter's Logical Take-Away: In this chapter, both conscious and subconscious motivations play a pivotal role in addiction. Responsibility and common sense are strongly encouraged to prevent unintended drinking or drug use. It is crucial to be aware that certain foods, such as fruit cakes with fermented fruit cuttings and some granola bars and cereals containing hemp seeds, may lead to a failed drug test.

EASIER TO STOP OR TO STAY STOPPED?

It isn't a weakness to struggle with stopping drinking or any addiction, but it is a weakness to relapse after a clean streak.

People who have already dealt with substance abuse or use disorders, including alcohol, are often asked the question: Is it harder to stop once or twice, or harder to stay stopped from drinking or using for good? Those who are alcohol or drug "dependent," engaging in daily use, cravings, and experiencing withdrawal symptoms leading to relapse will certainly want to stay away from the substance responsible for addiction once they've detoxified. For them, with medical treatment, it is easier than with addiction, where it may not be an everyday cycle of use. However, individual responses have not always been consistent with the universal data.

When it comes to making the commitment to quit drinking, stop using the substance altogether, or maintain abstinence, success varies from person to person[316]. Personally, I've always found quitting suddenly to be more difficult, regardless of the nature of my disorder. But once I decide to never indulge again, instead of forcing myself to quit, it becomes a relatively easy path for me. I remember my willpower, motivation, and desire to learn and understand! For others, though, it's quite the opposite. Everyone is different. They can stop immediately, but life's variables and other factors have too much influence on them, so they become powerless and drink or use again, giving in to the temptation. Regardless of which scenario you fall into, I firmly believe that the process of quitting constitutes merely 1% of long-term recovery, and living sober is 99% of the effort required to stay sober, regardless of what is harder for you.

After getting sober, the real challenge is to keep the streak going for the long term. Addiction treatment involves modifying one's mindset and behavior, learning new coping skills, forming new neural connections, and changing environments to reduce or remove the chance of relapse[317,318]. Having a close group of people who you can count on and regularly attending support group meetings as well as outside activities can also be very helpful in defending yourself against relapse. They can hold you accountable for your actions. You must never underestimate the power of accountability.

Chapter's Logical Take-Away: Recovery from addiction is a highly personalized experience. Some may find quitting relatively easy but struggle with relapse, while others may face a difficult time quitting initially but maintain sobriety once committed to recovery. In the end, achieving long-term sobriety or total abstinence from other addictions requires strong willpower and an even stronger dedication to your recovery program.

AVOIDING TRIGGERS AND CREATING BOUNDARIES

God doesn't let me buy lottery tickets because he doesn't want me to get hooked on Screamin' Eagle.

As one with an addiction, your ability to take on all the alluring forces of your surroundings can simply be narrowed down to timing. One's mood range varies all through a given day. They say "timing is everything," but with addictions, it involves variables. What is the timing we're talking about in this context, and what might those variables be? In twelve-step programs, the timing they are referring to is the "condition of your spiritual fitness," or simply the condition of your state of mind at a given moment, the level of your sanity[319]. This is derived from how well you know yourself and your limitations, as well as the current stage and severity of your addiction. The variables, as mentioned briefly in Chapter 28 "Avoidance," would be the surroundings or environment, which include people, places, and things that could draw you into the compulsion to engage in your addiction. I had someone say, "All the old playmates and playgrounds must go." I cannot be around people who are still in their active addictions when I am in recovery. If I want to change, I must let go of my old mindset that's holding me back. And I can't go to my old stomping grounds or any place that would trigger my addiction. Making and maintaining boundaries are seemingly imperative solutions at the beginning of abstinence from your addictions[320]. So, with boundaries, it is important to form the most impenetrable walls until you "know yourself." Stay away from "people, places, and things." Visual cues or any reminders "tease" your willpower to try a drink.

When I ask myself if there is even a 1% chance that where I am going or who might be there will tempt me to cave to my addiction, that 1% may as well be 99%, and the answer must be a hard pass! In these situations, employing logic with your hard-earned sobriety is paramount. Twelve-step programs stress the importance of prayer with a higher power or a God of your understanding[321]. I am a big proponent of willpower, so either, or both of these exercises must be an accompaniment to a little logic and common sense along the path to recovery.

Another safeguard against relapse might include activities with people who are also sober or in recovery programs, or close friends or family members who have never been involved with alcohol. This ensures disciplined accountability and sets a barrier to keep you away from the pull of temptation[322]. Boredom, a notorious precursor to relapse, is reduced by surrounding oneself with like-minded individuals so one can better assimilate into the open world and its endless possibilities.

Because people with addiction are people first, but only with an added layer that demands medical or therapeutic attention (similar to a diabetic, for instance), we can't, nor do we want to circumvent the rest of society. It's always advisable to surround yourself with people who care about your well-being. We must learn to sidestep potential harm until we regain our footing in the world, establishing ourselves as an integral part of society.

Just as individuals modify their diets, steer clear of racetracks and casinos, avoid bars, and quit smoking, the world once again appears vast with plenty to do and explore.

If there was a social gathering with a hundred people in a room, and fifty of them were casual drinkers and the other fifty were alcoholics in recovery, and there was no liquor being served, how many people could have a good time? The likely answer would be a hundred. The casual drinkers could take it or leave the liquor to have a social, good time, and the alcoholics who are in recovery would have to manufacture a good time because their lives depend on their sobriety. The point is that no one has to have alcohol, or anything, for that matter, to have fun!

Chapter's Logical Take-Away: The path to sobriety in addiction rehabilitation involves steering clear of triggers and establishing clear boundaries during the early stages of recovery. Engaging in sober activities, embracing rehabilitation, and filling boredom with productive activities are essential to preventing relapse. Sobriety can pave the way for a meaningful life ahead, and one can experience joy without the reliance on alcohol, even in social settings.

RELAPSE IS WEAK

I am too self-conscious to relapse.
And that is the only time
self-consciousness works for me!

Once again, the purpose of this book is to bring logical thinking and common sense to the recovery of your addiction or obsession. This chapter lends an understanding to meaning and causes for relapse. Relapse is giving in to your addiction after managing to control it for some time or to quit it completely[323]. I look at relapse as nothing more than a mere setback (a loss of a battle in the pursuit to win the war of addiction) if you are able to get back on track with your program of recovery.

We often hear in recovery circles that we plan our relapses. I believe this is only partially true and that it can depend on individuals at varying stages of their recovery. In those instances, what we're really saying is that whatever is bothering us might serve as a cause or justification for relapsing when faced with such challenges. It's like giving ourselves a pass or a "heads up" as we sense when a relapse is imminent and acknowledge its possibility according to the situation. This is where I say one is "weak".

There are many reasons why people relapse, but there is one and only one fundamental reason for relapsing: you chose to drink, drug, gamble, over-indulge, etc., period! The choice or decision was completely yours; no one is forced into relapsing. Your faculties were too weak to win against your impulses. The root causes behind this decision often involve underlying issues that act as triggers for relapse[324].

- One of the most common offenders is the stress induced by anxiety. High stress levels drain both mental and emotional energy, making it nearly impossible to maintain feelings of happiness and serenity[325]. And since individuals start to feel a sense of numbness due to those issues, they rely on substances to feel the emptiness.
- Depression, loneliness, personal tragedies, trauma, moments of happiness and celebration, can all push someone towards relapse.
- Sometimes, it can be as mindless as, "It was there (or I was where I shouldn't have been) and the urge was too strong for me to resist." In any case, it was a decision made in poor judgement, or a lack thereof. That is why twelve-step programs instill the importance of powerlessness and boundaries. And for me, being a big proponent of "knowing thyself," education and experience are always there to remind me of my strengths and weakness in every situation.
- One contributor to a possible relapse is "euphoric recall.[326]" Euphoric recall is a psychological term for the tendency of people to remember past experiences in a positive light while overlooking negative experiences associated with an event. This term often relates to substance abuse. Euphoric recall is also referred to as "memory bias." Euphoric recall, or memory bias, occurs most frequently when times are difficult for us[327]. When we are dealing with stressful and pressured situations, we reflect (recall) and

romanticize the good happenings in our lives to lift our emotions. But for those with addiction, this can be fatal.

With euphoric recall, a relapse is not planned; it is situational. You're out somewhere and are presented with the option to have a drink or participate in the use of a mood- or mind-altering substance. I would even include having a cigarette or laying down a bet on a game you're watching. What comes to mind is the remembrance of when these were fun times, when they used to be good, and you go for it. However, if only I had allowed thoughts of despair, depression, and emptiness back into my present state of mind, I might have been saved by morbid reflection and not relapsed. Euphoric recall and morbid reflection are adversaries combating each other in situations where relapse is most likely to occur.

Most people would agree, a decision is only a thought unless it's executed as an action. In the context of recovery, I believe this statement to be very true. If you've already made up your mind to carry out an action, then it's "in action" already. There's no need to consider semantics here. According to the twelve-step programs, separating the two phrases, "made a decision" and "I'm entirely ready," is trivial and pointless.

You may have heard the popular riddle: If three frogs are sitting on a log and one decides to jump off, how many are left? The answer is three because one only decided to jump, and "decided" does not equate to the action, jumping. And the Canadian rock band, Rush, has a thought-provoking line in their popular song "Free Will," "If you choose not to decide, you still have made a choice."

The frogs riddle is a metaphor for step 3 in twelve-step programs, which requires no action to be taken, whereas the Rush lyric reference is when an 'action' is carried out.

Usually, addiction is never the solution but a temporary fix or escape from harsh reality. So, there is always a high chance of an alcoholic being tempted to drink again when life becomes more challenging. This is because the disease never leaves us; we just learn how to manage it. It's just one simple decision away.

Chapter's Logical Take-Away: This piece discusses "Weak Relapse" and how self-consciousness can prevent it. Both positive and negative emotions can cause relapse during rehabilitation. Some of the common ones are stress, anxiety, tragedy, depression, loneliness, and joyous celebrations (positive emotions).

NEVER A SOLUTION

Alcohol is not the way to suppress our fears.

Your addiction can no longer be your solution, nor should it be your medium to process the difficulties you're going through. Time after time I have heard that drugs and alcohol are the suitable solutions for troubled individuals. Seasoned people in recovery know that's crazy talk. You should be trying to break the addiction habit, not use it as your escape from reality. It's like using a Band-Aid where stitches are called for—only a temporary fix, and what is more, a Band-Aid eventually falls off in the shower.

Throughout this book, you will be reminded that the purpose and end goal of its content is to help you understand and deal with underlying problems, so you never have to use drugs or alcohol again as an addict. In case you haven't yet realized it, this is, to a greater degree, a book on psychology, to penetrate the minds of those who can't live without substance, and not so much about specific addictions.

Here are a few reasons why alcohol and drugs are not healthy or effective solutions when dealing with life's difficulties:

- Health Risks[328]: Alcohol and drug abuse can lead to serious health issues like addiction, liver damage, weakened immune system, cancer risk, heart problems, and mental health disorders.
- Escapism[329]: Using substances to escape from problems does not address the root causes of those problems. They may temporarily numb the pain or stress, or offer a sense of isolation, but they do not provide lasting solutions.
- Addiction: Substance abuse can lead to addiction and obsession, which is a chronic disease. It is often characterized by compulsive indulgence of drugs and alcohol, without thinking about the harmful consequences it can leave in the long run.
- Legal Consequences: Many drugs are illegal and using them can result in legal problems like arrests, criminal charges, and imprisonment[330].
- Social and Relationship Issues[331]: Alcohol and drug abuse can strain and break relationships with family, friends, and intimate partners, leading to isolation and loneliness, which can further lead to mental disorders like depression.
- Financial Impact[332]: Maintaining a substance abuse habit can be expensive, leading to financial instability, loss of employment, and debt.
- Mental Health[333]: Substance abuse often worsens mental health issues rather than improving them. It can lead to anxiety, depression, and other mental health disorders.

It's important to seek healthier alternatives when faced with difficult life challenges or testing emotional times. These might include seeking support from friends and family, talking to a therapist or counselor, practicing stress management techniques like meditation or exercise, like mindfulness meditation, or finding constructive ways to address and solve the underlying issues causing distress. If you or someone you know is struggling with substance abuse or addiction, it's crucial to seek help from a healthcare professional or a support group to start the journey toward recovery and a better life.

The important thing is to make the most of where you are right now, regardless of your struggles, and to be grateful to just be alive. Today's reality is now, and escaping this moment with drugs or alcohol is not a sustainable solution. For instant gratification, we forget the long-term consequences. Learning to live with gratitude simply changes our attitude and outlook on life. As with any good thing, recovery from addiction takes time. It's a slow process, but if you stick to it, you'll succeed.

Chapter's Logical Take-Away: When adversity hits, suppressing feelings with substances should never be an option. Whenever you feel the urge to use drugs or substances when facing difficulties, remember the quote (*"Alcohol is not the way to suppress our fears."*), and recite it continuously until you believe what you are saying.

I NEEDED A MEETING – REALLY?

What I really need is friends I can count on.

often hear people in twelve-step program meetings say, "I need," or "I needed a meeting." Another very popular line is "I heard what I needed to hear today. It came at the right time." This could easily make a lot of sense with people new to the program and more likely with people just coming back to the program after a relapse. Nevertheless, in most cases those statements usually come from people who have sobriety in the program.

When I hear someone who has stayed clean for many years say, "I almost drank last night"; I can't help but scratch my head in disbelief. So, what about the relapse prevention skills/tools taught in the program and the knowledge learned about your addiction? How could you forget and almost drink? If you knew you had six months to live and decided to exploit your disease of addiction, you missed the boat with your program.

"I am one drink away from relapsing" is another one. Everyone who admits they are an alcoholic will always be one drink away from a relapse; alcohol is Kryptonite to the alcoholic. But this is supposed to get easier over time until the obsession and cravings fade; that's when we reach a level of manageability of our addiction and have total control over ourselves. The gas can won't explode if you don't light a match. It's simple as that.

When people "needed" a meeting, I hope what they're really implying is, "I needed to be here, in this building, with all my friends and the people who make me feel more comfortable." Remember, we are social beings, and your good energy is transferred to me when I am near you. Your energy stimulates me. It's contagious, in a good way. Whatever is troubling me is lessened when I'm around people, as opposed to being alone or isolating. So, when I say I need a meeting, I'm saying, "I need you [all] to help me through my addiction." I also believe what you "needed to hear" could be anything at all that is uplifting to take your mind off what's troubling you. And sometimes, out of pure coincidence, what's being discussed might be just what's bothering you.

> **Chapter's Logical Take-Away:** When people in any twelve-step program exclaim "they needed a meeting," what they are really saying is that they need to break away from the environment they're in and be around people they know and feel comfortable with.

ABSTINENCE AND SOBRIETY

*You can't have one
without the other.*

The definition of abstinence *is the practice of abstaining of not doing or having something that is wanted or enjoyable.* This may include any indulgence of a particular appetite, impulse, craving, or desire, such as from alcohol, sexual activity, social media, etc.[334]. In this chapter, you will be able to understand the commonly used (and confused) terms for abstinence or sobriety pertaining to drug and alcohol addiction.

The term **"clean"** usually refers to being **"abstinent"** (or absent) from substances, including alcohol.

The term **"sober"** is usually referred to as alcohol-free or drug-free for an extended period of time.

"Clean and sober" simply means without the presence of either drugs or alcohol in your bloodstream.

Yet another term like **"sobriety"** which is a broad statement for having both, **"physical sobriety"** (complete abstinence bodily), and **"emotional sobriety"** (mental resilience and with strong coping mechanism).

A life of sobriety is the grand accomplishment for a person with addiction or obsession issues[335]. With the help of a psychic change, you can reach the level of normalcy in life. The only stipulation to living this kind of life is to let go of all addictions and obsessive behaviors.

Sobriety is how you react emotionally when dealing with life's ups and downs, and of course, addiction or obsession. So, if you stopped drinking and using, and are now "clean and sober," but your personality is what it used to be while high or intoxicated, then you are not really living a life of sobriety. The process of recovery involves becoming a different—better—person altogether. You may be clean and sober, but you basically are in need of a personality makeover, or you'll never be happy regardless of whether you drink alcohol or not. That's where the psychic change is necessary. If no changes are made, you suffer from the "Dry Drunk" syndrome[336]. Chapter 43 just ahead is dedicated to dry drunk syndrome, or "untreated alcoholism.

Addiction recovery is all-encompassing. It needs unshakable commitment. The path to a clean and healthy lifestyle begins with detoxification and continues with self-examination, self-reflection, personal growth, and spiritual and/or religious awareness.

Clean is the trailer, and sobriety is the whole movie as you start to live a happy life. Though the threat of relapse will always keep you alert, never let yourself take your recovery for granted. But you must have something to recover from. It is not just all about substance abuse; recovery can also be about mental affairs. After all, mentality is everything. The identification and focus on removing anything that sets you back from being happy, social, and successful is the object of recovery.

> **Chapter's Logical Take-Away:** Abstinence and sobriety are more than just giving up drugs or bad habits. It is about taking back control of your life, being a better human being, and looking forward to a better future.

EMOTIONAL SOBRIETY

I can't will people into my happiness;
all I can do is share it.

As derived from the last chapter, emotional sobriety is the mental aspect of the two-part "sobriety." It is a combination of a way of living with an addiction and its absence without addiction actions. Emotional sobriety particularly includes the ability to cope with a spectrum of feelings in a healthy manner. Emotionally sober people experience happiness, sadness, rage, and other intense emotions, but they know how to them so that they do not rule their actions or become overwhelming[337]. They control their emotions, not the other way around.

Emotional sobriety also entails being able to completely experience feelings without needing to suppress them with drugs, alcohol, or other substances. This talent instills a deep sense of tranquility and strength within a person, allowing them to handle any difficulties that may arise in life. Other signs of emotional sobriety include[338]:

- Living fully in the present without harboring resentments from the past or over-planning for the future. It also includes less overthinking.
- Monitoring and controlling one's own actions.
- Being able to deal with life's difficulties, obstacles, and other conflicts with a strong mindset.
- Avoiding the use of drugs or alcohol or engaging in any other unhealthy or addictive activity to cope with feelings.
- Having a generally cheerful outlook on life.
- Embracing positive and meaningful interactions with others.
- Preventing powerful emotions from taking over.

It is critical to address the negative feelings that may have led to the development of addiction, to find the root cause. Furthermore, the feelings (self-loathing, guilt, shame, loss of self-esteem, etc.) that arose as a result of addiction must be addressed[339]. While unpleasant emotions can certainly cause a physical relapse, emotional sobriety is employed to regulate these feelings so that relapse does not occur. If someone is sincerely committed and determined to lead a sober life, they will try to achieve emotional sobriety.

The reason deer don't hit the trees isn't because they say "tree, tree, tree." It's because they say "path, path, path." Stay focused.

Behavioral therapy is a psychological treatment that aims to modify specific behaviors and reshape the way individuals think and understand the world and themselves[340]. One of the most widely recognized forms of behavioral therapy is Cognitive Behavioral Therapy (CBT)[341]. CBT sessions raise awareness of negative environmental influences. This is accomplished with techniques such as coping mechanisms and intervention sessions, with the ultimate goal of transforming behavior into positive thinking and a better outlook on life.

Chapter's Logical Take-Away: Emotional sobriety is all about the emotional balance and well-being of an individual. It involves self-awareness—recognizing, understanding, and processing all emotions without judgment and with an open mind.

UNTREATED ALCOHOLISM/DRY DRUNK

I don't regret the past, nor wish to dwell on it.

"Dry drunk syndrome" is a catchphrase used in the sober community for untreated alcoholism[342]. Both, passably interchangeable, are terms that refer to the same symptoms, whose risky conditions can traditionally mark the initial stages of relapse. Neither term is recognized in medical or psychological diagnosis, but rather a concept that has been used within the context of Alcoholics Anonymous (AA) and other addiction recovery communities.

Dry drunk syndrome, or untreated addiction, are used to describe a set of behavioral and emotional patterns that some individuals who have stopped drinking alcohol or stopped using drugs exhibit, even though the days of addiction are way behind them. They still behave in dysfunctional ways[343].

I've often heard the statement, "Every day I wake up with untreated alcoholism." Untreated alcoholism is commonly referred to as 'Dry Drunk Syndrome.' In my opinion, I strongly disagree with the idea that they are the same, and here's why:

If you wake up with untreated alcoholism, you are simply acknowledging that you are an alcoholic and must confront your condition as you face the day. Moreover, by waking up with untreated alcoholism, you are expressing the intention to address and treat your disease based on what you have learned.

On the other hand, waking up as a dry drunk signifies more than just being an alcoholic; it suggests living a life that lacks sanity. To truly recover, one must not only be aware of their disease but also actively work on restoring sanity to lead a normal life.

As the author of this book on addiction, I present this logical perspective. I propose replacing terms such as 'sober' (using abstinence), sobriety, "a life of sobriety," and "living sober" (despite it being my favorite book on alcoholic living) with the term "EMOTIONAL SOBRIETY." To me, nothing encapsulates the idea of living a normal life as an alcoholic more than these two words.

An alcoholic/addict who has not properly worked on their underlying emotional issues or behaviors during their recovery period will continue to experience negative attitudes and behaviors. These symptoms, despite being abstinent, impact their quality of life and often the people around them. Excessive anxiety and worry begin to seep into various threads of their lives. Feelings of being bored or dissatisfied with life begin to creep in over time. One becomes easily distracted from productive tasks. Remnant feelings of depression and anxiety surface even after stopping substance use. Negative thoughts are accompanied by negative feelings. Some people experiencing dry drunk syndrome may display intense anger, frustration, and resentment toward themselves and the world. They might struggle to manage their emotions and have difficulty coping with daily stressors. They might even develop a shortened temper. Many partake in isolated behavior and find life generally difficult, experiencing a sense of uneasiness and restlessness with life. They might feel a sense of alienation and struggle to connect with others. Questions like "What's the point in all of this?" might cross their minds.

People with dry drunk syndrome might find it challenging to accept that they have a substance problem, which can hinder their willingness to engage in proper treatment and recovery activities.

Remember, you are not a drunk now, you are a person in recovery. But always an alcoholic or a person with a substance problem if you can't be honest with yourself.

> **Chapter's Logical Take-Away:** In the sober community, "untreated alcoholism" or "dry drunk syndrome" refers to people who are clean and sober but are not living a life of sobriety. They have done nothing to improve themselves and are therefore no closer to living a better life than the day they put down the drink or drugs. They maintain negative attitudes and behaviors like anxiety, boredom, and dissatisfaction while living in isolation. Emotional instability can cause anger, frustration, and loneliness. In my view, equate to merely existing.

THE ROAD TO RECOVERY

"I have returned; therefore, I am restored."

What is "recovery?" The term "recovery" holds various applications, but for all intents and purposes of this book, a book about addiction, it simply means having a plan or program in place to overcome all related addictive disorders[344]. If we look back to the 13th century, "recovery" is referred to as a return to health after illness, injury, misfortune, etc., closely aligning with its significance in this book, which deals with addiction in a healthy and positive way. Thus, to recover something, a pre-existing condition must be in place, and in our case, it's addiction.

Every addiction is marked by a starting point and a destination in recovery. I am cautious not to label it as an "end" but rather a continuous process, extending until death, if warranted. I believe there is a singular beginning, like navigating a maze with twisted paths to traverse and challenges to face along the way.

In the foreword of the first edition of Alcoholics Anonymous's *Big Book*, it is written: "We, of Alcoholics Anonymous, are more than one hundred men and women who have recovered from a seemingly hopeless state of mind and body. To show other alcoholics precisely how we have recovered is the main purpose of this book." I do not subscribe to the notion of being "fully" recovered. Our disease remains within us and is kept at bay if we are diligent with our program of recovery. While some may identify as a "recovered addict" or "recovered alcoholic," I prefer the terms "recovering" addict, or "recovering" alcoholic, or "recovering" gambler, or a gambler "in recovery." Similarly, one can be a person "recovering" from an eating disorder; all these terms are considered politically correct (PC). It may be worth noting that if the obsession to engage in your addiction is no longer present and your body no longer craves your addiction/obsessions, it is up to you if you feel you have recovered from a hopeless state of mind and body. That's when you are able to let others know about the process of your recovery. Your experience can help many.

The disease of addiction persists for life and is never truly cured. The concept of never being "fully recovered" parallels the incurable characteristics of most addiction-related mental diseases, firmly rooted in the mind[345]. Much like we are never entirely mentally healed from physical injuries, though we learn to live with them, complete "recovery" from addiction is only idealistic. Diseases of addiction linger indefinitely, necessitating lifelong, successful management. Despite all that, people find a way to lead happy lives of contentment.

At about the age of fifteen, I vividly remember Olympic gymnast Nadia Comaneci's ambitious dismount on the balance beam. Although it seemed she might falter during the landing, the TV commentator praised her "nice recovery" as she secured the gold. I also had an experience with a fractured bone. I was in a car accident when I fractured my wrist. A cast was applied that I wore for five to six weeks to help the bones mesh together and fuse properly. When the cast was no longer needed, it was removed, and my wrist was healed. I was recovered, but only partially so. My mind would continue to caution me that it would never be the same and never function as it used to before the injury, and I had to treat it differently moving forward. Ironically, the same feelings occurred after back surgery. My body had healed, but my mind still carried the fear of reinjury. This is a psychological trauma.

A vital third component in many recovery programs is spirituality. Twelve-step programs, considering themselves "spiritual," integrate spirituality into the daily routine with the mind and body components working together[346]. This is based around the concept of a "spiritual malady" (malady: a disease or disorder of the body), an inner conflict causing restlessness, irritability, and discontentment, particularly recognized in spiritual programs like AA. So, addressing this spiritual malady is crucial for claiming full recovery.

Alcoholism and substance misuse or abuse, categorized as mental addictions, differ from spirituality, which pertains to the soul rather than the mind[347]. Therefore, addressing and rectifying this spiritual malady is imperative. I prefer terms such as "repair" or "fix," as well as "maintenance" or "maintaining control" over addiction. This approach is quite like managing chronic diseases like diabetes, obesity, arthritis, etc., where lifelong control through insulin or dialysis is essential to avert severe consequences. While alcoholism and substance addiction are incurable diseases, the focus centers on employing effective management strategies.

In my personal journey, I find AA (or any twelve-step program) to be the most beneficial. Although alcohol was not my primary addiction or DOC (drug of choice), it is the only path I have come to know in my journey to recovery. I enrolled in a treatment campus and was taken to an AA meeting on my first day, and for the next ninety consecutive days that followed.

Two years after understanding and living sobriety (referenced in Chapter 39 on sobriety), which occurred on October 12, 2019 (my sobriety date is October 12th, 2017), I received acknowledgment from "The Georgia Council on Substance Abuse" that I was now considered a person in long-term recovery (LTR). As of this writing, I have just received my six-year medallion, denoting six years clean and sober from all substances.

> **Chapter's Logical Take-Away:** The concept of "recovery" in addiction is a continuous journey with no absolute endpoint, rejecting the idea of being "fully recovered." This book reiterates the goal of achieving physical wellness and a diminished or nonexistent desire for one's addiction. However, it emphasizes that the struggle remains embedded within us as a reminder that we are never cured.

BE PATIENT

We're not all mind readers,
but we can sense it coming.

On page 164, the last page of the "basic text" in the AA *Big Book*, it says: "You will surely meet some of us as you trudge the Road of Happy Destiny." Because of its strategic location in the book and the ambiguity of its actual meaning for readers, I would bet that the word "trudge" has been looked up more than any other word in the book. There were a few on my list, and trudge was one of them. Because the book was conceived in the writing style of 1939, some words seem archaic to many readers. If you had to guess, most people would think trudge is to drag yourself through mud. But its true meaning is to walk slowly and deliberately, with more focus on thoughts than on feet. Furthermore, the metaphorical use of the word "trudge" in the *Big Book* is not about physical movement at all, but rather a slow and deliberate mental approach.

So, if you happen to be walking through the mud, that might be how you would choose to walk—slowly and carefully. But a better metaphor would be walking on ice and not in the mud. I hail from where it snows, and if you have ever walked on the ice, you move about slowly and plant each step down firmly in a robotic, surefooted manner so as not to slip.

Going back to what the book tells us on page 164, we go slowly and carefully in an unhurried way. Recovery from addiction is an ongoing and unending commitment, so what's the rush? Pardon the pun (about "rush" as it's attributed to dopamine release). Get it slowly, if necessary, but get it. The longer you remain conscious of your goal to be abstinent and mindful of the state of your addiction, the clearer the puzzle appears before you.

While walking or trudging implies a physical action, the message from page 164 of the AA's *Big Book* is one of mental implication. People with addiction might get frustrated when nothing makes sense. How do we handle the everyday setbacks (job, family, and other ventures) outside of our recovery? Everything becomes a juggling act. If you are struggling with a multitude of issues, I make a simple and relatable point: "If you have too many balls in the air, you won't be able to coordinate your hands to catch them all, and you will begin dropping them. Slowly begin taking some that are too much to handle out of the rotation and setting them on a table. Set them aside until you can manage the ones in the air." Give yourself achievable tasks.

There are dozens of quotes out there that include "Worth waiting for," and "Patience is the key." So, I am going to suggest the first one that comes to mind: "Anything worth having is worth waiting for." This tells me everything I need to understand about the complexities of recovery in so many ways. The new bike or car I saved up for as a kid. We usually think about material things, but what about the right person or job? Or, in the context of this book, my sanity and sobriety. Making a strong commitment and patiently enduring what I need to learn about myself and my recovery are worth waiting for, in my view. What about you?

In AA, they also say, "More will be revealed." I found that to be very true, so I had to be patient with the process. I was willing to wait for another piece to fit so I could see more of the overall recovery picture. The connectivity among individuals is *magical,* in a way. Like in a relay race where the baton from one area of recovery is connected to the next when the handoff is made.

The subtitle of this book is "Treating the cause, not the symptom." One of the reasons I chose it was because when you get down to understanding the root cause or reason for the happenings, you become more able to correct them and less likely to repeat the mistakes again. I give credit to the many learned parts of AA's twelve-step program to help me fix what needs fixing within myself. It takes time, but as you've also heard, "It's worth it." And it indeed is worth it.

Chapter's Logical Take-Away: If you've decided to eliminate addiction from your joyless life, there is an educational journey to embark on and so many things to be revealed and understood. As you witness measurable progress, clarity will gradually manifest, marking the beginning of positive changes in your life.

MULTIPLE PATHS TO RECOVERY

If you're heading for California, you can drive, fly, or hop on a train. Whichever you choose is up to you!

There are many pathways to recovery treatment that are recognized by various addiction communities. These are the most popular and successful recovery approaches:

<u>Natural Recovery:</u> This involves an individual taking their process of recovery into their own hands. In general, this is a more viable option for those in the early stages of drug or alcohol dependence. It's for those who exhibit more self-control[348].

<u>Support Groups:</u> Also called self-help groups. These are small, community-oriented groups where those struggling with addiction gather to provide support to each other under the guidance of an overarching framework. Examples include Alcoholics Anonymous or Narcotics

Anonymous. When it comes to dealing with alcoholism, the most successful support group is AA (Alcoholic Anonymous), the "Godfather," or the model for all the dozens of twelve-step programs today[349]. What success means to me is "return to service or society" as it used to be. When we stop drinking, we think all our troubles will miraculously disappear. That we won't have to face the consequences of our actions. I am reminded that the old timers (people with many years sober in the program) would begrudgingly say, if you go outside the program, you're not working our twelve-step program.

<u>Medication-Assisted Recovery</u>[350]: Those in the middle or later stages of addiction often find relief in the combination of behavioral therapies and counseling alongside medication, such as methadone or buprenorphine.

<u>Peer Recovery support:</u> Nonclinical, peer-led services such as recovery coaching and peer-led small support groups, providing friendly environment[350].

<u>Alternative and Holistic Recovery Methods</u>[351]: Alternative methods complement traditional recovery treatments with the aim of bringing holistic healing to the mind, body, and spirit. Examples could include yoga and mindfulness meditation.

<u>Inpatient Treatment:</u> Residential programs that include medical, therapeutic, and social support[352].

<u>Mental Health Services:</u> Services such as psychotherapy and cognitive-behavioral therapy.

<u>Self-Directed Recovery (DIY):</u> This is when you put together a program of recovery that works for you. This is my program of choice, which I've devoted the next chapter to in full detail.

I am here to tell you that recovery doesn't have to be your life, just whatever part you make it for your betterment. Being mindful or ever-conscious of your addiction or obsessions will help you keep your priorities straight. It does, however, require a commitment that includes abstinence from your addiction. You will undoubtedly make life changes and miss important events, but if successful, you'll never really care about "might have." Did you ever talk to someone who is newly retired? At first, they have said to themselves, "What am I going to do with all my free time?" Do you know what they all end up saying? "I am busier than before when I was working." Today, I say, "I have a lot of free time, but I am busy as hell." That translates to: "I have time to do whatever I wish, but I choose to fill my time with productive and healthy activities everyday now."

Chapter's Logical Take-Away: There are several addiction recovery choices for different stages and personal preferences. Addiction responsibility helps early-stage addicts recover spontaneously. Good rehabilitation should encourage lifelong abstinence and beneficial activities, along with healthy habits.

SELF-DIRECTED (MY) WAY OF RECOVERY

Outside AA is like home schooling

Let's first understand that recovery from anything in this world involves a meticulous process and constant action. We are a creative and innovative species, so there's assuredly more than one way of finding and developing solutions. Let's skip over recovery from physical ailments and injuries; that would be better served in the realm of medical doctors. The brain is at the helm of all obsessions and addictions, piloting the entire body and its functions, so the mental processes available to recover for those areas are vast.

In the previous chapter, we discussed how there were multiple pathways to recovery from addiction and obsessions, utilizing template-style programs. But a self-directed (custom-designed) program is more suitable for my makeup, as I mentioned.

Self-directed means by your own direction, similar to how people self-teach themselves some skills, or self-devised as in your program to manage your addiction or obsession. A multitude of sources, personal experience, twelve-step programs, treatment centers, clinical, social workers and counselors, friends, books & literature, tapes etc. are the likely ingredients for a successful, sober program. Even the Internet nowadays is a valuable resource. There's obviously an abundance of feeds to formulate an effective program that can work for you. What makes sense to you logically? What works for you? Don't discount your common sense and intuitions. Weigh the source. Is it trusted? Is it credible? I am a firm believer that knowledge doesn't come from only one source.

An ever-popular phrase used in recovery is "take what you need and leave the rest." "Consider only what aligns with you." "Salad bar" or "buffet style" style recovery is often publicized too.

Don't forget to consider your personal difficulties as an individual. Everyone's struggles are different. How will it affect your immediate and long-term health? E.g., If I am overweight and need to lose weight for my heart health, I probably need to diet before I can proceed with the workout. I may not be able to walk at first because of my weight, but if I lose weight by dieting first, my knees will be able to handle a lighter body. It's a cycle that, in this case, may lead to cycling.

As addicts or alcoholics, you do not have to buy into everything you are taught to heal yourself (as mentioned in the last page, take what you need, and leave the rest). Who can say that you don't already know more about a topic or subject than the one teaching you? You may genuinely desire to be fully versed in addictions and addictive behaviors before you dive in to analyze your own problems and want to know them so well that you can live by them. If you are even slightly unclear about the meaning of something, seek assistance from as many people or resources as you need until you are satisfied with the answer. While it's true that knowledge is one click away, that applies to misleading knowledge as well. Know it well enough with conviction that you can pass it on to others with total confidence. My attempt is not to oppose the ways of any recovery program but to point out mine, how my approach is slightly different from theirs, and the logical perspective of others in various addiction programs.

Chapter's Logical Take-Away: This chapter merely states that when in recovery from addiction, the individual chooses to source their education in whichever way works for them, no matter the origins. Think of a "buffet".

SECTION 4

FIXING YOURSELF

THOSE SOCIALLY INSIDE AND OUTSIDE THE CIRCLES

Ultimately, "the proof is in the pudding."

In the realm of addiction recovery and mental health, individuals often find solace and support within organized programs, forming a distinct social circle. Let's focus on individuals dealing with alcohol or drug-related problems for a moment.

As mentioned in Chapter 23, "What Kind of Drinker are You?" If you even have to ask yourself whether you have a problem with drugs or alcohol, you probably do. If you seek psychological help or a mental health practitioner, your solution will be looked upon favorably, as this would appear to be an acceptable protocol for rehabilitation——as long as you don't refer to them as a "shrink." It wouldn't appear to be invasive to talk to someone about your problems, right? However, if you choose to join a club, organization, or program as an alternative method of treatment, you will, in a sense, be joining the ranks as a lifetime member of the "damaged" in the eyes of all other outsiders. The reason for this perception by the non-afflicted is that support groups are essentially forever, in that you're never cured; substance disorders can only be managed or remedied. So "forever" is accurate, and the cold, hard truth is here.

Being part of a twelve-step program frequently brings a comforting sense of belonging and camaraderie. In this shared journey, individuals confront similar struggles, united in their quest to overcome addiction. This captures the nuances of these programs, highlighting the common goal of achieving a normal life free from mood-altering substances. Yet, it also reveals the internal divisions within the community, specifically in terms of differing perspectives on adherence to program principles.

The majority of twelve-step program members who make the choice on their own to join this way of life, which it becomes, are unwilling to accept any deviation from the program as it is outlined. These hardline members shun the remaining others in the program, who only choose to take what they need that the program has to offer. Personally, I am one of those.

While participating in many meetings, I share meaningful and helpful insights. My shares are generally met with a favorable reception. However, when asked about my sponsor, I revealed that I don't have one, surprising others. I have even heard, "how are you able to stand here"? I matter-of-factly respond, "there's nothing wrong with my legs." It's as if they can't believe I am even alive, to their dismay.

<u>Here is possibly the best metaphor this book has to offer:</u> I play a rock-style electric guitar. And probably ninety-five percent of all electric guitar players use a pick. Of the other five percent, Jeff Beck, who is arguably the best electric rock guitarist of all time, and Mark Knopfler from Dire Straits, Rolling Stone's #27 in their top 100 do not use a pick. As I say in my forthcoming book, *The Proof Is in the Pudding,* you can't argue with success.

I have lived in a custom-designed world and in my head since I was young. I adhere to the rules but prioritize what I believe is helpful for me. I consider myself the best kind of alcoholic because I can be myself without drugs or alcohol, never depriving myself entirely of anything any program offers. I am a one-chip wonder, as evidenced by the fact that my devised program is working for me.

In Chapter 40 I make reference to a few twelve-step groups and meetings I like, based on the format and the people attending. It has been written in a twelve-step textbook that "that we are people who would not normally mix." What they are simply saying is that we are not likely matches for each other in most capacities, coming from different geographic, demographic, and socio-economic backgrounds and surroundings. But we all gather in a program with a track record for success, willing to make it together by helping each other achieve one common goal: to stay clean and sober. I have also heard that "this [a twelve-step meeting] is the only group where a bunch of strangers can get together to reminisce."

We were created with the purpose of forming connections and equipped with social skills to cultivate friendships. So how, with our uniqueness, are we to have them beyond the invisible barriers that were unintentionally created and that separate us? Individuals of short stature often choose to marry others within their community who understand and share similar challenges. However, it is important to emphasize that love should transcend physicality or mental predispositions and should be based on a deeper connection with the individual. So, can we please get past the physical and mental uncommonness of the addict and the non-addict? These may all be the unwritten truths many hold inside.

We get to pick our friends and relationships,
but they can only be if they pick us back! So, like every
bond with another, they have to pick us back.

The idea of compatibility is something that I think about when I am considering friendships and significant partnerships. As a participant in a twelve-step recovery program, I occasionally wonder if I might be more likely to connect with people who don't struggle as much with substance addictions or who adhere to a more stringent program than the one I've created for myself from selected outside sources. This is something I've been contemplating lately, the more time I spend in the program.

Before entering any programs and achieving sobriety, my associations were often with individuals who brought no positive influence into my life. During that period, rational thinking eluded me, and my judgment was skewed, desperately needing recalibration. This transformation underscores the disarray of my past, marked by misguided pursuits of sex and drugs, against the backdrop of the clean living within the program.

However, stories develop of individuals who have turned their lives around. Athletes, distinct from those in positions of trust, especially concerning money and people's lives, seem to be absolved of their past addictions. In society, they are now revered, having overcome their challenges, and made a triumphant return.

Chapter's Logical Take-Away: This is a unique perspective from an individual who opts for a more personalized approach to recovery, choosing to "take what he needs" rather than strictly adhering to the prescribed guidelines. It captures the tension between collective adherence to program principles and the desire for individualized approaches. Through personal experiences and reflections, here lie valuable insights into the multifaceted social dynamics of twelve-step programs and the intricate balance between conformity and autonomy in the journey to recovery.

I WANT WHAT YOU GOT

I love your car, but mine's fine.

If I am somewhat jealous of you, it's because you have something appealing that I don't have. Perhaps you possess positive qualities, skills, and talents that may be viewed as enviable by others. But this is not limited to just the person themselves; it can include the lifestyle they have and the expensive things they own. I have never been married, so my friends, who are all married, have often said, "who has it better than you Rick?" And my response has always been, "How do you know that I don't want what you have? Maybe I would love for my child to leap onto the bed on a lazy Sunday morning and land square on my crotch (ouch!)." So, the grass is not always greener … as they say. Yet, when it comes to addiction, I find myself in a similar frame of mind. Such thoughts are only natural; it's a common human tendency. When I am around someone who is managing their addiction earnestly and has it all together, from a happy life to a fulfilling job, it fills me with hope.

Do you know when I can have a Ford GT? It's not when I have the money to afford one, it's when I have a garage to keep it in safely. And having hope tells me, if I want one bad enough, I should start saving for a home with garage. The time I get one is when it is supposed to be. That is what you can expect in the next chapter, "Promises that Make Sense."

But there is a flipside to every coin, as with everything in life. For every concept, there exists its polar opposite. For every problem there exists a solution. Just as there is hot and cold, fast and slow, there is also a flip side to what attracts me or repels me from others. There too, is at least something of theirs I don't want. Maybe it's their mannerisms, or even something as much as their appearance. It is quite reasonable to have these feelings. In such cases, I perform a little reverse engineering, which you will find in detail in my book titled, *Sales and Selling Yourself.* I put myself in the other person's shoes and say to myself: "Do I do that?" Sometimes it's the best way to see what is truly revolting about another person. What an enlightening lesson!

In Chapter 40, I wrote, "What have you learned for God's sake?" A significant aspect of this book revolves around cultivating improvement in individuals. While it's a book on addictions and how to overcome them, throughout the reading, you've probably started to realize, if we don't become better people, the prospect of living with addiction and finding happiness becomes virtually impossible.

Additionally, I talked about emotional sobriety in Chapter 42, turning negative thinking into positive with CBT. This transformation extends to converting healthy jealousy into a desire that fuels an individual positively or turns someone's character into acceptance.

> **Chapter's Logical Take-Away:** People are inherently jealous and seek what others have, or sometimes don't want. However, one should choose based on their values and needs. While this impulse can be heightened by addiction, seeing someone in recovery can change that.

CHAPTER 50

PROMISES THAT MAKE SENSE

Just remember, all promises come at a cost.

would like to begin with a logical analysis with the use of the word "promise."

"I promise you will lose weight if you burn more calories every day with a systematic workout regime." (**SCIENCE**).

"If you get caught with an unregistered firearm on your person, I promise, you might go to jail." (**THEORY**).

Do you follow?

Promises claimed in recovery programs really don't have the power to assure you of anything. The implication is that if you adhere to the program and remain clean and sober, you will experience nothing but positive results. In a nutshell, you are putting yourself in a better position to improve without drugs and alcohol interfering. Recovery programs provide emotional hope to help you maintain focus and to feel better as you move forward with the process. In my opinion, this is merely fundamental psychological marketing.

Therefore, now that you are clean and sober, you are much more employable and in a better position to land a decent job. Similarly, you are now in a much better position to attract potential mate. When you are sober, a sense of responsibility sets in that had been suppressed due to mental disorders like depression. You now pay all your bills on time, thereby improving your credit score. As a result, the house you have in mind has become more attainable. The world now looks very different from when it did during active addiction. You won't be plagued by your financial situation now that you're a contributing member of society. As I mentioned in several of the previous chapters, when you are living a life of sobriety, being physically and mentally sober, you become eligible for "that" job, the one you really want.

Twelve-step recovery programs also claim the fear you have of people leaving you forever. That excludes any sort of violent conflict. What this implies is that we have a newfound sense of inner pride and confidence about ourselves, and as a result are more assured around everyone.

Social anxiety is one of the greatest fears which many people suffer from. Without the physical aspects of our obsessions or addictions to contend with, we are better suited to dealing with society[353].

> *To paraphrase Jim Morrison of the Doors …*
> *"People are (no longer) strange when you're a stranger."*

The term egomaniac, one who is self-centered and looks out only for their own gain, with an inferiority complex, a person who feels inadequate, is constantly repeated ad nauseum in alcoholic recovery[354]. All that means is that the individual projects a "front of confidence" (false ego) in their mannerisms to compensate for their insecurities on the inside (inferiority complex).

When we maintain our sobriety and put a plan in place to better ourselves, we unintentionally attract better people into our lives. As we know, like attracts like. I might instinctively or subconsciously do good, estimable, selfless acts every day without a return. That is the meaning of altruism. Doing good deeds without ever expecting anything in return. But I need to "Keep the Faith" no matter what, because when I am expecting something good to happen for me, it just may happen! Perhaps one day I will be rewarded for being decent and fair, and that is "karma." Other days, not so much. Faith is also trust. It is hope with a good track record. Trusting that the program might work for you and taking a leap of faith. Evidence may help strengthen your faith with anything. If you think faith sounds too religious for you, substitute it with trust. In the chapters that follow, we'll focus a lot more on personal development.

Chapter's Logical Take-Away: This chapter offers personal and rehabilitation growth. It indicates recovery program claims are all about emotional support, not results. You make your breaks, which become apparently more likely when you are successfully dealing with addiction.

PAY CLOSE ATTENTION

Nothing I learned gets replaced until something better or more simplistic comes along.

I have often said that everything in this world has already been said before, just by different people in different ways. Nothing is truly original. It's through "standing on the shoulders of giants" that people come up with different variations of existing concepts or ideas. Are you merely reading words on a page, or are you truly reading and absorbing? Reading, reciting, or repeating (out loud, or in silence, with or without subvocalization), and comprehending can be challenging if you are not focused. With my ADHD (Attention-Deficit/Hyperactivity Disorder) I get easily distracted and even anticipate words that should come next in whatever I am reading. For me, it is important that I stay focused when it's my turn to read. It is also not uncommon for me to have to read things multiple times to strengthen my comprehension. Look around you.

If you have thirty years of experience in recovery, thanks; because I don't have thirty more years left to live.

Along with willpower, self-knowledge often receives a bad rep from scholars in twelve-step programs. However, I firmly align myself with logical reasoning on this matter. Self-knowledge, in essence, serves as a vault of all my life experiences stored in my brain as hard drive memory. Ultimately, everything comes from experience, both yours and my own. We are the sum total of our experiences. Once I learn something and can recall it when needed, the response I provide becomes my truth. In my forthcoming book, *The Proof Is in the Pudding*, everything I experience firsthand is "my truth." Self-knowledge comprises all my truths, including those I've accepted and embraced as others' truths from my own trusted sources. Even lies are truths until proven otherwise.

Julius Caesar said, "Experience is the best teacher." You can say I have a lifetime of self-knowledge within me from all that I learned from my experience. I carry, hold, and recycle the things that have come from those who have touched my life in their own ways. I get it, then you get it. That is the essence of progress and growth as we navigate the intricacies of life. And as a bonus, you don't have to make the mistakes I made, you can learn from them before it's too late and possibly do what I did better.

A head full of knowledge only makes you a nerd. No one likes nerds. A head full of knowledge that you utilize makes you a productive part of society.

When we face challenges, whether in addiction or during the process of recovery, or in our daily lives, in general, we must be available to unconventional solutions, thinking outside the box, to push beyond our comfort zones. We need to find the courage to try new approaches when our old ways have failed or are too outdated for the modern lifestyle. As I grew older, I learned to trust the opinions of wise and successful people. Surrounding myself with individuals of integrity became the cornerstone of my open-minded thinking. It's like having my very own board of advisors. This might sound a little crazy, but I believe it makes total sense now. If I want the best pizza in town, but I am new to the area, I will look for someone who paints themselves as a "foodie" (someone for whom good food is important), or someone who speaks Italian. In the case of the latter, I might need a translator at the same time. But you can see why I chose to mention an Italian to allude to good food. It might just be my preference. For others, it could be a Mexican or an Asian, but you get my point. This approach would apply to just about anything. It's a little bit of logic. Amazon reviews and ratings are the benchmark for everything they sell. Highly rated means higher sales, it's the consensus and simple as that.

So today, on many occasions I let others help me decide with my purchase when I think it's best. I have also said that "Two brains are better than mine." So, I have decided to let all my readers in on a secret about the books I write. I have a cover artist whose style suits my subject matter and my writing style. There are rock bands too that use this approach with their covers. Look at any Boston, Molly Hatchet, and many Yes album covers, the same unmistakable look, by the same artist from nearly the same era. My artist reads my introduction and whips up a dozen different covers for me to pick from based on the theme, mood, and tone of the book. I then narrow my choices down to six, and then take a poll on my six finalists from people who I trust for their honesty and integrity in my world. I tell them to pick their top three, their three favorites. Whichever gets the most points becomes my cover. I get a vote, and on my last three books, ironically, my favorite choice has never earned a cover. I look at this as a great lesson learned… "Everyone can't be wrong." Here I have displayed willingness, open-mindedness, acceptance, and humility, all which are discussed in this book. With addiction and recovery, one might have to come with an open mind to the possibility of a new approach right from the start. This perhaps is an instance of greater urgency than choosing a book cover.

Chapter's Logical Take-Away: Addiction treatment requires understanding and integrating others' knowledge and experience. It stresses learning from others to avoid mistakes.

ACCEPTANCE: YES, NO, MAYBE

"I may not control the wind,
but I can adjust my sails."

This won't blow anyone's mind, but it needs to be said. While we are here (on this planet, of course), we are on assignment. Time to work to keep this place up, to leave it in better condition for our next generations, and time to play to make it all worth the journey. Since I happen to believe in a creator, this all adds up to me. During our brief stay, we will be met with countless acceptances on a daily basis. The concept of acceptance is one of the greatest challenges we will ever face. In my opinion, we have 3 options regarding the prospect of acceptance:

- I can accept something flat out at face value, or disagree, but still go on and accept it. This is the famous "we agree to disagree" saying.

- I can make a change, but before that, I need to ask myself, "do I need to change anything here"? I have no power over my surroundings, but I do have the power to persuade people and, hence, make modifications to my surroundings. I can't stop the rain, but I can get out of it to seek shelter or grab an umbrella.

- I can decide to reject the idea of acceptance, move on, or walk away. Moving on here means removing myself from the situation. This is the most dramatic because I accept an impasse has been met in my decision to keep the situation unchanged.

I have a hard time accepting people who are never wrong.

In the context of this book, let's explore the role that acceptance plays in our recovery. Apart from acknowledging the possibility of having a problem with addiction, obsession, or habitual behavior (as evidenced by your purchase of this book), acceptance constitutes the first step towards wellness. It also provides a way out, at least for the present moment, in any situation. I've bulleted out above the most commonly adopted options we have when facing life's challenges, which are distinct from using substances to escape our unbearable reality. We cannot control society, much less the entire world, but we do have influence over certain aspects of our lives.

"Life on life's terms" involves dealing with things as they are in the pursuit of making them as they should be. Whatever unfolds does so for a reason. Therefore, accepting it and making the best of the situation is like learning to "go with the flow" whenever possible. Working on our character deficiencies to improve ourselves makes accepting "life on life's terms" much more bearable.

You don't have to accept that you're an alcoholic, you just need to acknowledge it. To accept it means I'm fine with it and with who I am, but I'm open to constructive suggestions. I must change me because my alcoholic behavior is unacceptable!

FABRICATED AND OVERPLAYED FEARS

*Fear doesn't mean you're scared,
it's just there as a reminder.*

It's astonishing how nearly every aspect of our lives can be traced back to fear. It lingers in the background, whether it's fear of failure or success, fear of rejection, or fear of acceptance, we concoct undue anxiety, stress, worries and concerns, all stemming from fear. Stress can ruin a good day. If you're on guard all the time, you are living a life of fear. As much as it keeps us safe, it could be our greatest barrier.

At the top of every poll regarding fear of addiction, individuals are most afraid of losing what they have and never getting what they want. There is one simple remedy for such fears: stop it! Comedian Bob Newhart performs a 6:17-minute skit called "Stop It," I highly encourage everyone to watch it if they get the chance. It is very funny and on-point with the one

I am making about "fabricated fears." Stop creating unnecessary problems for yourself—just stop it!

I recently had a conversation with a friend about a presentation I had to deliver. I'd rehearsed it multiple times, making sure I knew the content by heart. Yet, what caught me off guard was the fear of making a mistake in delivering it to a live audience. The inevitable happened, and I stumbled a few times. It made me realize that if I hadn't been so preoccupied with the fear of making a mistake, I probably wouldn't have made any at all. There's a saying that goes, "he who hesitates is lost," and indeed, I got lost in my self-created fear, struggling to recover from my blunders quickly enough to conceal them quickly under my nervousness (or stage fright).

Twelve-step recovery programs claim that fear is often cited as the root cause of all our troubles. The concept of its use is founded, but the word fear itself is freely overstated. Clearly, worry and concern are more fitting in less troublesome instances. I am afraid of heights. I also drive past tall buildings every day. In my case, I don't worry, nor am I concerned that I have a fear of heights when I look upward at their great stature towering over me. But should I wind up on the upper floors in one of those buildings, my fear of heights will begin to mount.

In one of my other books, I discuss how we can make a case for tying fear to anything and everything. Someone should create another card game like "Cards Against Humanity" called "10,000 Fears." You might never run out of cards on any given night."

And then there's the kind of fear we conjure when we are successful. I may fear that if I get the girl I dreamed about, how will I live up to her expectations? What if I'm not good enough for her? Similarly, how would I manage the many new responsibilities if I get that promotion I have been vying for? In my opinion, "worry" and "concern" better describe these instances, giving rise to anxiety in most cases. A friend in AA once told me that his success in recovery worries him and that he's expecting a "catch." The program was becoming easy for him now, which was something he was not used to. He said, "When is the other shoe about to drop? How do I not handle being challenged?" I said, One, you're overthinking things, which is prevalent with fear, and two, "You're supposed to get it; understanding the program is the goal!"

Overthinking, also referred to as rumination, is the repetitive dwelling on the same situation to the point that it disrupts your life. Overthinking usually falls into two categories: ruminating about the past (counterfactual thinking) and worrying about the future (anxiety). For me, overthinking is quite fundamental. It occurs when I start asking myself questions about something I have already said or done (oftentimes regrets) or when I wonder what might happen. The funny thing is, I can't take back what has been done, nor can I control what I dread could or might happen.

There is also great value in having healthy fears, which I like to think of as safeguards. These are fears born from experience, knowledge of what to expect based on past outcomes and being prepared to confront them when they recur, like having the answers to test in advance. There are evolutionary fears as well, like fear of snakes, loud noises, and height. My birth name is Frederick, but I go by Rick. Yet, whenever my mother called me by "Frederick," it was never a good sign, it was like a red light started to flash in my brain. You might think that I am "overthinking" in these situations, but experience tells me to prepare for the worst.

In Chapter 77, I talk about phobias as compared to fears. It's important to recognize the distinction between fears and phobias. Phobias are intense, irrational, and enduring fears that can profoundly disrupt someone's life. Conversely, fears are typical reactions to perceived threats and are usually controllable. It's necessary to understand that fears and phobias are not synonymous.

But the most prevalent, and quite the opposite of experience-based fears, are fears of the unknown. Being in the dark and with little to go on as you feel your way to the end of the room, you don't know what you'll run into. That's when we start manufacturing anxiety without good cause. Here's a common depiction of that. If my boss at work says to me, "Can I see you in my office?", I will undoubtedly experience a faster heartbeat, my palms might begin to sweat, and my breathing will quicken. I might begin to think, hmmm … since it's in his office, which is in private, I am about to be reprimanded or even fired. That would be my natural way of thinking. To prepare for the worst-case scenario. What wouldn't be natural for me is to think I am the only employee in the company getting a bonus, and it needs to be carried out behind closed doors.

"Your mind is playing tricks on you,
as long as you allow it."

All the fears, worries, or concerns occupying our heads, might be out to get us, but there are ways of overcoming them; one is with faith. Faith is the prospect of a way out of our fears. Faith is simply trusting God and in any higher power you entrust yourself to.

I was agnostic, not knowing if there was a God or not—that is, until I became spiritual and discovered faith and hope. I am not on the side of any religion, but I learned to believe in a creator, or *"my God"*. Together with His guidance and my new-found faith, I am able to accomplish so much. As an individual who has dealt with addiction, having faith, or trusting the system, in my case, has been a significant motivating factor in my recovery program. Alcoholics Anonymous adopted the "Serenity Prayer." As they did with the "Prayer of Saint Francis," due to their profound nature. I have included my interpretation of the Serenity Prayer in the back of this book. If you don't already know it, after reading, you will understand what faith means to all of us.

You may have heard the term "have faith." That might mean trust in God. "In God We Trust" is the motto of the United States and is on every form of US currency. Powerful enough for you?

Chapter's Logical Take-Away: Usually, moderate-to-extreme fear can create unnecessary concern and anxiety. Self-created worries like the thought of making mistakes or not meeting expectations can also threaten our program of recovery.

WHAT DID YOU EXPECT?

The level of one's expectations is commensurate to the likelihood of its results.

If I expect something, I am truly hoping for favorable results. And if I am expecting negative ones, then too, my motive must still be for reasons that favor me, though in that case, I'll be less disappointed with failure. If I am expecting failure or didn't expect to come out on top, then my thinking is skewed and probably needs an adjustment. So, if someone says, "It's no big deal, I didn't expect to win, or get the job anyway," to me, that sounds like it wasn't that important in the first place, so the person probably didn't try hard enough and wasted his time in the process. In my view, that's the wrong attitude. Similarly, if I anticipate receiving something in return, I could be setting myself up for disappointment. Even if such expectations seem reasonable to me, I must remember that not everyone thinks like I do. When there's a profit motive involved, expectations can escalate even further along the expectation scale.

But I must take responsibility for my own expectations, realistic or unrealistic. No matter what the cause, people, or nature, I am the setter of the expectations I put on everything. I expected you to be there, and you didn't show up. I counted on you, and you let me down. These are expectations we place on others. Perhaps that was poor judgement on my part to hold you in such high regard. I didn't expect that a cute little dog would bite me. Whose fault is that? Maybe I should have approached with caution since I just met the dog for the first time.

We often set our expectations for others unreasonably high, believing that this time things will be different. We expose ourselves to risks when we fail to consider all the facts, sometimes even accepting an outcome that contradicts our better judgment. What do our instincts tell us?

If we put ourselves as people with addiction in precarious situations, we are tempting fate and inviting poor outcomes. When we learn about our inner selves, we better understand our limitations. And beyond our limitations increases our chance of failure and disappointment, but so are the chances of success. And to repeat what I said above, we find ourselves saying: "I didn't expect this to happen". Well, what did you expect? Perhaps the odds were not so great to begin with. In twelve-step programs, we are reminded that high expectations can often lead to resentments towards oneself and others. We expect people to do what they say they will do, and then they don't deliver. Don't allow yourself to be put in that position where so many things are out of your control.

As I also mentioned earlier, trust your sources when you've done your research and follow your instincts. If you have a 1% bad feeling about something or are reluctant to make a decision, look toward alternative options.

*It's better to be pleasantly surprised
than to be knowingly wrong.*

Here are two ways of looking at expectations: If you enjoy gardening, your expectations do not have to be so high if you do not like tomatoes. On the other hand, if you are a farmer, then the tilling can be exhausting and arduous, but worth the effort.

It is normal to have reasonable expectations. Some people say expectations are resentments waiting to happen. I say, not if you check all the boxes before you make a decision. All this takes a little practice and patience.

Chapter's Logical Take-Away: It is important to assess everything and follow your intuition to manage expectations. Personal responsibility for setting expectations and avoiding disappointment is mainly stressed. False expectations, especially when instincts or better judgment suggest caution, must be avoided.

A PSYCHIC REVELATION

*The way you think has the
power to change your life.*

Psychology is the scientific study of the human mind and behavior. So, the science, or theory based on evidence, is simply learning how we think and act[355]. As we progress through various stages of our lives, our methods of thinking evolve. Our physical and emotional needs change as we grow. The carefree days of our younger years welcome us into a new era of maturity and responsibility[356]. We naturally begin to plan more to better navigate the next stage of our lives. Some individuals with the disease of addiction are fortunate enough to experience a psychic transformation, which those without the disease may also undergo for other reasons. This is also known as a philosophical paradigm shift or psychic change. But there is still another change all may experience, widely recognized by the recovery community as "awakening." I believe this is different from a psychic or philosophical change because it centers in the mind and spirit collectively. The spiritual awakening or change will be discussed in depth in the chapters ahead.

But a psychic or philosophical change, which I just mentioned, can happen to anyone. It's when you naturally begin to "do the next right thing." This revelation now gives us the power to change and the desire to become a better version of ourselves.

The Prayer of St. Francis is a fabulous example of unselfishness and what is righteous, or the next right thing.

Lord, make me an instrument of your peace: where there is hatred, let me sow love; where there is injury, pardon; where there is doubt, faith; where there is despair, hope; where there is darkness, light; where there is sadness, joy.

In the case of an addict, this new way of thinking represents a significant step toward recovery or getting well. A better method of thinking leads to an improved way of life. No longer will we fight any entities or demons that reside within us. Negative energy that brings us down is expelled by positive thought. And that downturn is like a mudslide soon taking the form of an avalanche. But our desire to achieve natural heights of success propels us. After a psychic change has occurred, which we'll refer to as a "mental change" going forward, something natural begins to happen. We discover how to "catch ourselves." We stop and momentarily pause just long enough to make sure what comes out is good and not negative. Or, what happens is for a reason. And if something is then repeated, we become mindfully aware without much thought. This change in our minds is a natural occurrence, but that doesn't mean you can't begin to make things better for everyone from this very day forward. I believe we can induce the state of being without undergoing a physical transformation ourselves. We don't necessarily have to be experts to impart knowledge. A person who is already spiritual practices righteousness.

Chapter's Logical Take-Away: Recovery, or getting better, is not far removed from having a positive mental attitude. When we finally wake up and realize that acting better with a positive mindset gets us well (not be mistaken with the "fake it 'til you make it" phrase), we can then go on to lead a better life. But none of this is possible without a strong desire to change for the better and a hunger for knowledge about our addiction.

TRANSFORMING CHARACTER

We are always around ourselves,
so it pays to have a clear conscience.

Throughout the book, I have emphasized the significance of self-improvement as a fundamental equation that leads to fewer problems, fewer concerns, and a more optimistic outlook on life. But how do we start this voyage of self-transformation? The discipline of rebuilding one's character and pursuing personal growth is a lifelong pursuit that requires self-awareness, self-reflection, and perseverance. Expect setbacks along the way, but keep in mind that dedication, fortitude, resilience, persistence, and self-compassion are the pillars of becoming the best version of yourself. Personal development, self-improvement, and behavior modification converge under the banner of "transforming human character." Listed below are some methods to accomplish this transformation[357]:

- Self-Reflection and Consciousness: Assess your current character (worldview, beliefs, values, etc.), habits, and behaviors to begin the process. What aspects of yourself do you wish to alter or improve? Consider constructing a personal ledger of assets and liabilities—a straightforward listing of your "virtues" on the left and your "deficiencies" on the right on a page.

- Recognize Your Motivation: Discover the motivations that are fueling your desire for change. Is it motivated by personal development, improved health, enhanced relationships, or career advancement, or perhaps a combination of these? All the above may apply in cases of addiction, as a complete character overhaul may be required to achieve long-term sobriety and escape the grip of addiction.

- Seek information and sources: Equip yourself with knowledge regarding the desired alterations. Read books (including the rest of this one, and my other works), enroll in courses (online and offline), and, most importantly, seek the insight and counsel of reputable individuals in the corresponding field.

- Exercise Self-Control: Self-discipline is essential to the process of character transformation. It requires unwavering dedication to your objectives, despite obstacles and diversions.

- Adopt healthier habits: replace old, undesirable routines that hold you back with new, beneficial ones. Consistency is the key to maintaining these healthy behaviors.

- Develop Emotional Intelligence: Mastery of emotional intelligence requires understanding one's own emotions and having empathy for those of others, as well as having self-awareness and self-regulation. People with high emotional intelligence are better equipped to handle tough societal situations. Essentially, it involves perceiving feelings and responding appropriately.

- Develop a Support System: Surround yourself with encouraging and accountable friends, family, or a support group during your transformation as you recover from your addiction. The previously mentioned sages and dependable individuals could very well serve this purpose.

- Engage in Self Care: Focus on your physical and mental health. This includes regular exercise, a healthy diet, adequate sleep, social connection, and stress management techniques like meditation and mindfulness. Recognize the close relationship between mental and physical health.

- Learn from Failures: Recognize that setbacks and failings are inherent to life and the process of transformation. Instead of dwelling on negative experiences, view them as a learning curve and development opportunities. It's easy to get hung up on failure, but don't forget to celebrate small progress and take responsibility for what went wrong.

- Maintain Patience and Perseverance: Transformation is a gradual process that is filled with obstacles and setbacks. Be patient and persistent with yourself in the pursuit of your goals.

- Seek Professional Assistance: Despite the fact that this book predominantly assists those battling addiction and obsessions in reclaiming their lives, it is essential to recognize that everyone, including yourself, has flaws and blind spots and can benefit from assistance. In this voyage, medical professionals, therapists, and counselors are invaluable resources.

- Giving Back: Sometimes, helping others or your community in various ways can be a potent way to reinforce your transformation of character. Twelve-step programs, for instance, emphasize community service as an essential element of recovery.

Each of us has a unique combination of character strengths and perceived "flaws" that collectively define our public persona. This persona is supported by a conscience chip that functions as a check valve or compliance department, regulating the flow of information between our interior thoughts and external actions.

Character development is a journey that is inherently unique, and there is no one-size-fits-all formula. Appreciate the trip with self-love and dedication to your individual path. You have the ability to mold yourself into the person you aspire to be, so long as you consistently cultivate your desire for change. We've established that many of our difficulties stem from our own imaginations (to quote Seneca, "We suffer more in imagination than in reality"), frequently fueling our addictions. Unquestionably, addressing these interior issues can significantly improve our overall mental health. According to Alcoholics Anonymous, our problems are largely the result of our own actions. Before we can undergo the essential psychic shift that is crucial to overcoming addiction or obsession, we must conduct a personal inventory a engage in deep self-reflection. Recovery circles have coined various acronyms and sayings over the years. Concepts such as "He's one of us," or "She's one of us," are identifiers for alcoholics. The term "normie" refers to a person who does not struggle with addiction issues, which might have an "othering" effect on normal people. Nonetheless, it is crucial to recognize that no one is completely "normal;" we all have flaws. Even the most ordinary of individuals struggle with some kind of psychological problem. I like to say affectionately, "We are all mental cases."

The program is a path to self-improvement regardless of a person's drinking behaviors; it is not exclusive to alcoholics. Anyone facing life challenges can benefit from the program I advocate for throughout this book.

Chapter's Logical Take-Away: Self-awareness and exploration are the foundations of character development and transformation. Your journey to becoming a better version of yourself begins with your decision to undergo this mental transformation today, paving the path for a better tomorrow.

DEBUNKING THE MYTH OF THE ADDICTIVE PERSONALITY

Addictive tendencies can be part of your makeup, but not by your personality.

You don't need to be an addict to ponder the possibility of having an addictive personality. It's a common refrain we hear regularly: "If I'm not addicted to this, I'm addicted to that." Too much involvement in anything could border on "addiction," but that isn't essentially bad. I, too, have embraced this notion for much of my life, proclaiming, "When I dive into something, I'm fully committed, for better or worse." This commitment can swing from positive pursuits like diet and exercise, creative hobbies, or any kind of personal growth endeavor to more detrimental ones like illicit substances. However, I've come to realize that not everything I claim to be addicted to truly fits the bill. Fig. 2, following Chapter 13 suggests that my involvement with something can range from mere curiosity or interest to full-blown obsession or addiction. So, I'm not addicted to everything I think I am. Some things simply spark my interest to different degrees.

I've always known I have a collector's tendency. I've pursued hobbies like guitars and guitar amplifiers, baseball cards of my favorite players, watches, and dress shoes. This demonstrates my ability to become deeply engrossed in items and activities that bring me satisfaction and fulfillment. For me, it's not solely about the end result, in fact, it's about the pursuit itself. The chase or the hunt. You could say it's all a bit of a game. How do I know this? Well, I grow bored and weary of an activity once I reach a certain level of contentment, and then I move on and get busy with life, and so it's quickly out of my system. That's never the case with addiction. With addiction, it's constantly asking for more (better substance, drinks with higher ABV [Alcohol by Volume], etc.).

Experts in the field of addiction assert that there's a long-standing fallacy suggesting that certain individuals possess an addictive personality—a personality type that renders them susceptible to addiction. However, professionals generally concur that addiction is a neurological disorder (as we have already seen, genetics can play a role in addiction too) rather than a matter of personality. While various factors can heighten one's susceptibility to addiction, there's no concrete evidence that a particular personality type directly leads to addiction.

As an illustrative example, when marketing the opioid prescription drug OxyContin, the American pharmaceutical company Purdue Pharma advised its representatives to inform doctors that only people with an "addictive personality" were at risk of developing addiction, despite their awareness of its high addictive potential and widespread abuse.

Psychologist Mark Griffiths emphasizes, "There is no personality trait that guarantees an individual will develop an addiction, and there is little evidence that an addictive personality alone predicts addiction[358]. In short, the concept of an addictive personality is a complete fallacy." Experts firmly believe that addiction primarily stems from brain-related factors, not one's personality traits. While people often use the term "addictive personality" to describe a cluster of traits and behaviors aimed at indicating a predisposition to addiction, there's no universally accepted definition.

In early 2018, when I committed myself to a treatment center in Atlanta, where professionals from various fields such as aviation, medicine, and business were undergoing rehabilitation, I had the opportunity to participate in a course on recovery psychology. I vividly recall the doctor who taught the class emphatically, stating that there's no such thing as an "addictive personality." I was immediately taken aback. Being an avid seeker of knowledge, especially in addictions and recovery, I considered this revelation a valuable nugget of wisdom, especially given his credentials in aviation psychology, ranking among the highest in the world. When I earned my degree in addiction in Atlanta, I proudly shared this newfound understanding, reinforcing the idea that the addictive personality myth had been debunked.

However, this doesn't imply that individuals can't develop other addictions or acquire additional bad habits alongside their primary addiction. With all the alluring fishhooks of modern life (social media, video gaming, shopping apps, workaholism, etc.), it's hard not to get snagged by some of them. Many people who quit drinking or using drugs may turn to smoking as a substitute, often to address an oral fixation, which can lead to weight gain for those who quit smoking. It becomes a never-ending cycle. Likewise, caffeine in coffee can provide the stimulation that an addict seeks. The key is moderation when substituting one habit for another; you don't want to replace one addiction with another. Productive habits might seem like a chore at first, which they are, but they're the most rewarding ones for the improvement of your life. Methadone has proven effective in helping people overcome heroin addiction but has also given rise to methadone addicts in the process. In the past, alcohol was used for medicinal purposes (tinctures and tonics), but it proved challenging to regulate its consumption because individuals react differently to alcohol. Next time you watch a classic western movie, observe the character taking a swig of whiskey straight from the bottle before a bullet extraction—a testament to the historical use of alcohol in medicine.

Chapter's Logical Take-Away: There is no such thing as an "addictive personality" since addiction is a *neurological condition (genetic)*. While specific character traits and behaviors may elevate the risk of addiction, there is no conclusive proof that a particular personality type is inherently prone to addiction. Our personalities are who you see on the outside through our actions (or a lack thereof). Our character is who we are on the inside. Our inner characteristics make up who we will be seeing. We can change our character and have addictive behaviors, but not addictive personalities. It's just the wrong way of saying it.

KNOW YOURSELF, LIVE AS YOU ARE

Intend to be, not pretend to be.

"Know yourself, live as you are" promotes self-awareness and authenticity. Understanding your strengths, weaknesses, values, beliefs, and goals can result in a more fulfilling existence. Accept your authentic self and make decisions consistent with your identity and objectives.

In our pursuit of realizing our full potential, we must acknowledge our limitations and maintain our expectations grounded in reality. Doing so will spare us from unwarranted disappointment. This approach also minimizes the mental, emotional, and physical risks we expose ourselves to. In other words, it'll help you take calculated risks.

> "A man's *gotta know his limitations*"
> —Clint Eastwood

This awareness is pivotal for personal growth and making sound decisions. Here are some steps to enhance your grasp of your limitations:

Self-reflection: Take some time to consider your strengths and weaknesses. Consider your talents, experiences, and areas in which you have previously struggled. Once you do this, the areas in which you excel will naturally start to surface in your awareness. The first step is to be honest with yourself about your limitations.

Feedback: Gather feedback from others, including friends, family, co-workers, and mentors. They can shed light on areas in which you may require development or where your limitations may be hindering your performance. There are some things about yourself or your activity that are hidden from you or that you often overlook. Exposing yourself to different ideas will help you see those parts of yourself.

Set realistic objectives: Setting goals that are attainable and taking into consideration your limitations can help you work freely, putting you in a better position to expand your boundaries as you improve yourself. Avoid setting objectives that are beyond your current capabilities. Humans can achieve anything they set their mind to, but they still need to start small.

Continuous Learning: Identify the areas in which you struggle and commit yourself to learning more about them. Formal education, online research, self-directed learning, and cognitive or logical understanding can assist in overcoming certain limitations and expanding your horizons. I have repeated this many times throughout my life: "Knowledge is powerful, knowledge is social." Because of my insatiable desire to fully comprehend why everything is the way it is, anything that catches my attention stays with me until I am satisfied with a logical comprehension of its function and existence. As a result, I am well-versed in the subject and capable of participating in any discussion that may arise.

Acceptance: It is essential to recognize that everyone has limitations. No one is flawless, and recognizing your flaws does not diminish your worth. Embrace your imperfections, as they make a person real, and focus on areas where you can excel. Naturally, our shortcomings, or flaws, if you will, are at bay when repairing is convenient. A human being, a perfect lump of clay at birth, is exposed to varying types of societal requirements as they grow. Conforming to every single requirement is humanly impossible. They also start to develop an idealized self-image. Both of these factors contribute to a person being perceived as "flawed," in their own mind and in the minds of society. But little do we know that that very thing makes us human.

Recognize that you cannot do everything alone. Delegate or collaborate, whichever is more suitable. Teamwork is the best work. When I was young, my father used to tell me, "Work smarter, not harder."

Keep in mind that recognizing and addressing your limitations demonstrates self-awareness and maturation. It is a journey that requires time and effort, but it can lead to improved decision-making and an overall more fulfilling existence. Self-improvement is a life-long process, not a destination.

> **Chapter's Logical Take-Away:** Promoting a happier life can be achieved through honesty in recognizing your strengths, weaknesses, values, and goals. Personal growth requires accepting your limitations. One can accept their limits through constructive self-evaluation, self-reflection, setting reasonable goals, constant learning, and accepting and fixing the mistakes made.

FINDING BALANCE: EGO, PRIDE, AND SELF-WORTH

"It's not that you're a guy, it's your ego is too big to ask for directions."

Life is an intricate balancing act, an interdependence of various facets of events, navigating the visible challenges, and for some, the temptations and mounting habits that turn into addictions. Is there a way to maintain a crafted persona without facing the truth of addiction? Or are you too proud and lack a level of humility to admit you have an addiction problem? Do I view myself above the belief of others that I am too perfectly created to have a disease, especially one of addiction? Doesn't the world know I have an image? A reputation to maintain? When there's no escape from the truth of an addiction, it's time to put aside the ego until we learn how to safely control it.

In my view, the foundation of most addiction recovery programs begins with personality and character development. Which is all about self-improvement. When we think of ego, we often associate it with a "big ego". This glaring ugliness can be overbearing, conceited, arrogant, and perhaps even narcissistic. E.g., "He is so full of himself." But the bottom line is: "overly" in any aspect of something will make the whole thing out of proportion. And we know what a disproportionate object looks like.

> *People sometimes say: "I love being wrong."*
> *I would rather say:*
> *"I like when someone is more right."*

I have often contended that ego and pride get a bad name in programs of recovery. And rightly so, because some mentors might come across as condescending to the support groups. Here's why I have an adverse opinion on the two: My rationale for this stance remains in my search for balance and moderation, our ultimate objective. I come from just outside of New York City. It is like a different world to some, especially those who have never been there, and so are the attitudes of its citizens. There is a touch, and perhaps a bit more of an ego and level of pride innate or developed by "big city" folks. If you possess too little, you will be run over where you stand. You must keep pace with the ever-changing lifestyle of NYC. No one stands still there; the city is always in motion, and most survive the lifestyle of the surroundings, living on the outskirts, like Jersey City or Hoboken. Therefore, as we strive for self-improvement within the framework of our addiction recovery program, we must also acknowledge the skills necessary to navigate the world outside of our addiction. Sometimes, as we adapt to one environment, we find ourselves lagging behind in the other.

> *Not all our flaws are of our making.*
> *Don't be so proud not to let them lie.*

Chapter's Logical Take-Away: Here, addiction can be compared to a person's fully formed ego. It's possible that pride and a lack of humility are preventing people from getting help for their addiction. People sometimes overestimate themselves. With addiction, that shouldn't be the case. Rehabilitation for addiction aims to balance that self-image and ego.

UNDERSTANDING HUMILITY

*Once you say you're humble,
you're already not.*

Humility is a character trait characterized by modesty, selflessness, and a lack of arrogance or pride. It involves recognizing one's own limitations. Being willing to acknowledge our mistakes or shortcomings[359]. When we struggle with addiction, we learn humility by accepting it. Thus, humility often involves a deep sense of inner peace and contentment, regardless of external circumstances.

Additionally, nothing and no one is beyond our willingness when we are asked or forced to do what we think is above us. Humility involves doing what makes us uncomfortable, shamelessly exposing ourselves to what others might find embarrassing[360]. Humility is just living it—not hiding from who you are. I believe humility is when you feel good about yourself just the way you are … comfortable in your own skin, with nothing to feel embarrassed about.

In another one of my books, I recounted how I worked a retail job where I had to wear a name badge on my shirt. At first, I was so embarrassed every time I looked down at my name below my chin. I would think to myself: how did I ever wind up working at such a menial job for minimum age at this age (59 years old); I used to earn that much in minutes! But after a few weeks, I reached a point where I never looked down at my name again. I learned the "feeling" of humility having learned it first-hand.

Humility entails being open to learning, or, as they say in the program, "remain teachable." And because acknowledging the problem doesn't yet involve action but is merely the first step, taking responsibility and then admitting it to others might be a slow process, depending on the audience you are reaching out to. It might seem awkward, humiliating, and even deeply embarrassing, as you're exposing the darkest part of yourself to others, but that is also humility. It has been said: "Humility is not thinking less of yourself; it's thinking of yourself less." But I have a better one:

> *"Humility is not thinking less of yourself*
> *but thinking you're not above others."*

We often hear "being humble" when talking about humility; however, being humble and feeling humility are not the same thing. People get them mixed up or use them interchangeably, but there is a small difference between the two[361].

Being humble is an action or behavior that reflects humility. It involves showing modesty, deference, and respect toward others. Being humble means not seeking attention or praise for oneself but instead recognizing and valuing the contributions and perspectives of others. It often manifests in acts of kindness, generosity, and empathy towards others. I liken being humble to being a team player.

When you are humbled, you find yourself "right-sized," (reduced-to-size) as they say in twelve-step programs, placed on equal footing with others and given the same treatment without any impartiality. It involves swallowing your pride when you'd rather be the center of attention. Thus, when you no longer covet the spotlight all the time and think others deserve an equal chance, you've found true humility. Humility is the entry level to becoming humble. Pride is putting my name on everything that is good. Humility is putting my name on what might not be my best.

There is also false humility; here is an example: people in twelve-step programs who say, "I don't know anything." That is a ridiculous statement if the person doesn't truly lack self-esteem. I want to say to them: "So you're a block of clay, huh?" Or when someone else says: "If I had your talent …" What they are really doing is downplaying what they don't believe is true. The truth is, they are fishing for you to say: "Aw heck, you are one of the most talented people around!" What would undoubtedly end this charade is if you said: "You could have my talent if you practiced more!" This might sound harsh, but it is honest and sends a necessary message in a positive way. Hopefully, being straightened out enough times when they take that tack will teach them true humility. And to appease them doesn't bolster your integrity, either. To me, false pride is intentionally putting yourself down about all the things that have come from your accolades or accomplishments when you don't believe it all. This is always to get a reaction that builds you up after you have falsely put yourself down. This is also false humbling in the form of self-deprecation. It is also almost always ego-driven, looking or fishing for compliments and praise, rooted in the hunger for validation.

> **Chapter's Logical Take-Away:** Humility is being comfortable with something you believe is above you. Humility is being impervious to embarrassment. Being humble is letting someone else lead when you know you easily can. Not needing to be the main focus.

SELFISH WAYS

The next time you want to know what being unselfish and having humility feels like, drive someone in the opposite direction from the way you're going.

There was a time in my life when I thought I had my own world, my own space to conduct myself in any way I saw fit. If you didn't like me or agree with me, I didn't need you anyway. I would even go so far as to say: "It's my world and if you don't like the way I am, you can go back to yours. I wasn't trying to be mean; I just thought everyone had their own too. When I became wiser and more spiritual, I started to realize that we were meant to share this place and all its resources with each other. So, it is fair to take what you can carry, but everyone else gets their share too. This could be viewed as my connection with the creator: "All that is seen and unseen." I believe the "Creator," or God, if you will, instills a permissible level of selfishness in all of us.

Often throughout my life, I have maintained, "I am the person and everything I was ever meant to be," to justify my ways of behaving on some of my bad days. Like the title of my book: 'I Didn't Ask to Be Me.' That mindset worked wonders whenever others disagreed with my outlook. It's simply me being me. When I was in my active addiction, I was incredibly selfish. It's not that I wanted to be or even realized I was so self-centered. My immediate needs were all that concerned me. Your needs would only be considered once mine were met.

You see, selfish and self-centered people are not able to care about others; they lack compassion. I have always been compassionate, good-hearted, and generous. I was just overdue for an awakening. The way I share and divide my time with others supports those attributes. All we possess has no value unless those attributes of our being are shared. Moreover, giving goodness is unselfish, no matter what the return or lack thereof. A good example of being unselfish is passing up certain pleasures of our own to be there for others.

It's not always selfish to put your needs first, though. The operative word here is "needs." We have basic needs, life-operating skills (hunger, thirst, social interaction, etc.), and God-given instincts that are encompassed for our survival. We must take care of ourselves first before we can help others. (Quote: Fill your own cup so that you can overflow into the lives of others.) People who are self-centered think that the world revolves around them only. I began this chapter with "… I thought I had my own world." That would be that of a selfish and self-centered person. Apparently, I was ignorant all this time. But we must know the difference between helping someone and enabling them. Recently, I was asked to lend $30 to a person I knew from a twelve-step meeting I go to. He texted me on Thursday night, telling me he would repay me on payday; I'm sure he didn't realize payday was only 8 hours away on Friday. I did some quick math, hmmm … twenty-four-pack of beer, cigarettes … Immediately, my intuition kicked in and convinced me it was a bad idea. Helping for the wrong reason is not helping at all. Instead, we should give some tough love to these individuals.

When we get out of our heads or think less about ourselves, focusing on the world around us, our ways of self-centeredness are mitigated. At the same moment, we are feeling a sense of humility, which was just covered in the last chapter.

Chapter's Logical Take-Away: My ego and selfish thinking brought me unsustainable happiness. It turned out to be more damaging to my health, personality, and well-being. When I became spiritual, I realized there's so much contentment to find in sharing what's ours, and collectively and co-operatively, I am in a better place today for having realized prior ugliness.

UNDERSTANDING RESENTMENTS

*If I resent you, I will probably
judge you until you change my mind.*

We all have resentments, but before I entered the world of recovery, I had never heard the word used so much. Resentment is a feeling of angry displeasure directed towards someone or something perceived as wrong, insulting, or injurious. Or, as simple as, "I am bitter towards…." For instance, when I become complacent and am not as productive as I would like to be, I get mad at myself and develop resentment. When we grieve, we may also experience self-resentment. Grieving individuals also develop a sense of resentment toward the world. They might feel a sense of unfairness, injustice, and even powerlessness. In these instances, we are harsh on ourselves for not doing more, even though we know we could have. Keep in mind that, whomever or whatever you have resentment to-wards, everyone has a part that brings on the resentment. And unless you were not present, then you have a part in everything, for better or worse.

If my boss fires me, it's only normal to hold resentment against him/her. I then use logic to investigate why I was fired, or simply "my part." Was I often late for work? Did I steal from the company? Did I make a lot of mistakes, or perhaps I just didn't work hard enough? Was it because of my misdemeanor? When I am able to see my part more clearly, is it really fair to harbor resentment toward my boss?

The same could be said of failed relationships. Who left who? Why didn't it work out the way I had hoped it would? Was it infidelity, boredom, incompatibility, differences of opinion, or a lack of emotional connection? Any number of factors could be the reason for the breakup. And in some cases, both sides take responsibility for it not working out, and then the split is amicable, and when we part, we stay friends. But it doesn't always go so smoothly. When emotions run high after such unpleasant situations, our first thought might be to take comfort in drinking or getting high.

So, what is resentment in the context of recovery? I found this to be much deeper than I expected. Resentments can be traced all the way back to the psychological burdens that we continue to carry around today. They can be the lingering feelings of anger, bitterness, unfairness, or blame we hold towards people, organizations, groups, ourselves, or even toward a higher power, like God[362]. The cause of our ongoing anger and bitterness is quite possibly linked to resentments from the low moments of our past or mistakes we made in those instances, but there is still no reason to drink or drug to try to forget them. Even though they are from our past, we carry these resentments into the present, leading some of us who are trying to recover from addiction to relapse.

According to twelve-step recovery programs involving alcohol and substance abuse, resentments are the number one cause of relapse[363]. I personally don't share that belief. But I could make a case for it being high on the list. During pre-recovery, I have only heard, "I resent that," but that's the extent of its usage. It's like saying, "I take offense…." Personally, when

I feel I was wronged, I am inclined to despise or hold a grudge against the person. I may even be upset, disappointed, mad, or angry with that person. They also say you can resent institutions or organizations like the company you work for or the IRS. I am not angered, nor do I harbor resentment toward the owner of my local gas station or Exxon/Mobil for the rising prices of gas. I am incredibly enraged when I identify the source of an issue, as writing this book teaches me to do.

Chapter's Logical Take-Away: Resentments are considered a significant relapse trigger in recovery programs, as unresolved negative emotions from the past can linger in people's minds during such a vulnerable period in their lives. Addressing these complex emotional burdens is crucial for lasting sobriety.

CHAPTER 63

AMENDS IN RECOVERY: A STEP TOWARDS SOBRIETY

"Mistakes are a part of life; what truly matters is the effort we put into making them right."

In the previous chapter, we talked about resentments. The downside of holding onto resentment is that until I make amends, I find myself often revisiting how negatively or angry I feel about that person or situation. It continues to gnaw at me, making it hard for me to focus. Until I do my part and make amends, I will not be able to shake the lousy feeling I have about them that keeps popping into my head throughout the day or from time to time when I hear the name of the person who wronged me or the organization that treated me unfairly. This is not going to get me back on my "doing the right thing" campaign toward being a better person.

Another term for amends is restitution for a wrong. It is, in a sense, "mend" as in mending. That would make sense because both are an act of repairing. Another good word for amends, like make it right, or make good, is "pardon." An amend is not a simple apology, but it can be where it's fitting. Often sorry doesn't cut it when repairing a big damage caused by a terrible mistake. Sorry is only a statement. The victim receiving the apology might not always think that the offender truly means it. If my seventeen-year-old kid backs over your mailbox, to make it right you might approach the homeowner and work it out, or even better, send your kid over. You might say, or in the latter case, have your kid say, "Do you want me to get the same one you had and have someone install it?" He might say, "Give me $100 and we'll call it even." As it turns out, he wanted to replace it anyway with a better model, and the reimbursement will help pay for the more expensive one. So, it's a win-win, and both sides walk away happy. And if you're happy with the way you handled it, then you can close the case on this amends. But guess who is still on the hook for the $100 and any damage to your back bumper? Now is the perfect time to send an amends message to your seventeen-year-old kid. Sometimes you want to get that big amends on your list out of the way, since it took so long and now you finally have the courage to say it. But sometimes they are not ready for your plea. Remember everyone has a life and emotions of their own, so be patient, you only want to do this once, when they're ready.

After a psychic change (a better, new way of thinking) as a result of getting clean and now beginning to live a life of sobriety (responsible, societal living), we take on the task of self-improvement by going back to those we have done harm to and making amends. What about amends that have nothing to do with being under the influence? Perhaps you were just a jerk or a bad person? Yet this could even be when we were selfish due to an addiction, as it drained us not only emotionally but financially too, but now we have experienced the psychic change. Despite its title, this book isn't solely about addiction; much like my previous book, "I Didn't Ask to Be Me," it encompasses living a fulfilling life while navigating through addiction. The causes of addiction go much deeper than just having them, and so does this book. And so, the process of making amends, although a win for both sides, is mainly for our own good by removing guilt and the weight of ill feelings we are burdened with. It also removes the fear of ever having to worry about running into them again. Now you've eliminated another "fear."

We make amends to lift our emotional condition or balance. The amends process is about reaching out to those you have wronged in some way, whether big or small, and attempting to "make things right" or to repay your figurative debt[364]. Making a list is probably the best way to be the most thorough. When dealing with addictions, making amends is a vital part of personal growth and healing. By making amends, you will have a chance to reconnect with family, friends, etc. that you hurt while you were not completely yourself when you were using substances or drinking alcohol. Using or being under the influence is key. After which, a sense of closure and peace will naturally occur.

I have learned that making amends can be now, later, or maybe never. I don't believe you have to go back to the kid you hit with the kickball when you were in second grade. That kid will be a grown-up by now, as you are. Let's employ some logic here. If I have to dig up an old grave to decide whether I have to plan an amend, it is obviously not gnawing at me to warrant an amend. I don't want to bring up resentments that have already healed. Why stir it up again if it's trivial? If something comes to the surface of my thinking more often than not, amends are probably necessary, as that particular action of mine might have been severe. It makes no sense to bring up a "closed case." I think leaving old unresolved issues that are over-the-dam or water-under-the-bridge is best. I offer this: time heals everything. And if so much time has gone by since you have already forgotten the harm caused, there's a possibility it has also been forgotten by the other party. I see no value in stirring up old wrongdoings, especially when you're digging for them.

There is also "living amends" which literally means amending the way you live. Living amends also means creating real changes through true and honest behaviors and actions through deep self-examination, as well as following an emotionally sober path[365]. Commit to living a sober and healthy life. This means committing to never go back to the old ways that originally hurt those close to you or yourself. It also means to stop reminding your loved ones of past hurts. Fulfill a promise that you made to someone in the past but that you did not keep because you forgot about it due to addiction, or maybe you weren't up to the mark to live up to it, emotionally and financially, again. Living amends means proactively improving relationships in your life with a concerted and focused effort. It's about not taking people in your life for granted. Regarding living amends, don't wait; start this now! It is a good start and an exercise that will last forever when you make that psychological change to practice good moral principles.

The difference between direct amends and indirect amends: direct is confronting and reconciling. It's restitution. Indirect amends is when the damage cannot be undone, so you do good deeds like volunteering and helping others[366]. E.g., since direct amends you know won't make things right, as the damage done by you is too inexcusable, you can benevolently do something like support one of their causes, like a charity.

Sometimes we hear something in a twelve-step meeting that has never been stated before. Recently, I stumbled on one such, which I believe has never been discussed before. I am going to refer to it as a "third party amends." This is taken from a personal experience at a meeting. The chairperson that day wrongfully cut me off, apparently without any reason. I can easily say I was bothered by her actions. After the meeting, though, another person who always appreciates my opinions came up to me to side with my commentary. He said to me that she was out of line and outright disrespectful. By him pointing out how wrong she was, I decided to acknowledge his words as an unknowing amend that should have come from her instead. Just someone else seeing I was right made me feel much better about myself, enough to let it go. Ironically, the same woman got my phone number and asked if I would substitute for her as chairperson for the upcoming two Thursdays. Apparently, she either has some respect for me after all, unwavering gumption, or is having a hard time finding a replacement. But no matter, both she and I can thank my supporter (call him "Jo") for helping me see why I should step up and fill the position for those two Thursdays.

In any situation where an amend might be called for, it is most important to look at the situation from every angle to see how you might also be responsible. I believe, like in the case of a car accident, if someone hits you from behind, it's probably 90% their fault, but you must own something in the accident. You may have been stopped, but your brake lights weren't working. Or you were on a hill and rolled into the other car behind you. In that case, it might be 80% your fault for rolling downhill into the other car. The other driver might have to take 20% of the blame for possibly not being at a safe car distance apart, and there is a good chance that the insurance company is also going to see it that way. In either case, *you have a part,* and you need to reconcile, own up to it, and work it out. Your job is to make your part right with the other person. The automobile scenarios were only used as an example of how we are involved in any unfavorable situation.

In this book, I discuss how fears can be linked to every situation you can imagine. Here, I draw a parallel and connect this idea to our perceived involvement in every resentment. The prevailing notion suggests that we play a role in every resentment, a claim with which I completely disagree. If one can link fear to every conceivable circumstance, following that logic means tying my part to everything, even when it lacks coherence. It's like saying my role is simply being present on the planet when an event occurs. The absurdity of this notion becomes evident when taken to the extreme.

Chapter's Logical Take-Away: To make amends in order to bury grudges, foster a sense of forgiveness, and promote personal development, especially in addiction recovery. This entails more than simply apologizing; it involves repairing the emotional damage caused to others, with or without meaning to. Overall, the chapter emphasizes the importance of making restitution for personal development and recovery.

THE NEWCOMER MEETING

"Pay attention, today my wisdom is free."

For the purpose of this book, we are going to refer to the "newcomer" as an individual who is new to any recovery organization. At the beginning of every meeting, the chairperson will undoubtedly ask if there is anyone there for their very first day; that person is the newcomer. The chairperson might also inquire if anyone is in their first week or has less than thirty days in the program; these individuals might be newcomers, but only the first-ever attendee is a "true" newcomer. Of course, the term "newcomer" could also refer to someone new or unfamiliar to a geographic region or activity, such as being new in town or new to a sport.

I attend many twelve-step meetings, and whenever there is a newcomer present, the theme of the meeting almost inevitably and purposefully shifts from whatever the topic would have been to a "newcomer meeting.". A newcomer meeting follows the same format as the regular meeting group but focuses on themes similar to those in a beginner's meeting. Just like in school, we must start slowly to avoid missing the very important rules or messages.

When any member of the group so much as brings up "'the steps'," sponsors, home groups, God, or higher power, which happens in every newcomer meeting, they create a wave of uneasiness. It's like telling a first grader to first add or subtract what's in the brackets and then multiply the sum by what's outside the brackets on the left. This is not a cult, but it sure sounds like one when members choose this tact when welcoming a newcomer.

In my view, it's best not to bring up any of those things at all. It's unimportant to even get into the problems that brought them there in the first place; it's too early for that. The best way to entice someone, especially with an ongoing program, is to make them feel comfortable from the very beginning. All that other information is overwhelming. When things sound too complicated all at once, they are more likely to give up before really getting started.

Also, when referring to the newcomer, another phrase often repeated in meetings is, "You are the most important person in the room.". The recurrent emphasis on this phrase might be an attempt to convey that those vocalizing it have more experience than the newcomer. Consequently, our collective "focus" and sense of value or importance" are intended to be extended to you today. Regrettably, by default, tomorrow you will assimilate into our collective experience.

Chapter's Logical Take-Away: The only thing that changes at a Newcomer 12-twelve-step meeting is the topic, or lack thereof. There's no need to overwhelm someone who is just starting; doing so might scare them off. The session should consist of nothing more than a warm welcome and a clear mission statement. When this simple approach brings them back, the program will gradually unfold as they continue to attend meetings, regardless of time or place.

NAVIGATING CROSSTALK IN MEETINGS

Nodding your head "yes" in agreement is OK but shaking your head "no" is not OK. Similarly, eye-rolling constitutes a form of body language that can be as disruptive as direct crosstalk.

The focus of this discussion pertains specifically to one of the guidelines in twelve-step programs during meetings. I decided to bring this up as I've observed one form or another of "cross-talking" occurring at every meeting I attend. I believe some people don't understand the rules well enough, or they are not big rule-abiding folks. This may have prompted me to compile a refined meaning and offer my interpretation on the subject. I believe that my observations could be valuable to all meeting attendees.

So, let's explore the logical interpretation of cross-talking:

- First and foremost, it revolves around respect. When the chairperson signals the start of the meeting, silence should prevail, like in a courtroom or a church. In simpler terms, no talking is allowed unless a question has been posed.

- No side conversations, these are disrespectful and disruptive. Remember, court and church.

- There are no interjections of approval or disagreement while someone is sharing their experience. In some meetings, where there are many "old-timers" (people with many years of sobriety under their belt) who consider themselves twelve-step superstars (thumpers), you hear them say "yes," or "correct," or even "amen," which is unnecessary and wrong.

- They just don't say it once during another's share; they await their cue to squeeze them in to an excessive degree. This is disruptive as it slows down the person sharing, and, their approval of your share is completely ego-driven on their part, like you're correct, because I personally agree with what you're saying, and I am a scholar here.

- When it's your turn to share, it's acceptable to reference something positive from a previous share. You can even go so far as to mention the individual's name you're crediting or quote their valuable lines. While some opt for more general acknowledgments like "like someone said," it's perfectly fine to use their name specifically when giving credit. As they say, credit where credit is due. In my research on the subject, I read somewhere: "It displays love and support."

- Disputing someone's opinion or displaying disagreement through body language is inappropriate. Like "acceptance" in the program has taught us, simply agree to disagree without explicitly expressing it.

- Crosstalk also includes giving advice or making direct suggestions to another person, calling that particular person out, rather than addressing the group. Instead, we are encouraged to preface our statements with phrases like "in my opinion" or "for me" to avoid being directive. Even if you possess professional credentials (e.g., CAC, LSW), the meeting rules take precedence within the meeting's confines. You can offer advice when the meeting is over, but always use wise judgment and sensitivity wherever you are. Understand that not everyone may be receptive to your opinion. Meetings are not group therapy.

Chapter's Logical Take-Away: Avoiding crosstalk is all about creating a courteous and friendly meeting environment where everyone can speak without interruption or judgment while respecting the group's guidelines.

SECTION 5
SPIRITUAL BY NATURE

THE CREATOR

If God didn't put birds on earth,
we would never have airplanes.

Many addicts and problem drinkers who find their way into organized recovery are told that the only way to get and remain sober for a long time is to believe in a higher power or God of their understanding[367]. That seems to be a non-negotiable trend. They stress the importance of prayer and having a connection to a source greater than man as a higher power or Creator for their recovery.

It's hard to escape the thought of religion when you constantly hear the word "God." The unchanging factor in every twelve-step anonymous program is their "steps to success." The steps themselves are nearly identical except for the name of the disorder (Alcohol, Narcotics, Gambling, Overeaters, Thrill-seeking, etc.) which is simply substituted across programs. Moreover, every twelve-step list reference God or a higher power, which to me would indicate that these programs are loosely religious-based, and that's fine. Even so, these twelve-step programs claim to be spiritual by nature given they deal with the human psyche.

In my justified belief, the "God" word scared away so many would-be members in the early years of the organization. I'm sure brainstorming brought about a new, and more acceptable term for the concept of God, a "God of your understanding" so you could pick your *own* God, if you don't already follow a religion. I found that so many people like me don't want to pick a god or include a "higher power" in their lives. I am settled on my "Creator." Yet, as a tactic of persuasion by other believers, I hear them repeatedly ask: "Do you believe that I believe?" I never got that one. Of what esteem are those who ask? If my answer is "yes" that gets me no closer to believing.

"God" is just a word devised for communication, and its interpretation is unmistakably recognized in every part of the world, in every walk of life. Thus, "Creator" could have been chosen if the word "God" was settled on first. The point remains, this was still not good enough for those who flat out reject religion. In one of my other books, I state that religion is a choice, having idols and a place to worship them. Whereas I believe spirituality is embedded in all of us, for us to discover when we need it the most. Bringing forth an understanding of a "creator" and an awareness of your part with nature. Of course, you can reject that premise too. Like I said, it's all about choice.

I attend more AA meetings than most. As a writer, it allows me to get inspiration and ideas to write about later. Besides the customary readings, I hear some things almost every day. Someone always says gratefully: "I am sober today by the grace of God." And like I said above, that's fine, but you can't change my mind about that not being a religious inference.

There are active twelve-step programs based on religion. AA is one whose foundation is based on spirituality and claims not to be a religious program.

Sounds counterintuitive, right? But it's true. The program was also positioned as a "spiritual" program to reaffirm its direction. Spiritual awakening rather than a religious experience was more tolerable and accepted by most active and would-be members. I believe that it is both a religious and a spiritual program, as evidenced in its texts, then and even today. The mixing and use of both concepts appear to work well. I myself have a different concept that favors spirituality, not only with my recovery but with the person I have become too.

I once encountered a simple yet profound way to understand "my higher power" or "God of my understanding." Someone asked me, "Did you create yourself?" I answered, "No." Then they asked, "Did you create me?" Again, I replied, "No." They concluded, "Well, something made us so, we have a creator." I expanded on this theorem by acknowledging that I had created nothing in nature, only reshaped the growth of plant life, but that's hardly a creation, only a fabrication. I also recalled a phrase from my church days: "Maker of heaven and earth, all that is seen and unseen." This realization was a breakthrough; I no longer needed to visualize or define my higher power or creator. What a discovery, which was my spiritual awakening!

My creator, and creator of the universe created me to do some of his work. And apart from a few "realistic" prayers of guidance and thanks, that is the extent of my connection with God, my Creator. I thoroughly believe I was made to be everything I am capable of being. I believe that I am supposed to fulfil my God-given abilities to my fullest to carry out a mission here and live amongst others in harmony. Anything less than the is a shortcoming, falling short of my Creator-given abilities. I don't ask my God to hold my hand every step of the way, but I've reached the point of praying only for guidance when absolutely necessary, and the strength to endure the pitfalls and highs life throws in my path. Today I owe my clean and healthy way of living to the creator who delivered me. It's not the medical professionals, fellowship groups, or my family and friends. It was my creator who gave me just enough to help myself, and to put these people in my life to make it all possible.

Chapter's Logical Take-Away: When people say, "God first," what they are implying is that they are religious. Religion is a choice. Its structures are enforced. Spirituality is merely a feeling and an understanding that you are part of the world with a purpose. I say this because twelve-step programs claim to be spiritual, when in fact they are both spiritual and religious at the same time. "Give it to God" and "God's will" clearly have religious undertones.

A SPIRITUAL AWAKENING – SPIRITUAL AWARENESS

No one has to be religious;
you just have to believe in yourself.

In the preceding chapter, I talked about my spiritual awakening. How settling on having a "creator" could also be the god of my understanding. This brought me to the understanding that spirituality is the connection with a creator, and your intended purpose for being a part of this planet and its place in the universe. How we're all here fleetingly in the cosmic scale, and what kind of legacy we leave.

Spirituality is interdependence and interaction with others. It is systematically and harmoniously orchestrated in unison. Spirituality is about finding yourself upon years of self-reflection, often accomplished through deep meditation. It is a sense of connection to something bigger than us, something we can't quite understand, but believe in it notwithstanding, and it typically involves a search for meaning in life[368]. The flip side is to suffer from existential crisis. As such, it is a universal human experience, something that touches us all. People may describe a spiritual experience as sacred or transcendent or simply a deep sense of aliveness and interconnectedness. I believe it can only be a one-time occurrence, an awakening or revelation when we start to see everything in a new light.

Others may pray or find comfort in a personal relationship with God or a higher power. Still, others wait for spirituality to come to their senses. Spirituality is not religion. If someone asks, "Are you religious?" you can say no, but still be spiritual (also known as *spiritual but not religious* [SBNR]). Religion is to worship, whereas spirituality is a state of mind, as a connection with the universe and existence. I remind you of the spirituality that resides in us all. But only with an open mind you can establish a connection with the creator and nature. After all, nature is "natural," or God-given!

While the subject of God and religion is notorious for dividing any group, a spiritual approach will bring more people together. Spirituality is a state of mind, whereas religion is a class, an order, or organization with idols and venues for worship. Sacred texts and religious scriptures provide guidance to their believers. With religion it's easy to attract controversies, but with spirituality, you can give your own exclusive opinion without offending anyone.

Here is a spiritual notion and a test. Look outside during daylight, preferably on a sunlit day. I challenge you to identify ten distinct colors in less than a minute. Limit your search to elements untouched by human hands. Man-made objects, such as painted, stained, or dyed items, don't count in this exercise, whose raw pigments were also delivered. Our existence is not confined to a black and white world, it is bursting with vibrant colors.

Chapter's Logical Take-Away: An awakening is a first-time experience, or revelation. A spiritual awakening occurs when one day the reality of something you never knew existed or have always known but ignored hits you. I prefer to think of it as when you understand your role and existence, and everything around you that was created by a "higher power," or in my case, "the Creator."

CHAPTER 68

SIGNS THAT MAYBE I'M BEING TESTED

I don't believe I have any special powers,
but I am reminded something does.

In the closing three paragraphs of Chapter 66, "The Creator," I shared my personal concept of God as my Creator. With the help of a friend in the program, we came up with this idea of "my God" to justify my existence. I'm sure many people are on board with my approach; it's not any more improbable than all the religious theories about God. However, over the past few years, particularly due to my involvement with AA, I've found myself becoming more intrigued and open to concepts like fate, karma, and even faith. This shift, albeit subtle, marks a significant departure from my self-proclaimed "realist" attitude. This may seem insignificant to many people hoping to get a grasp on an obsession or addiction, yet the most successful programs rely on spirituality to deliver their message. And a god of your understanding, or higher power, is essential in all these twelve-step programs.

Today I'm faced with a conundrum that I'm eager to unravel and would love to explain to you in detail. There is no sense of urgency, and from what I gather, the answers to my quandary often come gradually. It seems as though my Creator is gently beckoning me to become more of a believer, which includes daily prayer and meditation as well as frequent contact with Him. I've heard it said many times before that God speaks through others. They'll send you a message or sign in the most unexpected of ways. If this is true, I also have to believe his messages come in many forms. The terms "God shot," "coincidence," and "serendipitous moment" are likely to be used for individuals finding themselves in the right place at the right time.

Just recently, I was telling a friend on a drive somewhere about the remarkable WWII Corsair airplane and its speed, maneuverability, and so on. Then I noticed a sharp SUV in my rearview mirror. "Wait until you see this SUV coming up behind us," I told my friend. "It's probably one of those new Lamborghinis or Aston Martins." I slowed to a stop at the next traffic signal, knowing he'd take the vacant lane next to me. I looked over at the vehicle's insignia on the front fender as he pulled up alongside me. It said, "Lincoln Corsair." "That has to be a sign," I said.

When I am writing a book, I follow a specific format and methodology in assembling and working on the chapters. Think of it as a puzzle where one might begin by creating the entire border with the straight edges to form a frame (framework). Depending on the subject matter, I might then work inward from the frame or lay out the objects (chapters) inside the frame. In the latter case, it's probably because I can visualize enough of an object (chapter) to maintain momentum, or I might get bored and decide to bounce around to avoid getting stuck, as with writer's block. I set this up to say that after a year and a half of work on this book, I was putting the finishing touches on a couple of chapters. I had my music playlist playing softly in the background, as I do, but only sometimes when I am merely copying notes or reviewing what was already written.

I was rereading Chapter 55 when I came across the word "demons." I remember only using it once in the entire book, and as I was reading it again to myself, Kiss, in the song "God of Thunder," sang the lyrics: "I was raised by the demons" at that exact moment, not two seconds before or after, but in unison. Because I always hit shuffle on my playlist to prevent myself from getting tired of any songs, "If Looks Could Kill" by the band Heart came on next just as I read through the word "heart" in the manuscript. Now I realize that the word "heart," which is repeated fifteen times throughout the book, might seem like a stretch, but I have hundreds of songs and only two by Heart on my playlist. By the way, these two paragraphs, starting with "When I am writing a book …" were last-minute additions as this book goes in for proofreading tomorrow. If it didn't just hit me, it wouldn't hit you, readers!

These recent occurrences have astounded me. They are not spectacular windfalls for me, but rather signs of my creator's presence to draw my attention. They occur with increasing frequency, often becoming part of my daily life. Sometimes it's a song on the radio, a passage I've recently read brought to life in an unexpected conversation, a billboard message in the form of an advertisement, or a specific animal crossing my path. For me, the occurrence of coincidences is more than a human's ability to notice mundane patterns in daily life. I guess I'm just waiting for one more "big encounter" as proof or a "breakthrough" moment for me to cross over and join the ranks of higher-level believers.

I'm left wondering whether I am being prepared for a deeper understanding of the intricacies of spirituality. Perhaps, in doing so, I am merely confronting the challenges of living life on life's own terms, charting my own path, but also asking God to guide me. It's possible that these experiences are tests meant to gauge how best I can handle life's adversities and successes. Let us not forget that success affects our emotions too. Like I mentioned earlier, upon succeeding, people often fear not living up to the expectations. Tempting our memory and willpower in the face of addiction. Testing our patience and tolerance with people too. Ultimately, it's all about composure and balance.

Chapter's Logical Take-Away: As you remember, I stated that these programs are both spiritual and religious at the same time. To be spiritual, and to paraphrase AA, you would have a conscious with God as you understand Him. It seems that I didn't have a relationship with my creator, just an understanding, a sense of vagueness about His existence. But with all the happenings mentioned in this chapter, perhaps this is the level of contact I was to learn about?

MENTAL FITNESS

Mentally able is like stretching before a race.

The main foundation for twelve-step programs is a connection with God, or a higher power, if you will, developed through spirituality. They declare their spiritual nature and underscore their reliance on a higher power to be effective[369]. The term they use is spiritually fit. And what that means in the context of these programs is being balanced and living according to God's will. The term I would like to throw into the ring is "mentally fit." I define that as a condition of sanity, soundness, and unwavering mental fortitude arising from achieving a certain level of spirituality.

With a stable mind, we can efficiently deal with anything life has to offer, wise enough to call on innate logic and common sense in any situation. Also, there is a willingness in seeking the guidance of a god of your understanding, or a higher power, to pray for a sign, or just a calmness to endure the downturns a time may bring.

These programs speak of the importance of being "in a spiritually fit condition" when entering an environment that might test our sobriety. This holds true for gamblers and people with eating disorders, along with addicts and alcoholics alike. If we are "spiritually fit," being well-trained, level-headed, even-tempered, and without fear, we are probably well-equipped to face an environment that might break us otherwise. A significant aspect of this approach revolves around self-awareness and recognizing our limitations. It is like the drug user remembering that "a monkey can't sell bananas."

Chapter's Logical Take-Away: Being "mentally fit," is having a steady and logical mindset that you can expertly utilize, and to integrate logic and common sense to handle life's issues and seek divine guidance. Mental fitness helps people with addiction, gambling, eating disorders, and other concerns that face challenges to be overcome once and for all. Self-awareness and limitations are stressed as tools to help achieve this.

THE "WE" IN POWERLESS

Don't always try to be cute,
life is mostly taken at face value.

So much has been said about the first word in the first step of twelve-step programs being "we." Let's roll back the clocks. I truly believe that everyone has said to themselves "I" am powerless over my addiction, and consequently "my" life has become unmanageable. I say this because if you are in any group larger than one, "we" is plural for "I," especially when recited with others in unison. I remember our Creed in the Catholic Church by heart; "*We* believe in one God, father almighty …." Said aloud, it's the "We" version, but to myself it is "I." Over the years, the "we" in "We admitted we were powerless…" has been adopted as a subliminal message because one person helping another is better than trying to do it on my own. And as I've often stated, two brains are better than one. That is, we need to support each other to excel on this journey to recovery. But if truth be told, the "We" in "We admitted we were powerless[370]…" has no hidden message behind it at all. The "We" is We, the first hundred or so people in the program from late 1934. So, "We" as in "us!"

We should not get too cute or clever with every hidden might-be message in recovery terms and conditions. Nostradamus didn't write the book. Playing a Beatles album backwards is what you want to make of it. Coincidence or intentional? More like a coincidence, and usually a stretch at that.

However, the real issue with the "we" message lies in another area altogether. Every program will tell you that you need to be selfish about your recovery and that your sobriety, or any addiction, must come first.

> **Chapter's Logical Take-Away:** It's clear to me that too much emphasis is put on the word "We," as being the first word in the first step of the most important guides in all twelve-step programs. Focusing on hidden messages or interpretations in recovery literature is pointless and often a stretch.

"...THIS IS YOUR BRAIN ON DRUGS"

"We're alcoholics, that's what we do" ...
totally absurd!

In 1987, the Partnership for a Drug-Free America (PDFA) rolled out a very memorable, and wildly successful TV commercial, "This Is Your Brain on Drugs.[371]" If you've never seen the video, there are several versions on YouTube which I'll recommend you to watch. It portrays a comparison of the brain on drugs to the egg as it fries in a pan.

I have always maintained that "you are a person first, before you are anything else. The addict or alcoholic is still a human being, but also given an additional layer of flaws (addiction) that requires attention, unlike that of an ordinary, or non-diseased person (though their flaws might be totally different). And, despite the fact that I've been advocating for this concept since I began my recovery research studies five years ago, I've established a new theory that is consistent in a variety of settings.

I believe that people with SUDs (substance use disorders) can become permanently mentally impaired to some extent as a result of prolonged drug or alcohol abuse. I used to tell my sister, the psychologist, why my memory was fading, "I think I killed way too many brain cells with drugs." She would reply, "Rick, it wasn't the drugs—you're getting old." I believe my sister was only partially correct. My thoughts led me to the conclusion that since cocaine was my DOC (drug of choice), the chemicals used to create the "finished" product would be as lethal as it is with other drugs.

For instance, if you mix kerosene, solvents, and acids used in the production of cocaine or crack and pour the concoction on the back of your hand, the flesh will be severely burned. Therefore, you can't tell me that drugs, that is, the chemicals used to produce them, don't cause harm to brain cells before harming the digestive system and other vital organs.

When we have a psychological shift and make the decision to change our attitude and thinking in order to heal ourselves and become better people, we can only accomplish so much. Therefore, it is important to note that the damage caused by the continuous exposure of these poisonous substances to the brain tissue is irreparable.

You've probably heard the term "scrambled" or "fried" like the egg in the TV commercial above, well I believe that's what we're seeing here: damaged or "fried" brain cells. This lends credence to my theory on brain damage caused by prolonged substance abuse. If you shape a ball of putty into a square and put it away for a year, or two, or five. When you come back it's not going to be a ball, it is going to be a square, just the way you left it.

I discovered that former drug users who are now leading sober lives tend to forget things or are unreliable. These are two areas where I've seen these tendencies most prominently.

IT JUST MAKES SENSE

When someone says: "you could use a drink"
(like they say on TV), or "I could use a
drink," they don't mean a soda can!

Some of the most memorable marketing slogans in history are succinct, catchy, and immediately resonate with people. Phrases like "Just do it," "Just say no," and "Be the best you can be" are deserving of recognition. As a former businessman, I appreciated one in particular from a New Jersey-based off-priced clothier, Sy Syms: "An educated consumer is our best customer." Its profundity endures, even though his chain of stores is no longer in business.

The program's primary textbook was written by someone from a previous generation along with a few collaborators; it may have an archaic writing style, but it contains enduring wisdom that stands the test of time. When combined with the collective insights of millions of students of this literature, its meanings have evolved in today's language just like every piece of classic literature. The wealth of information available, in online and offline texts, and the lack of urgency to publish allows for continual refinement and growth.

Have you ever had a brilliant insight as an afterthought, perhaps as you were already heading out the door or sitting in your car, or taking a shower? This is exactly why there are second, third, fourth, and many more book editions, especially in non-fiction space, as the contents need to be updated in step with time. The purpose of the subsequent publications of the same book is to accommodate and combine past thoughts with the appropriate changes in the present.

Numerous lives have been saved by various twelve-step programs. Note that people often end up at Alcoholics Anonymous (AA) because it is the most well-known. Also, treatment centers and the legal system often endorse the AA approach. Therefore, those who can afford treatment or have insurance tend to enter programs that eventually introduce them to AA. If you can't afford formal treatment and are seeking recovery, there are free AA meetings you can attend. For those facing DUI charges, AA may be offered as an alternative to incarceration to rehabilitate the individual serving as a form of rehabilitation.

"AA never told me anything I didn't already know." I've shared these sentiments countless times at AA meetings over the years. It continually emphasizes the importance of maintaining a clean and sober lifestyle. These mindsets reflect my own behavior from the past. I would buy a piece of furniture that arrived unassembled in a box, bubble-wrapped with instructions. Initially, I'd lay out all the pieces on the floor and convince myself that I could figure it out just by looking at the box's picture. Some people might even disregard the step-by-step instructions that come with the booklet and solely rely on intuition to assemble the pieces. But half-way through, I'd realize that the back should have been attached before the top, which was already in place. I'd reluctantly admit, "That makes sense." Now, regardless of what had transpired, I would have to remove the top to properly attach the back, as instructed by the manufacturer. So, do you take off the top and follow the instructions or consult them to see what comes next? In this case, logic dictates following the instructions. Similarly, in recovery from any issue, many of us believe we can go it alone without guidance.

Not long ago, during a twelve-step program meeting, someone exclaimed, "Logic doesn't work!" I had made a comment about using common sense and logic when a woman was distressed over her overheating car. To numb her frustration, she was tempted to drink. I suggested that since the car was the clear problem, not the individual, and pouring alcohol into its fuel tank wouldn't help either, she should address the underlying issue causing it to overheat. I called it the "logical approach." Perhaps it was a radiator leak, low antifreeze, a faulty thermostat, or a malfunctioning water pump. In any case, liquor wouldn't fix the car, nor its owner. I said, "Sometimes you need to use a little common sense and logic." The person who followed my shared advice responded, "To Rick's point, common sense and logic doesn't work for us; we are alcoholics." Another participant echoed this sentiment, suggesting that alcoholics lack the capacity for rational thinking. It's baffling to think that they believe they've lost their humanity, and their optimism in the process, simply because they identify as alcoholics.

Let's consider a hypothetical scenario that relies on logic and common sense. If you are new to recovery and your struggle is with alcohol, embarking on a cruise or visiting an all-inclusive resort might not be advisable. I share this in Chapter 3 as FOMO. These locations typically offer overflowing amounts of free alcohol at every turn, including during meals and in minibars. Unless they are in recovery themselves, most people on these cruises or at resorts are likely to be intoxicated. Try as they might, they can't help but be influenced by the general mood of the cruisers. Furthermore, all-inclusive resorts are enclosed compounds, and once you're there, leaving the premises or avoiding alcohol becomes challenging. On board a cruise ship, there's no escape either, unless you are to the point of stealing a lifeboat.

In Chapter 31, focusing on anonymity, I discuss the importance of presenting oneself as a person before acknowledging the identity as an alcoholic in twelve-step program. One might assume that using the name you've carried throughout your entire existence should take precedence in any introduction, as it represents you to everyone you meet, because anyone would see you as a human being before getting to know you. This also serves to reaffirm that this is who you are. Addiction does not define me, but rather, it is a part of my makeup that I'm striving to manage. I often express to my peers that the efforts dedicated to achieving wellness in recovery can be applied to self-improvement as well. This concept can be likened to the age-old question, "What came first, the chicken or the egg?" Consider this: if we trace back to early civilization, there were people, not alcoholics. We are people first!

Chapter's Logical Take-Away: Having a problem with addiction doesn't absolve you from possessing and utilizing your brain to make life decisions, especially when you are clean and sober for some time. We acquire common sense and logical thinking in the earliest stages of our development. It doesn't matter where you get your knowledge from; just exercise what continues to work for you.

GIVING IT TO GOD IS NOT ENOUGH

*Magic is deception, don't be fooled
by what is expected of you!*

Often people who have a problem pray to God to take it all away. I've heard this referred to as "foxhole" prayers. "God, please get me out of this …" "God, please get me out of that…" I even heard, "God, please get me out of this, and I will never do it again." But it's slightly different for people with an addiction. If they are struggling with addiction, they may ask for help to break it once and for all. But if they are in a program based on spirituality like most twelve-step programs are, you will often hear, "When I have a problem, I just give it to God, and the problem is lifted by His grace." Really? You see, they are taught to let God handle their lives through His will.

In my 2022 book, 'I Didn't Ask to Be Me,' I discuss all the 'wills': 'my will,' 'God's Will,' and 'free will' with great depth and analysis. To fully understand the content of this chapter, it is important to provide you with an overview of how they impact my life, and most likely, yours too.

"Pick a thought, any thought." I can influence your thinking to some extent, but only you can truly create your thoughts, even when others fill your head with ideas. It is important to remember that you have the power to shape your own ideas. There are thoughts that require decision-making, and some of them may result in taking action. This process inspires 'my will.'

However, before I cast my decision, I have the comfort of knowing that my God is there for me, ready to guide me and listen to my prayers. He acts as a second opinion, a sounding board, or a lifeline before I decide what is necessary or best for me. This is where free will comes into play. Now that I have all the information I think I need, I am ready to jump into action. It is worth noting that the outcome of events, at least here on Earth, is believed to be predetermined by God's Will. If I made the correct decision, I could attribute it to my God-given brains or my trust in Him. If things didn't go as I hoped, it means my desires were not in alignment with God's will.

Moving the queen and then letting go could result in losing it. However, it's worth considering that your God might favor using the rook at this moment to gain better access to the king.

I personally believe things do happen for a reason, which is by God's will, but I also believe we are given the power from our Creator (my God) to get mature to an extent and use our innate wisdom to figure things out on our own.

So, this creator of mine empowers me to explore and understand myself well enough to effectively manage and deal with the problems I encounter.

I don't see a quick fix or for anything to be removed without utilizing my God-given abilities.

Let's say the problem is with a traffic violation that can only be taken care of at the Motor Vehicle office. Are you expecting your God or higher power to materialize and accompany you there to straighten out the summons? My God is my creator, who made me everything I am today. And since I was given the ability to drive to the Motor Vehicle office, wait in line, and pay the fine, all I have to do is say "thank you, God, for making me a responsible person. When you pray to God, I believe you should only ask for guidance and thanks, good counsel, and blessings, not to expect to receive the results you seek on a silver platter.

Here's an example: Imagine you are taking an important test and have studied hard like you should. Now that you've done your part, you can pray that you remain focused, calm, and confident enough to manage the time efficiently when the test starts. However, I believe that it would be illogical to expect the answers to come to you like an epiphany if you didn't prepare for the test. So, before you ask God to take away your problems, why not ask him to help you look for a possible solution?

Chapter's Logical Take-Away: I am strongly opposed to relying on God alone. I may have been created to do God's bidding, but I have a part in the outcome too, as I do the thing of my own volition, and so we have a partnership of sorts. With His guidance, I am directed to be responsible and actively do my part.

SECTION 6

A LIFE WORTH LIVING

BUILDING INTEGRITY RESPONSIBLY AND RELIABLY

"We're alcoholics, that's what we do"…
totally absurd!

What does it mean when I give you my word? For me, it's straightforward; my word is my bond. When I make a promise, consider it as good as done. Even if it's the last thing I do, I'll keep my promise. Yet if you offer me yours, it depends on how well I know you. Do we have a history? If we're total strangers, I might get some informal testimonials, especially if it's important. I call this the word-of-mouth approach; there is nothing genius about that. If I can't find much about you, then I'll trust my judgment. If you're not a responsible and reliable person, as evidenced by your initial reaction, your word has little value because, in my view, your integrity score is low. It's the same principle as a credit score. If you always pay your bills on time, you earn a high credit score. So, if you want to be the one everyone knows they can always count on, you need to maintain a high integrity score.

Having integrity, being reliable, and being responsible are completely up to you. These attributes are earned when someone vouches for your credibility. And I can't teach you to possess any of these qualities. I can, however, impart the importance and long-term value that can be gained with these and other admirable attributes. People of higher authority can influence your quest to become such. They constantly course-correct their pupils so they don't stray down dark paths like addiction and obsession. Observe and follow through!

But what if my life's messed up? Then you might hear me say, "Well, whose life isn't?" How am I supposed to use good judgment if I've lost the ability due to illness or disorder? Remember all the things we missed, blew off, shrugged off, or ignored, all because we didn't see their value at the time? Deep down, that wasn't really our intention. However, our creditors couldn't have known as much.

We usually don't want anyone to know why we did or didn't do the things we did; most times, our illness controlled us as though we were its puppets. So, when we finally commit to wellness, we leave behind a life of chaos to become a totally different person.

However, note that commitment is also a promise. We're not just starting anew; it's about self-awareness and becoming a better version of yourself. Remember, the path to becoming "best" must be trod via "better."

Feeling responsible is uplifting, a sign of sanity and clear thinking, the right ingredients to become a good human being. This transformation is a sort of mental house cleaning in order to make room for being responsible and reliable once again now. At this stage, our minds are no longer influenced by obsessions and addictions as we have exercised stronger control over ourselves. You are back for as long as you keep your word.

Chapter's Logical Take-Away: If you want to enjoy being liked, keep your integrity score high. When you make a commitment, others expect nothing less than the promises you make and how you stay true to them. You are being trusted. Seeing your commitment through builds trust and integrity.

CLEAN LIVING AND SELF CARE

"I have a lot of time, but I am as busy as hell."
I just choose how to be productive and
healthy as ways to fill my days.

First, we get clean and/or sober (or abstinent) then we embark on a life of "sobriety" (lifestyle changes). Yet at first, like everything we do, it's a bit of a challenge since every change is uncomfortable at first. So, whatever your habit or addiction is, it gets easier to manage as long as we stay committed. If we become distracted and lose focus, we can still maintain our newfound path to wellness as long as we stay true to the AA program. Recovery gets easier and life gets better.

Our brain tends to choose good over bad (not to be mistaken with its tendency to seek the path of least resistance), bridging the gap between abstinence from addiction and reintegration into the everyday world we were once separated from. Like the typical hard-working human who is responsible and loving, we strive to be more active, to break out of isolation, and to be a participant in things we once loved to do. So, what can we do as an alcoholic or substance abuser? It is best we cross over to the world of emotional sobriety (which is stated above as a "life of sobriety).

Self-care is the practice of taking an active role in protecting one's own well-being and happiness. This is really all about getting back to living life happily and sanely. What do you like to do with your free time, and where do you get pleasure, satisfaction, and contentment? Self-care activities are essential for maintaining physical, emotional, and mental well-being. Engaging in self-care can help reduce stress, improve overall health, and enhance your quality of life[372]. Remember that self-care is individualized since everyone's needs are different, and what works for one person may not work for another. It's important to listen to your own needs and make self-care a regular part of your routine to maintain balance and well-being.

There is a connectivity between our mind, body, and soul, or figuratively speaking, mental, physical, and spiritual health. Along the same lines, there are self-care activities that we should practice regularly as part of our daily routine. Here are suggestive areas to consider in relation to self-care[373,374]:

- Exercise should be a part of everyone's life for all the benefits it offers. It can improve mood, energy, and overall health. Consider joining a gym, or just walking every day like I do. Or consider jogging or running. Perhaps you like to bike, play tennis, swim, or kayak. There are countless indoor and outdoor activities that you can explore.
- Eat a balanced diet and drink plenty of water daily; it's good for the skin too. Also, sleep well so that you can face each day refreshed.
- Meditation is a good way to relax. Yoga can also help reduce stress because it promotes relaxation, which is the opposite of stress.

- Take warm, fragrant, or effervescent (bubbly) baths.

- Nature walks are assuredly peaceful. I discussed how I came to enjoy feeding horses, birds, and squirrels in another book. I didn't see that coming, but my new-found spiritual awareness led me to that peaceful place.

- As I mentioned, I am a "spiritual person." I don't subscribe to any organized religions, but I do pray. I believe prayer is often associated with religion, and when in line with one's beliefs, praying or engaging in spiritual practices is undoubtedly healthy for one's peace of mind.

- Follow your passions, like gardening, cooking, or crafting. Often I brag to people how big my plants are growing.

- I am a writer, but I wasn't always one. I discovered writing to be a fantastic exercise for the mind. It has pushed me to use my brain and to learn so much about who I am. I challenge my readers to write a poem or at least one short chapter about their lives. Try a stream-of-consciousness exercise. You will thank me for having done it!

- Don't forget to read anything that interests you. Expand your horizons. Brain games like puzzles and crosswords will also expand your mind.

- Express your creative side by painting, crocheting, or playing an instrument.

- Enjoy your favorite music to boost your spirits. You can also watch a movie or TV show to unwind and relax.

- One area that may be overlooked in self-care is therapy or counseling. Sometimes, we need someone to share our thoughts with, someone to listen to, and, by the way, these can be the closest people in your life to confide in your vulnerable secrets.

- Join social groups that match your interests.

In case you haven't figured it out, self-care is all about doing things that make you happy, relaxed and feel better about yourself.

Chapter's Logical Take-Away: Enjoying and lowering stress to boost happiness, sanity, and self-care. By exercising, eating healthy, meditating, going on nature walks, being spiritual, pursuing your passions, reading, being creative, and going for therapy, we create a healthy balanced program for our mind, body, and soul that can greatly impact our lives.

DEMONSTRATING GRATITUDE

"I suppose I am grateful when I get only one flat tire at a time."

For those who struggle with an addiction, there is no finish line. It's a life-long journey. We are never cured. Instead, the goal is to manage addiction successfully. I prefer to use the term "managing" rather than "overcoming" addiction, recognizing that problems and obstacles are a part of life that one cannot avoid entirely "We can't circumvent the world just like we cannot run from life." But this doesn't mean we have to face everything that troubles us. We do have freedom to distance ourselves from bad things. Logic and common sense tell me to avoid what has been historically harmful. Boundaries, as discussed in previous chapters, are seen as valuable tools to keep oneself away from precarious situations.

When we reach a point where our addiction or disorder is under control and being managed, we are fit to get back in the race with the rest of the world. We are prepared to welcome the psychological change talked about in parts of this book. I believe it is the key measure to virtuousness and the new beginning of a productive position in society. It is described as the "high" that comes from replacing selfish behavior with gratitude and a renewed sense of purpose when we are treading uphill in our lives. It is the restoration or resurrection of a contented character of what was me. So, I am very grateful now.

But there is a practice that you've still not cultivated. Being built up with gratitude is considered just a one-way street. You now have the ability to make this gift even more meaningful by spreading it to others. Think of grateful in, and gratitude out. What you give to others builds your legacy. In twelve-step programs, "pass it on" is repeated to keep the organization thriving. And now the new phrase is "pay it forward." By sharing your good fortune, you offer hope to those who haven't yet reached this point. It might be just what they need. In my opinion the most valuable form of hope comes through experience.

In Chapter 50, "Promises That Make Sense," I touch on the concept of altruism. Very simply, altruism is the act of being selfless, or, more accurately, less selfish, and putting others' needs over your own. When we experience gratitude, altruism comes naturally; it becomes our way of being and the conduit for expressing our gratitude.

Being an active member of the addiction recovery community, I often hear how grateful people are to be addicts and alcoholics. Some say, "I am a grateful addict or alcoholic." I prefer, "I am a grateful *recovering* addict or alcoholic." Or "I am grateful *to have found help* in overcoming my disease of addiction or obsession." I find it justifiable to understand how some people with problems in general are grateful for having had them and to come out clean and sober, inspiring success stories, but what about the people who never make it out, and continue to struggle?

Gratitude can't be linked to those who failed, it just doesn't equate. I do know individuals who had to go through all that they did to reach the point of desperation until they chose rehabilitation. For me, though, I prefer to say that I am a grateful person who was fortunate enough to find a solution with the help of AA, which has enabled me to become an author at fifty-nine.

You may recall from other areas of this book where I've reiterated that I am not a fan of the exact term "grateful alcoholic." I am, however, very much in favor of the usage of "recovering alcoholic" … there's no mistaking, "I am what I am."

A fellow member in a recovery program shared with me what had been told to him. Due to a life of total unmanageability, he was told, "if you weren't an alcoholic, you would be nothing at all." What he was saying is that the only thing you've made of yourself is an addict and alcoholic. These are harsh words of wisdom and real enough to provoke a change in his troubled life.

He goes on to say, "… so if I wasn't an alcoholic (grateful alcoholic), I would never be anything but, and probably be dead by twenty-five." In this case, I (the author), have to go along with the individual's sentiments.

I am not a "grateful alcoholic." I never asked to be one. But I can appreciate finding my true bottom which led to the help I needed before I died.

Chapter's Logical Take-Away: Recovery from addiction marks a new beginning and personal growth. When people with addiction find joy, an organic equation emerges: "grateful in, gratitude out," through sharing and helping others. Gratitude possesses the transformative power to inspire by sharing experiences.

LIVING WITH ADDICTION TODAY

"Remember to be Mindful."

This book aims to encourage a new mindset based heavily on logic and common sense. Those managing an addiction or anything habitual don't have to try so hard to live a normal life that they start to lose their sense of self. Instead of viewing disorders so negatively, we should consider them only as an additional layer compared to those without addictive disorders. Underneath that layer, we're still the same person. Why should we have to put so much thought into living a life of conformity? There's no need to put extra pressure on ourselves.

For instance, I don't think about my fear of heights when I drive past tall buildings, but I do become more mindful if I am at a rooftop restaurant, overlooking the sprawling cityscape. And if I know this will bring me anxiety, I just won't sit still, much less eat there. It also takes time to know yourself and your limitations. I remember going to a football game at a new stadium. I prefer to sit down on the lower level close to the field so I can see the players up close, since I don't have the greatest eyesight. When it comes to open-field games like football and soccer, I prefer the expansive view of the whole field. Nevertheless, this stadium was poorly designed whereas the pitch of the upper levels tested my phobia of heights. Well, I caught up with some friends after the game, one whose wife is also afraid of heights. They happened to sit a level above mine and didn't enjoy the game at all due to the critical angle of the seats and stairs. These illustrations are about knowing yourself and using common sense and logic.

Today I don't think about all the things I can't do, but all that I am capable of doing. I don't even think about drugs or alcohol at all; the obsession has been lifted for me. But if I were in a situation or setting where I felt uncomfortable and was reminded of my addiction, I would just exit the scene. Knowing yourself is paramount and goes hand in hand with logic and common sense. I strongly believe you can't have one without the other, either.

Gene Simmons from KISS was asked by a fan when they decided to unmask, "How are you going to play without makeup?" It's like asking someone who is healing from a leg injury, how are you going to be able to walk without shoes? Similarly, the alcoholic might ask how can I function without alcohol?

Moving forward, you are not going to be able to do everything you used to do. For the most part, I have learned to steer clear of my fears and phobias; that's what you should effortlessly be able to accomplish now. Simply, I don't eat what I don't like. I have never had tripe or liver but know I don't like them. Sounds crazy, right?

Also, there are people who have never tried drugs or alcohol and just know they're not for them. They are either happy where they are mentally or have been told about the dangers that come from them. In my case, enough people who have experienced liver and tripe said I would not like them either … and that's enough for me to not even want to try them. The good thing is that there are so many other foods I do like.

If obsessive tanning is your problem, the cause for it is mental, a problem driven by low self-esteem and insecurity. It's not the sun or tanning beds that's your problem here, it's a mental obsession. This gets tricky because the cure is some form of therapy, not to stop tanning. Of course, tanning poses health risks and associated hazards, such as skin cancer, associated with excessive tanning. Going overboard to the point of excessiveness is what addiction is really all about.

You'll discover that you can't always be in control or act moderately. After fixing the self-esteem and insecurities issue, as it pertains to your appearance, you may be mentally equipped to control your obsession to tan again. Any medical professional will tell you too much sun is not good for you. So as a healthier alternative, there are self-tanning lotions, sprays, and serums. But it is most important to always treat the root cause and not the symptom.

> **Chapter's Logical Take-Away:** This chapter promotes self-awareness and common sense pertaining to addiction, habit management, and repetitive behaviors. Therefore, avoiding triggers and fleeing harmful situations should always be a mindful reserve so as to never challenge your addiction.

FINAL STATEMENT

If you are struggling with addiction, or less to the point of obsession, there is a better way. We learn how to survive. We all just don't lay down and prepare to die. We make the necessary changes to cope with and even overcome our afflictions. We go from bad to good, worse to better, and negative to positive in the way we think. The actions that follow are the solutions to all the problems we face. In the meeting rooms, there are recovery superstars, "thumpers", and the self-entitled ones. But there is also a real world outside, and they may not be the same people in that environment. You see, social skills are as much a necessity to thrive where they count. "It's not *always* easy being me" Rick B.

MAGIC WORDS

MAGIC WORD	RECOVERY Meaning
Acceptance	Going along with something, but not necessarily agreeing with it. "Agree to disagree".
Action	Taking the initiative to make a change in my life to improve myself.
Amends	Making things right for wrongs caused.
Blackout	Incapable of short term memory caused by alcohol or substances.
Bottom	When you reach your low point of total despair.
Boundaries	Devising mental barriers or restrictions to protect us.
Change	It's time to make a change within ourselves.
Courage	Willingness
Ego	Having false courage. Being overly and excessively confident.
Expectations	Constantly anticipating a favorable outcome.

MAGIC WORD	RECOVERY Meaning
Faith ----------►	Having trust everything will work out. This may be believing in God or Higher Power other than you.
Fear (s) ---------►	Stressing over the unknown. Self-induced worrying. Afraid of failure or success.
Gratitude --------►	Very fortunate, displaying gratefulness.
Guidance --------►	God's Will for us.
Humble--------►	Learning to seek without recognition. "right-sized"
Humility --------►	Not embarrassed. Comfortable in own skin.
Judgement -------►	Taking other people's inventory. Comparing them to you.
Mindful --------►	Awareness when things happen. Catching yourself.
Paradox --------►	Something bad must happen to result in a favorable outcome.
Perfectionism -----►	Remember: only God is perfect.

MAGIC WORD	**RECOVERY Meaning**
Pride -------►	Too proud to do something in the view of others.
Recovery -------►	A program to get well from addiction.
Resentment ------►	Me being the one who disapproves the action of a person towards me.
Self-pity -------►	Looking to blame anyone or anything for the troubles I caused myself due to my addiction. "Poor me".
Serenity -------►	Peaceful easy feeling. Calmness about yourself.
Service --------►	Giving back to to the program of yourself without expecting anything in return.
Shortcomings -----►	As opposed to character defects (flaws). Falling short of your God-given abilities.
Spirituality ------►	One with the creator and nature.
Strength -------►	Fortitude, will, desire.
Surrender ------►	Conceding to being defeated by my addiction. I am ready to make a change.

<u>MAGIC WORD</u>	**<u>RECOVERY</u> Meaning**
Tolerance - - - - - - ▶	Enduring patience. A diminished to a drug or alcohol.
Will - - - - - - - ▶	With addictions, "will" or "my will" means controlling. Getting my way.
Willingness - - - - - ▶	Open-mindedness. To give something a try. What do you have to lose?

ANONYMOUS SUPPORT GROUPS

Support Groups for Addiction

- Alcoholics Anonymous (AA)
- All Addicts Anonymous (AAA)
- Association of Recovering Motorcyclists (A.R.M.)
- Caffeine Addicts Anonymous (CAFAA)
- Chemically Dependent Anonymous (CDA)
- Cocaine Anonymous (CA)
- Crystal Meth Anonymous (CMA)
- Heroin Anonymous (HA)
- International Doctors in Alcoholics Anonymous (IDAA)
- International Lawyers in Alcoholics Anonymous (ILAA)
- Marijuana Anonymous (MA)
- Narcotics Anonymous (NA)
- Nicotine Anonymous (Nic A)
- Pharmacists Recovery Network
- Pills Anonymous (PA)
- Recoveries Anonymous (R.A.)

For Families & Others Impacted by Addiction & Mental Illness

- Adult Children of Alcoholics (ACA)/Dysfunctional Families
- Al-Anon/A-lateen (For Family and Friends of Alcoholics)
- Codependents of Sexual Addiction – COSA (For Those Whose Lives Have Been Affected by Another's Compulsive Sexual Behavior)
- Families Anonymous (FA)
- Gam-Anon (For Families and Friends of Gamblers)
- NAMI Family Support Group (For Adults with Loved Ones Who Have Experienced Mental Health Symptoms)
- Nar-Anon (For Family and Friends of Addicts)
- Parents Anonymous
- S-Anon/S-Ateen (For Family and Friends of Sexaholics)

Secular Alternatives

- Life Ring Secular Recovery
- Secular AA
- Secular Organizations for Sobriety (SOS)
- SMART Recovery (Self-Management and Recovery Training)
- Women for Sobriety

Faith-Based Alternatives

- Addictions Victorious
- Alcoholics for Christ
- Alcoholics Victorious
- Buddhist Recovery Network
- The Calix Society
- Celebrate Recovery
- Christians in Recovery
- Dharma Recovery

- Jewish Alcoholics, Chemically Dependent Persons, and
- Overcomers in Christ
- Overcomers Outreach
- Refuge Recovery
- Significant Others (JACS)

Additional Support Groups & Organizations

- Adult Survivors of Child Abuse Anonymous (ASCAA)
- Clutterers Anonymous (CLA)
- Co-Dependents Anonymous (CoDa)
- ‘Debtors Anonymous (DA)
- Depressed Anonymous
- Dual Recovery Anonymous
- Eating Disorders Anonymous (EDA)
- Emotions Anonymous
- Food Addicts Anonymous (FAA)
- Food Addicts in Recovery Anonymous
- Gamblers Anonymous
- Grow in America (Peer Support for Mental Illness)
- Hearing Voices Network
- Internet & Tech Addicts Anonymous (ITAA)
- LDS Family Services
- Obsessive Compulsive Anonymous
- Obsessive Skin Pickers Anonymous (OSPA)
- Offenders Anonymous
- Online Gamers Anonymous (OLGA)
- Overeaters Anonymous (OA)
- Porn Addicts Anonymous (PAA)
- PTSD Anonymous
- Recovery from Food Addiction
- Reentry Anonymous

- Self-Mutilators Anonymous
- Sex Addicts Anonymous (SAA)
- Sexaholics Anonymous
- Sex and Love Addicts Anonymous (SLAA)
- Sexual Compulsives Anonymous (SCA)
- Sexual Recovery Anonymous (SRA)
- Social Anxiety Anonymous
- Spenders Anonymous
- Survivors of Incest Anonymous
- Underearners Anonymous (UA)
- Violence Anonymous (VA)
- Workaholics Anonymous

ENDNOTES

1   Sussman, S., & Sussman, A. N. (2011). Considering the definition of addiction. *International Journal of Environmental Research and Public Health*, 8(10), 4025–4038. https://doi.org/10.3390/ijerph8104025

2   Dennis, M., & Scott, C. K. (2007). Managing addiction as a chronic condition. *Addiction Science & Clinical Practice*, 4(1), 45–55. https://doi.org/10.1151/ascp074145

3   Rutgers Researchers Delve Deep Into the Genetics of Addiction. (2022, November 9). Retrieved from https://ritms.rutgers.edu/news/rutgers-researchers-delve-deep-into-the-genetics-of-addiction/

4   NIDA. (2021, April 13). Why is there comorbidity between substance use disorders and mental illnesses? *National Institute on Drug Abuse*. Retrieved from https://nida.nih.gov/publications/research-reports/common-comorbidities-substance-use-disorders/why-there-comorbidity-between-substance-use-disorders-mental-illnesses

5   NIDA. (2018, June 6). Understanding Drug Use and Addiction DrugFacts. *National Institute on Drug Abuse*. Retrieved from https://nida.nih.gov/publications/drugfacts/understanding-drug-use-addiction

6   Butler Center for Research. (2015, September 1). Drug Abuse, Dopamine and the Brain's Reward System. *Hazelden Betty Ford Foundation*. Retrieved from https://www.hazeldenbettyford.org/research-studies/addiction-research/drug-abuse-brain

7   Daniell, M. (2021, December 30). Gene Simmons uncensored: KISS icon talks vodka, anti-vaxxers and final tour. *Toronto Sun*. Retrieved from https://

torontosun.com/entertainment/celebrity/gene-simmons-uncensored-kiss-i
con-talks-vodka-anti-vaxxers-and-final-tour

8   Paton, A. (2005). Alcohol in the body. *BMJ (Clinical Research Ed.)*, 330(7482), 85–87. https://doi.org/10.1136/bmj.330.7482.85

9   NIDA. (2024, January 5). Drug Misuse and Addiction. *National Institute on Drug Abuse.* Retrieved from https://nida.nih.gov/publications/drugs-brain s-behavior-science-addiction/drug-misuse-addiction

10 Schuckit, M. A. (1996). Alcohol, Anxiety, and Depressive Disorders. *Alcohol Health and Research World,* 20(2), 81–85.

11 Felman, A. (2023, May 31). What is addiction? *Medical News Today.* Retrieved from https://www.medicalnewstoday.com/articles/323465

12 Petry, N. M., Zajac, K., & Ginley, M. K. (2018). Behavioral Addictions as Mental Disorders: To Be or Not To Be?. *Annual Review of Clinical Psychology,* 14, 399–423. https://doi.org/10.1146/annurev-clinpsy-032816-045120

13 Goh, C. M. J., Asharani, P. V., Abdin, E., Shahwan, S., Zhang, Y., Sambasivam, R., Vaingankar, J. A., Ma, S., Chong, S. A., & Subramaniam, M. (2022). Gender Differences in Alcohol Use: a Nationwide Study in a Multiethnic Population. *International Journal of Mental Health and Addiction.* https://doi.org/10.1007/ s11469-022-00921-y

14 National Institute on Drug Abuse. (30 May. 2023). NIDA. "Preface." https:// nida.nih.gov/research-topics/addiction-science/drugs-brain-behavior-science-o f-addiction Accessed 7 Mar. 2024.

15 American Addiction Centers [Editorial Staff]. (2024, March 1). Signs & Symptoms of Addiction (Physical & Mental). Retrieved from https://american- addictioncenters.org/adult-addiction-treatment-programs/signs

16 Davies, G., Elison, S., Ward, J., & et al. (2015). The role of lifestyle in perpetuating substance use disorder: the Lifestyle Balance Model. *Substance Abuse Treatment, Prevention, and Policy,* 10(1), 2. https://doi.org/10.1186/1747-597X-10-2

17 Ma, Z., Liu, Y., Wan, C., & et al. (2022). Health-related quality of life and influ-encing factors in drug addicts based on the scale QLICD-DA: a cross-sectional study. *Health and Quality of Life Outcomes,* 20(1), 109. https://doi.org/10.1186/ s12955-022-02012-x

18 Griffin, J. B. Jr.. (1990). Loss of Control. In H. K. Walker, W. D. Hall, & J. W. Hurst (Eds.), Clinical Methods: The History, Physical, and Laboratory Examinations (3rd ed., Chapter 204). Boston: Butterworths. Retrieved from https://www.ncbi.nlm.nih.gov/books/NBK317/

19 Edwards, S., & Koob, G. F. (2013). Escalation of drug self-administration as a hallmark of persistent addiction liability. *Behavioural pharmacology*, 24(5-6), 356–362. https://doi.org/10.1097/FBP.0b013e3283644d15

20 Bezinović, P., & Malatestinić, D. (2009). Perceived exposure to substance use and risk-taking behavior in early adolescence: cross-sectional study. *Croatian Medical Journal*, 50(2), 157–164. https://doi.org/10.3325/cmj.2009.50.157

21 Oxford Treatment Center. (2023). Common Drug Withdrawal Symptoms. Edited by L. Close & Reviewed by R. Kelley, *NREMT*. Retrieved from https://oxfordtreatment.com/addiction-treatment/detox/withdrawal-symptoms/

22 Popescu, A., Marian, M., Drăgoi, A. M., & Costea, R. V. (2021). Understanding the genetics and neurobiological pathways behind addiction (Review). *Experimental and Therapeutic Medicine*, 21(5), 544. https://doi.org/10.3892/etm.2021.9976

23 Ducci, F., & Goldman, D. (2012). The genetic basis of addictive disorders. *The Psychiatric Clinics of North America*, 35(2), 495–519. https://doi.org/10.1016/j.psc.2012.03.010

24 Mayo Clinic. (2024). Cold sore. Retrieved from https://www.mayoclinic.org/diseases-conditions/cold-sore/multimedia/cold-sore-/img-20005981

25 American Addiction Centers. (2024, March 1). Alcohol moderation management: Programs and steps to control drinking. Edited by A. Sharp. Retrieved from https://americanaddictioncenters.org/blog/alcohol-moderation-management

26 Grant, J. E., & Chamberlain, S. R. (2016). Expanding the definition of addiction: DSM-5 vs. ICD-11. *CNS Spectrums*, 21(4), 300–303. https://doi.org/10.1017/S1092852916000183

27 Zou, Z., Wang, H., d'Oleire Uquillas, F., Wang, X., Ding, J., & Chen, H. (2017). Definition of Substance and Non-substance Addiction. *Advances in Experimental Medicine and Biology*, 1010, 21-41. doi:10.1007/978-981-10-5562-1_2

28 Brewer, J. A., & Potenza, M. N. (2008). The neurobiology and genetics of impulse control disorders: relationships to drug addictions. *Biochemical Pharmacology*, 75(1), 63–75. https://doi.org/10.1016/j.bcp.2007.06.043

29 National Institute on Drug Abuse. (2011). Prescription drug abuse (NIH Publication No. 11-4881). Retrieved from https://nida.nih.gov/sites/default/files/rxreportfinalprint.pdf

30 Bruce, D. F. (2022, March 17). Prescription drug abuse: Addiction, types, and treatment. *WebMD*. Reviewed by S. Bhandari, MD. Retrieved from https://www.webmd.com/mental-health/addiction/abuse-of-prescription-drugs

31   NIDA. (2021, April 12). Is nicotine addictive? Retrieved from https://nida.nih.gov/publications/research-reports/tobacco-nicotine-e-cigarettes/nicotine-addictive on 2024, March 15

32   Pierce, J. P. (2022). Quitting smoking by age 35 years—A goal for reducing mortality. *JAMA Network Open*, 5(10), e2231487. doi:10.1001/jamanetworkopen.2022.31487

33   United States Public Health Service Office of the Surgeon General; National Center for Chronic Disease Prevention and Health Promotion (US) Office on Smoking and Health. (2020). Smoking Cessation: A Report of the Surgeon General. Chapter 6, Interventions for Smoking Cessation and Treatments for Nicotine Dependence. Available from: https://www.ncbi.nlm.nih.gov/books/NBK555596/

34   Dima, R., Tieppo Francio, V., Towery, C., & Davani, S. (2018). Review of literature on low-level laser therapy benefits for nonpharmacological pain control in chronic pain and osteoarthritis. *Alternative Therapies in Health and Medicine*, 24(5), 8-10. PMID: 28987080.

35   Pittman, G. (2010, September 29). Can lasers help you stop smoking? Check the data. *Reuters*. Retrieved from https://www.reuters.com/article/idUSTRE68S3TM/

36   Jazaeri, S. A., & Habil, M. H. (2012). Reviewing two types of addiction - pathological gambling and substance use. *Indian Journal of Psychological Medicine*, 34(1), 5–11. https://doi.org/10.4103/0253-7176.96147

37   Hasanović, M., Kuldija, A., Pajević, I., Jakovljević, M., & Hasanović, M. (2021). Gambling disorder as an addictive disorder and creative psychopharmacotherapy. *Psychiatria Danubina*, 33(Suppl 4), 1118-1129. PMID: 35354178.

38   Koomson, I., Churchill, S. A., & Munyanyi, M. E. (2022). Gambling and financial stress. Social Indicators Research, 163, 473–503. https://doi.org/10.1007/s11205-022-02898-6

39   National Research Council (US) Committee on the Social and Economic Impact of Pathological Gambling. Pathological Gambling: A Critical Review. Washington (DC): National Academies Press (US); 1999. Chapter 5, Social and Economic Effects. Available from: https://www.ncbi.nlm.nih.gov/books/NBK230628/

40   Gateway Foundation. (2021). Gambling and Depression [Mental Health Treatment]. Retrieved from https://www.gatewayfoundation.org/addiction-blog/problem-gambling/

41 Marionneau, V., & Nikkinen, J. (2022). Gambling-related suicides and suicidality: A systematic review of qualitative evidence. *Frontiers in Psychiatry*, 13, 980303. https://doi.org/10.3389/fpsyt.2022.980303

42 Hagen, A. E. F., Nogueira-Arjona, R., Sherry, S. B., Rodriguez, L. M., Yakovenko, I., & Stewart, S. H. (2023). What explains the link between romantic conflict with gambling problems? Testing a serial mediational model. *Frontiers in Psychology*, 14, 1018098. https://doi.org/10.3389/fpsyg.2023.1018098

43 Forsström, D., Lindner, P., Månsson, K. N. T., Ojala, O., Hedman-Lagerlöf, M., El Alaoui, S., Rozental, A., Lundin, J., Jangard, S., Shahnavaz, S., Sörman, K., Lundgren, T., & Jayaram-Lindström, N. (2022). Isolation and worry in relation to gambling and onset of gambling among psychiatry patients during the COVID-19 pandemic: A mediation study. *Frontiers in Psychology*, 13, 1045709. https://doi.org/10.3389/fpsyg.2022.1045709

44 Syvertsen, A., Leino, T., Pallesen, S., Smith, O. R. F., Sivertsen, B., Griffiths, M. D., & Mentzoni, R. A. (2023). Marital status and gambling disorder: A longitudinal study based on national registry data. *BMC Psychiatry*, 23(1), 199. https://doi.org/10.1186/s12888-023-04697-w

45 Parhami, I., Siani, A., Rosenthal, R. J., Lin, S., Collard, M., & Fong, T. W. (2012). Sleep and gambling severity in a community sample of gamblers. *Journal of Addictive Diseases*, 31(1), 67–79. https://doi.org/10.1080/10550887.2011.642754

46 Parhami, I., Siani, A., Rosenthal, R. J., & Fong, T. W. (2013). Pathological gambling, problem gambling and sleep complaints: An analysis of the National Comorbidity Survey: Replication (NCS-R). *Journal of Gambling Studies*, 29(2), 241–253. https://doi.org/10.1007/s10899-012-9299-8

47 Fong, T. W. (2005). The biopsychosocial consequences of pathological gambling. *Psychiatry (Edgmont (Pa. : Township))*, 2(3), 22–30.

48 Mestre-Bach, G., Steward, T., Granero, R., Fernández-Aranda, F., Talón-Navarro, M. T., Cuquerella, À., Baño, M., Moragas, L., Del Pino-Gutiérrez, A., Aymamí, N., Gómez-Peña, M., Mallorquí-Bagué, N., Vintró-Alcaraz, C., Magaña, P., Menchón, J. M., & Jiménez-Murcia, S. (2018). Gambling and impulsivity traits: A recipe for criminal behavior? *Frontiers in Psychiatry*, 9, 6. https://doi.org/10.3389/fpsyt.2018.00006

49 Theoharis, M. (2022). What is illegal gambling? Criminal Defense Lawyer. Retrieved from https://www.criminaldefenselawyer.com/crime-penalties/federal/Illegal-Gambling.htm

50 Latvala, T., Lintonen, T., & Konu, A. (2019). Public health effects of gambling – debate on a conceptual model. *BMC Public Health*, 19, 1077. https://doi.org/10.1186/s12889-019-7391-z

51 Latvala, T. A., Lintonen, T. P., Browne, M., Rockloff, M., & Salonen, A. H. (2021). Social disadvantage and gambling severity: A population-based study with register-linkage. *European Journal of Public Health*, 31(6), 1217–1223. https://doi.org/10.1093/eurpub/ckab162

52 Choi, J., & Kim, K. (2021). The relationship between impulsiveness, self-esteem, irrational gambling belief and problem gambling: Moderating effects of gender. *International Journal of Environmental Research and Public Health*, 18(10), 5180. https://doi.org/10.3390/ijerph18105180

53 Pilver, C. E., & Potenza, M. N. (2013). Increased incidence of cardiovascular conditions among older adults with pathological gambling features in a prospective study. *Journal of Addiction Medicine*, 7(6), 387–393. https://doi.org/10.1097/ADM.0b013e31829e9b36

54 Wagenaar, W. A. (1988). Paradoxes of Gambling Behaviour (1st ed.). *Routledge*.

55 Brewer, A. (2023, November 6). Opioid vs. Opiate: What's the Difference? *GoodRx*. Retrieved from https://www.goodrx.com/classes/opioids

56 Santos-Longhurst, A. (2022, February 17). Opiate vs. Opioid: What's the Difference? *Healthline*. Retrieved from https://www.healthline.com/health/opiate-vs-opioid

57 Shafi, A., Berry, A. J., Sumnall, H., Wood, D. M., & Tracy, D. K. (2022). Synthetic opioids: A review and clinical update. *Therapeutic Advances in Psychopharmacology*, 12. https://doi.org/10.1177/20451253221139616

58 World Health Organization. (2023, August 29). Opioid overdose. *World Health Organization*. Retrieved from https://www.who.int/news-room/fact-sheets/detail/opioid-overdose

59 Judd, D., King, C. R., & Galke, C. (2023). The opioid epidemic: A review of the contributing factors, negative consequences, and best practices. *Cureus*, 15(7), e41621. https://doi.org/10.7759/cureus.41621

60 Kampman, K. M. (2008). The search for medications to treat stimulant dependence. *Addiction Science & Clinical Practice*, 4(2), 28–35. https://doi.org/10.1151/ascp084228

61 Hanson, D. M. (2007, November). The Meth Lab Menace. *HMP Global Learning Network*. Retrieved from https://www.hmpgloballearningnetwork.com/site/emsworld/article/10321509/meth-lab-menace

62 De Luca, V. (2022, December 27). Understanding how plants produce cocaine. *Proceedings of the National Academy of Sciences*, 119(52), e2218838120. https://doi.org/10.1073/pnas.2218838120

63 Suescun, L. (2021, April 1). International Tables for Crystallography, Volume H, Powder Diffraction. First edition. Edited by C. J. Gilmore, J. A. Kaduk, & H. Schenk. *Wiley*. https://doi.org/10.1107/S1600576720015666

64 American Psychological Association. (2011, October 1). The danger of stimulants. *Monitor on Psychology*, 42(9). Retrieved from https://www.apa.org/monitor/2011/10/stimulants

65 American Addiction Centers Editorial Staff. (2023, December 1). Stimulant detox, withdrawal symptoms, and addiction treatment. Retrieved from https://drugabuse.com/stimulants/detox-withdrawal/

66 Lockett, E. (2023, June 16). What research says about the long-term effects of MDMA use. *Healthline*. Retrieved from https://www.healthline.com/health/substance-use/mdma-long-term-effects

67 NIDA. (2021, April 13). What are the effects of MDMA? *National Institute on Drug Abuse*. Retrieved from https://nida.nih.gov/publications/research-reports/mdma-ecstasy-abuse/what-are-effects-mdma

68 Vidyasankar, G., Souza, C., Lai, C., & Mulpuru, S. (2015). A severe complication of crack cocaine use. *Canadian Respiratory Journal*, 22(2), 77–79. https://doi.org/10.1155/2015/263969

69 Cleveland Clinic. (2023, October 23). Cocaine (Crack). *Cleveland Clinic*. Retrieved from https://my.clevelandclinic.org/health/articles/4038-cocaine-crack

70 Stuart, A., & Booth, S. (2023, September 28). Caffeine myths and facts. *WebMD*. Retrieved from https://www.webmd.com/diet/caffeine-myths-and-facts

71 Striley, C. L., Griffiths, R. R., & Cottler, L. B. (2011). Evaluating dependence criteria for caffeine. *Journal of Caffeine Research*, 1(4), 219–225. https://doi.org/10.1089/jcr.2011.0029

72 Meredith, S. E., Juliano, L. M., Hughes, J. R., & Griffiths, R. R. (2013). Caffeine use disorder: A comprehensive review and research agenda. *Journal of Caffeine Research*, 3(3), 114–130. https://doi.org/10.1089/jcr.2013.0016

73 Hartney, E. (2023, August 16). Caffeine addiction symptoms and withdrawal. *Verywell Mind*. Retrieved from https://www.verywellmind.com/caffeine-addiction-4157287

74 Poison & Drug Information Service, Alberta Health Services. (2023, June 1). Substance use: Common drugs. *Alberta Health Services*. Retrieved from https://myhealth.alberta.ca/Alberta/Pages/Substance-use-caffeine.aspx

75 Czarniecka-Skubina, E., Pielak, M., Sałek, P., Korzeniowska-Ginter, R., & Owczarek, T. (2021). Consumer choices and habits related to coffee consumption by Poles. *International Journal of Environmental Research and Public Health*, 18(8), 3948. https://doi.org/10.3390/ijerph18083948

76 Verma, H. V. (2013). Coffee and tea: Socio-cultural meaning, context and branding. *Asia-Pacific Journal of Management Research and Innovation*, 9(2), 157–170. https://doi.org/10.1177/2319510X13504283

77 Bickel, J. (2020, December 28). Tea bringing people together (just less literally lately). *T Ching*. Retrieved from https://tching.com/2020/12/tea-bringing-peopl e-together-less-literally/

78 Dwyer, K. (2020, August 18). What is tea culture? Lessons from around the world. *Pique Life*. Retrieved from https://blog.piquelife.com/tea-culture/

79 Institute of Medicine (US) Committee on Military Nutrition Research; Marriott, B. M. (Editor). (1994). Food components to enhance performance: An evaluation of potential performance-enhancing food components for operational rations. *National Academies Press (US)*. Retrieved from https://www.ncbi. nlm.nih.gov/books/NBK209050/

80 Budney, A. J., & Emond, J. A. (2014). Caffeine addiction? Caffeine for youth? Time to act! *Addiction*, 109(7), 1085-1086. https://doi.org/10.1111/add.12594

81 Yoshimura, H. (2023, November 17). Sugar cravings: Unraveling the mystery of our sweet addiction. *Rupa Health*. Retrieved from https://rupahealth.com/post/ sugar-cravings-unraveling-the-mystery-of-our-sweet-addiction

82 Polk, S. E., Schulte, E. M., Furman, C. R., & Gearhardt, A. N. (2017). Wanting and liking: Separable components in problematic eating behavior? *Appetite*, 115, 45–53. https://doi.org/10.1016/j.appet.2016.11.015

83 Misra, V., Shrivastava, A., Shukla, S., & Ansari, M. I. (2016). Effect of sugar intake towards human health. *Journal of Medical Sciences and Health*. doi:10.21276/ sjm.2016.1.2.2

84 Drewnowski, A., Mennella, J., Johnson, S., & Bellisle, F. (2012). Sweetness and food preference. *The Journal of Nutrition*, 142, 1142S-1148S. doi:10.3945/ jn.111.149575

85 Jacques, A., Chaaya, N., Beecher, K., Ali, S. A., Belmer, A., & Bartlett, S. (2019). The impact of sugar consumption on stress-driven, emotional and addictive behaviors. *Neuroscience & Biobehavioral Reviews*, 103. doi:10.1016/j. neubiorev.2019.05.021

86 Westover, A., & Marangell, L. (2002). A cross-national relationship between sugar consumption and major depression? *Depression and Anxiety*, 16, 118-120. doi:10.1002/da.10054

87 Westwater, M. L., Fletcher, P. C., & Ziauddeen, H. (2016). Sugar addiction: The state of the science. *European Journal of Nutrition*, 55(Suppl 2), 55–69. https://doi.org/10.1007/s00394-016-1229-6

88 Ma, X., Nan, F., Liang, H., Shu, P., Fan, X., Song, X., Hou, Y., & Zhang, D. (2022). Excessive intake of sugar: An accomplice of inflammation. *Frontiers in Immunology*, 13, 988481. https://doi.org/10.3389/fimmu.2022.988481

89 "Your Brain on Chocolate." (2012). *Genetic Engineering & Biotechnology News*. Retrieved from https://www.genengnews.com/news/your-brain-on-chocolate/

90 Terenius, L. (2011). From Opiate Pharmacology to Opioid Peptide Physiology. *Upsala Journal of Medical Sciences*, 105(1), 1-16. https://doi.org/10.1517/03009734000000043

91 DiFeliceantonio, A. G., Mabrouk, O. S., Kennedy, R. T., & Berridge, K. C. (2012). Enkephalin surges in dorsal neostriatum as a signal to eat. *Current Biology*, 22(20), 1918–1924. https://doi.org/10.1016/j.cub.2012.08.014

92 Bruinsma, K., & Taren, D. L. (1999). Chocolate: Food or Drug? *Journal of the American Dietetic Association*, 99(10), 1249–1256. https://doi.org/10.1016/S0002-8223(99)00307-7

93 Katz, D. L., Doughty, K., & Ali, A. (2011). Cocoa and chocolate in human health and disease. *Antioxidants & Redox Signaling*, 15(10), 2779–2811. https://doi.org/10.1089/ars.2010.3697

94 Parker, G. (2006). "Mood state effects of chocolate." *Journal of Affective Disorders*. Retrieved from https://doi.org/10.1016/j.jad.2006.02.007.

95 Wolz, I., Sauvaget, A., Granero, R., et al. (2017). Subjective craving and event-related brain response to olfactory and visual chocolate cues in binge-eating and healthy individuals. *Scientific Reports*, 7, 41736. https://doi.org/10.1038/srep41736

96 Casperson, S. L., Lanza, L., Albajri, E., & Nasser, J. A. (2019). Increasing Chocolate's Sugar Content Enhances Its Psychoactive Effects and Intake. *Nutrients*, 11(3), 596. https://doi.org/10.3390/nu11030596

97 Hardi, M. (2020). "Chocolate and Endorphins." Retrieved from https://remix-snacks.ca/blogs/remix-blog/chocolate-and-endorphin.

98 Minowa, Y., & Belk, R. W. (Eds.). (2018). *Gifts, Romance, and Consumer Culture* (1st ed.). Routledge. Retrieved from https://doi.org/10.4324/9781315144658.

99 Nasser, J., Bradley, L., Leitzsch, J., Chohan, O., Fasulo, K., Haller, J., Jaeger, K., Szulanczyk, B., & Parigi, A. (2011). Psychoactive effects of tasting chocolate and desire for more chocolate. *Physiology & Behavior*, 104, 117–121. https://doi.org/10.1016/j.physbeh.2011.04.040

100 Smit, H., Gaffan, E., & Rogers, P. (2004). Methylxanthines are the psycho-pharmacologically active constituents of chocolate. *Psychopharmacology*, 176(3-4), 412-419. https://doi.org/10.1007/s00213-004-1898-3

101 Marcucci, M. C., Ferreira da Silva, A. G., Gonçalves, C. P., Sawaya, A. C. H. F., Alonso, R. C. B., Oliveira, M. M. de, & Barbin, D. F. (2021). Quality parameters, caffeine and theobromine contents and antioxidant activity of artisan and commercial chocolate from Brazil. *Open Access Library Journal*, 8(5). https://doi.org/10.4236/oalib.1107377

102 Kazemi, F., & Esmaeili, M. (2010). The role of media on consumer brand choice: A case study of chocolate industry. *International Journal of Business and Management*, 5. https://doi.org/10.5539/ijbm.v5n9p147

103 Seçuk, B., & Seçim, Y. (2024). Concept of artisan chocolate from the perspective of chocolatiers. *International Journal of Food Design*, 9, 27-52. https://doi.org/10.1386/ijfd_00064_1

104 Coe, S. D. (2023). The True History of Chocolate [Summary]. Retrieved from https://www.bookey.app/book/the-true-history-of-chocolate#freePdf

105 Locke, A., & Arnocky, S. (2020). Eating disorders. In *Encyclopedia of Evolutionary Psychological Science* (pp. 1-8). https://doi.org/10.1007/978-3-319-16999-6_696-1

106 Bulik, C. M. (2005). Exploring the gene-environment nexus in eating disorders. *Journal of Psychiatry & Neuroscience*: JPN, 30(5), 335–339.

107 Jain, A., & Yilanli, M. (2023). Bulimia Nervosa. In StatPearls [Internet]. Treasure Island (FL): *StatPearls* Publishing; 2024 Jan-. Available from: https://www.ncbi.nlm.nih.gov/books/NBK562178/

108 Sheehy, K., Noureen, A., Khaliq, A., Dhingra, K., Husain, N., Pontin, E. E., Cawley, R., & Taylor, P. J. (2019). An examination of the relationship between shame, guilt and self-harm: A systematic review and meta-analysis. *Clinical Psychology Review*, 73, 101779. https://doi.org/10.1016/j.cpr.2019.101779

109 Cipriano, A., Cella, S., & Cotrufo, P. (2017). Nonsuicidal Self-injury: A Systematic Review. *Frontiers in Psychology*, 8. https://doi.org/10.3389/fpsyg.2017.01946

110 Moutier, C. (2023). Nonsuicidal self-injury (NSSI). *American Foundation for Suicide Prevention*. Retrieved from https://www.merckmanuals.com/

professional/psychiatric-disorders/suicidal-behavior-and-self-injury/
nonsuicidal-self-injury-nssi

111 Klonsky, E. D., Victor, S. E., & Saffer, B. Y. (2014). Nonsuicidal self-injury: What we know, and what we need to know. *Canadian Journal of Psychiatry. Revue Canadienne de Psychiatrie*, 59(11), 565–568. https://doi.org/10.1177/070674371405901101

112 Waals, L., Baetens, I., Rober, P., et al. (2018). The NSSI Family Distress Cascade Theory. *Child and Adolescent Psychiatry and Mental Health*, 12, 52. https://doi.org/10.1186/s13034-018-0259-7

113 DeCamp, W., & Bakken, N. W. (2016). Self-injury, suicide ideation, and sexual orientation: Differences in causes and correlates among high school students. *Journal of Injury & Violence Research*, 8(1), 15–24. https://doi.org/10.5249/jivr.v8i1.545

114 Hagan, E. (2021). Four reasons why individuals engage in self-harm. *Psychology Today*. Retrieved from https://www.psychologytoday.com/us/blog/happiness-is-state-mind/202103/four-reasons-why-individuals-engage-in-self-harm

115 Russell, K. R., & Hartung, S. Q. (2016). Identifying the signs of self-harm in students. *NASN School Nurse*, 31(2), 121–124. https://doi.org/10.1177/1942602X15574776

116 Bjornsson, A. S., Didie, E. R., & Phillips, K. A. (2010). Body dysmorphic disorder. *Dialogues in Clinical Neuroscience*, 12(2), 221–232. https://doi.org/10.31887/DCNS.2010.12.2/abjornsson

117 Sindi, S. A., Alghamdi, M. K., Sindi, E. E., Bondagji, M. F., Baashar, D. S., Malibary, J. A., & Alkot, M. M. (2023). The prevalence and characteristics of body dysmorphic disorder among adults in Makkah City, Saudi Arabia: A cross-sectional study. *Cureus*, 15(2), e35316. https://doi.org/10.7759/cureus.35316

118 Taqui, A. M., Shaikh, M., Gowani, S. A., et al. (2008). Body dysmorphic disorder: Gender differences and prevalence in a Pakistani medical student population. *BMC Psychiatry*, 8, 20. https://doi.org/10.1186/1471-244X-8-20

119 Mayo Clinic Staff. (2022). Cosmetic surgery. *Mayo Clinic*. Retrieved from https://www.mayoclinic.org/tests-procedures/cosmetic-surgery/about/pac-20385138

120 Gatkine, T., Shete, V., Mahajan, N., & Mahajan, U. (2019). Potential of phyto-constituents as skin tanning agents. *Research Journal of Topical and Cosmetic Sciences*, 10, 34. doi:10.5958/2321-5844.2019.00008.6

121 Kosut, M. (2015). Tattoos and body modification. *International Encyclopedia of the Social & Behavioral Sciences, 2nd edition*, 24, 32–38. https://doi.org/10.1016/B978-0-08-097086-8.64027-8

122 Carmen, R. A., Guitar, A. E., & Dillon, H. M. (2012). Ultimate answers to proximate questions: The evolutionary motivations behind tattoos and body piercings in popular culture. *Review of General Psychology*, 16(2), 134–143. https://doi.org/10.1037/a0027908

123 Sarwer, D. B., & Crerand, C. E. (2008). Body dysmorphic disorder and appearance enhancing medical treatments. *Body Image*, 5(1), 50-58. https://doi.org/10.1016/j.bodyim.2007.08.003

124 Castle, D. J., Phillips, K. A., & Dufresne, R. G., Jr (2004). Body dysmorphic disorder and cosmetic dermatology: More than skin deep. *Journal of Cosmetic Dermatology*, 3(2), 99–103. https://doi.org/10.1111/j.1473-2130.2004.00105.x

125 Mundada, P., Kohler, R., Boudabbous, S., Toutous Trellu, L., Platon, A., & Becker, M. (2017). Injectable facial fillers: Imaging features, complications, and diagnostic pitfalls at MRI and PET CT. *Insights into Imaging*, 8(6), 557–572. https://doi.org/10.1007/s13244-017-0575-0

126 Knoedler, L., Ruppel, F., Kauke-Navarro, M., Obed, D., Wu, M., Prantl, L., Broer, P. N., Panayi, A. C., & Knoedler, S. (2023). Hair transplantation in the United States: A population-based survey of female and male pattern baldness. *Plastic and Reconstructive Surgery. Global Open*, 11(11), e5386. https://doi.org/10.1097/GOX.0000000000005386

127 Kyle, D., & Mahler, H. I. M. (1996). The effects of hair color and cosmetics use on perceptions of a female's ability. *Psychology of Women Quarterly*, 20(3), 447-455.

128 Arora, S., & Gulhima, A. (2014). Laser hair removal. Retrieved from https://doi.org/10.13140/2.1.2589.0887

129 Thappa, D. M. (2022). Body contouring (sculpting) – Why are non-invasive techniques preferred? *Journal of Clinical and Scientific Dermatology*, 2, 86. https://doi.org/10.25259/CSDM_99_2022

130 Al-Ghanim, D. A., Al-Salat, G. M., & Al-Shaikh, R. S. (2018). The role of cosmetic dentistry in restoring a youthful appearance in Saudi population: An overview. *World Journal of Pharmaceutical Research*, 7(10), 249-258. https://doi.org/10.20959/wjpr201810-12312

131 Marwah, M., Kerure, A., & Marwah, G. (2021. Microblading and the science behind it. *Indian Dermatology Online Journal*, 12(1), 6-11. https://doi.org/10.4103/idoj.IDOJ_230_20

132 Kumar, H., & Aagrwal, M. (2023). Filtering the reality: Exploring the dark and bright sides of augmented reality–based filters on social media. *Australian Journal of Management.* Advance online publication. https://doi.org/10.1177/03128962231199356

133 Emini, N. N., & Bond, M. J. (2014). Motivational and psychological correlates of bodybuilding dependence. *Journal of Behavioral Addictions, 3*(3), 182–188. https://doi.org/10.1556/JBA.3.2014.3.6

134 Sun, M., & Wang, L. (2022). Effect of bodybuilding and fitness exercise on physical fitness based on deep learning. *Emergency Medicine International, 2022,* 3891109. https://doi.org/10.1155/2022/3891109

135 Maffetone, P. B., & Laursen, P. B. (2017). The prevalence of overfat adults and children in the US. *Frontiers in Public Health, 5,* 290. https://doi.org/10.3389/fpubh.2017.00290

136 Melmer, A., Kempf, P., & Laimer, M. (2018). The role of physical exercise in obesity and diabetes. *Praxis, 107,* 971-976. https://doi.org/10.1024/1661-8157/a003065

137 Osborn, C. O. (2023). How do muscle and fat affect weight? [Reviewed by Jake Tipane, CPT]. *Healthline.* Retrieved from https://www.healthline.com/health/does-muscle-weigh-more-than-fat

138 The Social and Health Research Center. (2016, October). Fat versus muscle? Retrieved from https://sahrc.org/2016/10/fat-versus-muscle/

139 Fletcher, J. (2022). What to know about hypersexuality. *Medical News Today.* Retrieved from https://www.medicalnewstoday.com/articles/hypersexuality

140 Alavi, S. S., Ferdosi, M., Jannatifard, F., Eslami, M., Alaghemandan, H., & Setare, M. (2012). Behavioral addiction versus substance addiction: Correspondence of psychiatric and psychological views. *International Journal of Preventive Medicine, 3*(4), 290–294.

141 Pozza, A., Coluccia, A., Gualtieri, G., Carabellese, F., Masti, A., & Ferretti, F. (2020). Post-traumatic stress disorder secondary to manic episodes with hypersexuality in bipolar disorder: A case study of forensic psychotherapy. *Clinical Neuropsychiatry, 17*(3), 181–188. https://doi.org/10.36131/cnfioritieditore20200306

142 Chaudhary, S., Singh, A. P., & Varshney, A. (2022). Psychodynamic perspective of sexual obsessions in obsessive-compulsive disorder. *Annals of Neurosciences, 29*(2-3), 159–165. https://doi.org/10.1177/09727531221115305

143 Fong, T. W. (2006). Understanding and managing compulsive sexual behaviors. *Psychiatry (Edgmont (Pa. : Township)), 3*(11), 51–58.

144 van Tuijl, P., Tamminga, A., Meerkerk, G. J., Verboon, P., Leontjevas, R., & van Lankveld, J. (2020). Three diagnoses for problematic hypersexuality; Which criteria predict help-seeking behavior? *International Journal of Environmental Research and Public Health*, 17(18), 6907. https://doi.org/10.3390/ijerph17186907

145 Goerling, E., & Wolfe, E. (2022). Introduction to human sexuality: Chapter 16 - Variations in sexual behavior. *Open Oregon Educational Resources*. Retrieved from https://open.umn.edu/opentextbooks/textbooks/1273

146 Maguire, L. C. (1922). Nymphomania. *The Veterinary Journal*, 78(8), 272-283. doi:10.1016/S0372-5545(17)53017-5.

147 Walker, J. M. (2018). Anxiety, stress, depression, and addiction of the US celebrities at the light of the Creative Economy Era. Retrieved from https://www.academia.edu/35986276/Anxiety_Stress_Depression_and_Addiction_of_the_US_Celebrities_at_the_light_of_the_Creative_Economy_Era

148 Burd, E. M. (2003). Human papillomavirus and cervical cancer. *Clinical Microbiology Reviews*, 16(1), 1–17. https://doi.org/10.1128/CMR.16.1.1-17.2003

149 Duffy, A., Dawson, D. L., & das Nair, R. (2016). Pornography addiction in adults: A systematic review of definitions and reported impact. *Journal of Sexual Medicine*, 13(5), 760-777. https://doi.org/10.1016/j.jsxm.2016.03.002

150 Camilleri, C., Perry, J. T., & Sammut, S. (2021). Compulsive internet pornography use and mental health: A cross-sectional study in a sample of university students in the United States. *Frontiers in Psychology*, 11, 613244. https://doi.org/10.3389/fpsyg.2020.613244

151 Privara, M., & Bob, P. (2023). Pornography consumption and cognitive-affective distress. *The Journal of Nervous and Mental Disease*, 211(8), 641–646. https://doi.org/10.1097/NMD.0000000000001669

152 Gilliland, R., South, M., Carpenter, B., & Hardy, S. (2011, March 8). The roles of shame and guilt in hypersexual behavior. *Sexual Addiction and Compulsivity*, 18. https://doi.org/10.1080/10720162.2011.551182

153 Okechukwu, C. E. (2021). Does frequent pornography use adversely affect men's sexual health? A call for clinical investigation. https://doi.org/10.4103/MTSM.MTSM_20_20

154 Muratovic, N. (2023). Porn addiction and productivity: Understanding the link. Retrieved from https://americanaddictioncentersreviews.com/porn-addiction-and-productivity/

155 Yoder, V., Virden, T., & Amin, K. (2005). Internet pornography and loneliness: An association? *Sexual Addiction & Compulsivity*, 12, 19-44. https://doi.org/10.1080/10720160590933653

156 Villena, A., & Actis, C. (2019). Consequence of pornography use: Brief report. *Cuadernos de Medicina Psicosomática y Psiquiatría de Enlace.*

157 Sharpe, M., & Mead, D. (2021). Problematic pornography use: Legal and health policy considerations. *Current Addiction Reports*, 8(4), 556–567. https://doi.org/10.1007/s40429-021-00390-8

158 Siegel, A. (2024). Role of adrenaline in addiction: Definition, function, production, release, and its connection to addiction. *Olympic Behavioral Health.* Retrieved from https://olympicbehavioralhealth.com/rehab-blog/adrenaline-in-addiction/

159 Heirene, R. M., Shearer, D., Roderique-Davies, G., & Mellalieu, S. D. (2016). Addiction in extreme sports: An exploration of withdrawal states in rock climbers. *Journal of Behavioral Addictions*, 5(2), 332–341. https://doi.org/10.1556/2006.5.2016.039

160 Adrenaline addiction 101: How, what, who? (2020). Retrieved from https://rosglasrecovery.com/adrenaline-addiction-101/

161 Chu, B., Marwaha, K., Sanvictores, T., & Ayers, D. (2022). Physiology, stress reaction. In *StatPearls*. Treasure Island, FL: StatPearls Publishing. Available from: https://www.ncbi.nlm.nih.gov/books/NBK541120/

162 Rowden, A. (2021). What is an adrenaline junkie? *Medical News Today.* Retrieved from https://www.medicalnewstoday.com/articles/adrenaline-junkie

163 Picard, G. (2023). 50 Best Adrenaline Activities for Thrillseekers. Retrieved from https://tourscanner.com/blog/best-adrenaline-activities/

164 Thompson, K., & Tieperman, J. (2024). How to Get an Adrenaline Rush: At-Home Ideas. Retrieved from https://www.wikihow.com/Get-an-Adrenaline-Rush

165 "Am I an Adrenaline Junkie? Read This if You Are!" (2023). Retrieved from https://kentuckycounselingcenter.com/adrenaline-junkie/

166 Kasia. (2020). 18 Adrenaline Adventures: Activities For The Ultimate Rush. Retrieved from https://kasiawrites.com/adrenaline-adventures-activities-for-bucket-list/

167 Raypole, C. (2019). How to Tell if You're an Adrenaline Junkie. *Healthline.* Retrieved from https://www.healthline.com/health/adrenaline-junkie

168 WebMD Editorial Contributor. (2023). What to Know About an Adrenaline Rush. Retrieved from https://www.webmd.com/a-to-z-guides/what-to-know-adrenaline-rush

169 Hua, K., Zulkefli, Z., & Lim, C. (2022). Voice of Academia: The Langkawi Island Market Potential for Extreme Outdoor Sports Tourism.

170 Perry, E. (2022). How to use fear as a motivator. *BetterUp*. Retrieved from https://www.betterup.com/blog/fear-as-a-motivator

171 King, D., & Delfabbro, P. (2020). Video game addiction. *In Clinical Psychology of Internet Addiction* (pp. 185-213). doi:10.1016/B978-0-12-818626-8.00007-4

172 Lelonek-Kuleta, B., & Bartczuk, R. P. (2021). Coping Strategies and Motivation to Play Determinants of Behavioral Patterns of Playing Pay-to-Win Games. https://doi.org/10.31234/osf.io/t86er

173 Griffiths, M., Kuss, D., & King, D. (2013). Video game addiction: Past, present and future (Vol. 8). *Current Psychiatry Review.*

174 Beckhusen, B. (2016). Mobile Apps and the ultimate addiction to the Smartphone. Retrieved from https://www.diva-portal.org/smash/get/diva2:950846/FULLTEXT01.pdf

175 Nikolic, A., Bukurov, B., Kocic, I., Vukovic, M., Ladjevic, N., Vrhovac, M., Pavlović, Z., Grujicic, J., Kisic, D., & Sipetic, S. (2023). Smartphone addiction, sleep quality, depression, anxiety, and stress among medical students. *Frontiers in public health*, 11, 1252371. https://doi.org/10.3389/fpubh.2023.1252371

176 Jniene, A., Errguig, L., El Hangouche, A. J., Rkain, H., Aboudrar, S., Ftouh, M., & Dakka, T. (2019). Perception of sleep disturbances due to bedtime use of blue light-emitting devices and its impact on habits and sleep quality among young medical students. *BioMed Research International*, 2019, 1-8. doi:10.1155/2019/7012350

177 Rosenfield, M. (2016). Computer vision syndrome (a.k.a. digital eye strain). *Optometry in Practice*, 17, 1-10.

178 Mongkonkansai, J., Madardam, A. P. U., & Veerasakul, S. (2020). Smartphone Usage Posture (Sitting and Lying Down) and Musculoskeletal Symptoms among school-aged children (6-12 years old) in Nakhon Si Thammarat, Thailand. doi:10.21203/rs.3.rs-51245/v1

179 Shoukat, S. (2019). Cell phone addiction and psychological and physiological health in adolescents. EXCLI Journal, 18, 47–50.

180 Lu, X., Watanabe, J., Liu, Q., Uji, M., Shono, M., & Kitamura, T. (2011). Internet and mobile phone text-messaging dependency: Factor structure and correlation with dysphoric mood among Japanese adults. *Computers in Human Behavior*, 27, 1702-1709. Retrieved from https://api.semanticscholar.org/CorpusID:19610431

181 Kuldip Singh, M., & Samah, N. (2018). Impact of Smartphone: A Review on Positive and Negative Effects on Students. *Asian Social Science*, 14, 83. doi:10.5539/ass.v14n11p83

182 Ling, R. (2004). *The Mobile Connection: The Cell Phone's Impact on Society.* ISBN: 1558609369.

183 Zhao, J., Jia, T., Wang, X., Xiao, Y., & Wu, X. (2022). Risk Factors Associated With Social Media Addiction: An Exploratory Study. *Frontiers in Psychology,* 13, 837766. https://doi.org/10.3389/fpsyg.2022.837766

184 Ji, Y., Liu, S., Xu, H., & Zhang, B. (2023, February 7). The Causes, Effects, and Interventions of Social Media Addiction. *Journal of Education, Humanities and Social Sciences,* 8, 897-903. https://doi.org/10.54097/ehss.v8i.4378

185 Onifade, T. (2022, January 5). Effects of Social Media Validation. *Journal of Social Media Studies,* 1.

186 Ballara, N. B. (2023). The Power of Social Validation: A Literature Review on How Likes, Comments, and Shares Shape User Behavior on Social Media. *International Journal of Research Publication and Reviews,* 4(7), 3355-3367. https://doi.org/10.55248/gengpi.4.723.51227

187 Burhan, R., & Moradzadeh, J. (2020). Neurotransmitter Dopamine (DA) and its Role in the Development of Social Media Addiction. *Journal of Neurology & Neurophysiology,* 11(7), 507.

188 Wu, X. (2023). Research on the Ways to Overcome Social Media Addiction. *SHS Web of Conferences,* 155, 02023. https://doi.org/10.1051/shsconf/202315502023

189 Adelabu, O. (2015). Social Media, Advertising Messages and the Youth: Any Influence? *New Media and Mass Communication,* 39, ISSN 2224-3267.

190 Dhingra, M., & Mudgal, R. (2019). Historical Evolution of Social Media: An Overview. *SSRN Electronic Journal.* https://doi.org/10.2139/ssrn.3395665

191 Ahmad, A. (2011). A Short Description of Social Networking Websites And Its Uses. *International Journal of Advanced Computer Sciences and Applications,* 2. https://doi.org/10.14569/IJACSA.2011.020220

192 Liappis, E., Papadeli, C., Tselekidou, E., Chaidemenos, I., Korsavvidis, D., & General Dentist. (2024). FOMO Social Phenomenon: How and to What Extent Does It Affect Dental Students? A 2022 Research. *Global Journal of Clinical Medicine and Medical Research (GJCMMR).* ISSN: 2583-987X

193 Gupta, M., & Sharma, A. (2021). Fear of missing out: A brief overview of origin, theoretical underpinnings and relationship with mental health. *World Journal of Clinical Cases,* 9(19), 4881–4889. https://doi.org/10.12998/wjcc.v9.i19.4881

194 Izul A., Hidayah N., & Lasan B. (2020). *Fear of Missing Out (FoMO) in Analysis of Cognitive Behavior Therapy (CBT).* https://doi.org/10.2991/assehr.k.201204.040

195 Jaworska, D., & Iwanicka, K. (2024). Exploring the role of fear of missing out in coping and risk-taking among alcohol use disorder and general young adult

populations. *Addictive Behaviors Reports*, 19, 100532. https://doi.org/10.1016/j.abrep.2024.100532

196 Laurence, E. (2023). The psychology behind the fear of missing out (FOMO). *Forbes*. Retrieved from https://www.forbes.com/health/mind/the-psychology-behind-fomo/

197 Griffiths, M. D., Demetrovics, Z., & Atroszko, P. A. (2018). Ten myths about work addiction. *Journal of Behavioral Addictions*, 7(4), 845–857. https://doi.org/10.1556/2006.7.2018.05

198 Sussman, S. (2012). Workaholism: A Review. *Journal of Addiction Research & Therapy*, Suppl 6(1), 4120. https://doi.org/10.4172/2155-6105.S6-001

199 Power of Positivity. (2017). 10 Behaviors Of An Egomaniac (And How To Avoid Having Them). Retrieved from https://www.powerofpositivity.com/egomaniac-behaviors/

200 Milosevic, T. (2011). Workaholism in America: A European's Perspective. HuffPost. Retrieved from https://www.huffpost.com/entry/workaholism-america-europe_b_805975

201 Sharma, R., Tyagi, P., Singh, U., Khatter, A., Sharma, A., & Kumar, K. (2020). Exploring shopaholics' attitudes and behaviors: A dose, defense, or disorder? *Indian Journal of Health Social Work*.

202 Zayed, A. (2023). Compulsive buying disorder (CBD): Is it really an addiction? Retrieved from https://diamondrehabthailand.com/what-is-compulsive-buying-disorder/

203 Nyrhinen, J., Lonka, K., Sirola, A., Ranta, M., & Wilska, T. A. (2023). Young adults' online shopping addiction: The role of self-regulation and smartphone use. *International Journal of Consumer Studies*. https://doi.org/10.1111/ijcs.12961

204 Salma, H. (2014). Online Shopping Addiction: The Case of Malaysian Youth Consumers. Retrieved from https://www.academia.edu/9954154/Online_Shopping_Addiction_The_Case_of_Malaysian_Youth_ Consumers_2014

205 Chen, T., Samaranayake, P., Cen, X., Qi, M., & Lan, Y. (2022). The Impact of Online Reviews on Consumers' Purchasing Decisions: Evidence From an Eye-Tracking Study. *Frontiers in Psychology*, 13. https://doi.org/10.3389/fpsyg.2022.865702

206 Chen, Z., Xing, Y., & Zhang, Z. (2021). *The Review of Antisocial Personality Disorder*. Advances in Social Science, Education and Humanities Research, Volume 586. https://doi.org/10.2991/assehr.k.211020.192

207 Sloan, E. (2021). How To Differentiate Between a Pathological and Compulsive Liar—And Navigate a Relationship With Either One. *Well+Good*.

Retrieved from https://www.wellandgood.com/difference-between-compulsive-pathological-liar/

208 Fariba KA, Gokarakonda SB. (2023, August 14). Impulse Control Disorders. In: *StatPearls*. Treasure Island (FL): StatPearls Publishing. Available from: https://www.ncbi.nlm.nih.gov/books/NBK562279/

209 MacKey, B. (2020, October 29). The Addiction Cycle. *Rehab 4 Addiction*. Retrieved from https://www.rehab4addiction.co.uk/resources/addiction-cycle

210 Henden, E., Melberg, H. O., & Røgeberg, O. J. (2013). Addiction: choice or compulsion? Frontiers in psychiatry, 4, 77. https://doi.org/10.3389/fpsyt.2013.00077

211 Lüscher, C., Robbins, T. W., & Everitt, B. J. (2020). The transition to compulsion in addiction. *Nature reviews. Neuroscience*, 21(5), 247–263. https://doi.org/10.1038/s41583-020-0289-z

212 Gupta, S. (2022, September 30). Substance use vs. substance abuse: What are the differences? *Verywell Mind*. Retrieved from https://www.verywellmind.com/substance-use-vs-substance-use-disorder-whats-the-difference-6385961#citation-2

213 Pedersen, T. (2023, December 1). What is a controlled substance? *Healthline*. Retrieved from https://www.healthline.com/health/what-is-a-controlled-substance

214 Office of National Drug Control Policy. (2024). Congressional Budget Submission FY 2024. Retrieved from https://www.whitehouse.gov/wp-content/uploads/2023/03/FY-2024-ONDCP-CONGRESSIONAL-BUDGET-SUBMISSION-FINAL.pdf

215 Timeline of State Marijuana Legalization Laws. (2016, May 2). *Third Way*. Retrieved from https://www.thirdway.org/infographic/timeline-of-state-marijuana-legalization-laws

216 Drug Enforcement Administration. (2023, January). Fentanyl (Trade Names: Actiq®, FentoraTM, Duragesic®). Drug & Chemical Evaluation Section. Diversion Control Division. Retrieved from https://www.deadiversion.usdoj.gov/drug_chem_info/fentanyl.pdf

217 NIDA. (2021). Is marijuana addictive?. Retrieved from https://nida.nih.gov/publications/research-reports/marijuana/marijuana-addictive on 2024, March 21

218 NIDA. (2023). Is marijuana a gateway drug?. Retrieved from https://nida.nih.gov/publications/research-reports/marijuana/marijuana-gateway-drug on 2024, March 21

219 Ramos-Matos, C. F., Bistas, K. G., & Lopez-Ojeda, W. (2023, May 29). Fentanyl. In *StatPearls*. Treasure Island (FL): StatPearls Publishing. Retrieved from https://www.ncbi.nlm.nih.gov/books/NBK459275/

220 Treadwell, S. D., & Robinson, T. G. (2007). Cocaine use and stroke. *Postgraduate Medical Journal*, 83(980), 389–394. https://doi.org/10.1136/pgmj.2006.055970

221 KidsHealth Medical Experts. (2023). What Is MDMA (Ecstasy)? Retrieved from https://kidshealth.org/en/parents/drugs-ecstasy.html

222 Editorial Staff. (2023, July 19). Salvia vs. DMT: Effects & Differences. Retrieved from https://oxfordtreatmnt.com/substance-abuse/hallucinogens/salvia-vs-dmt/

223 Cleveland Clinic medical professional. (2023, April 18). Hallucinogens. Retrieved from https://my.clevelandclinic.org/health/articles/6734-hallucinogens-lsd-peyote-psilocybin-and-pcp

224 Mars, S. G., Bourgois, P., Karandinos, G., Montero, F., & Ciccarone, D. (2016). The Textures of Heroin: User Perspectives on "Black Tar" and Powder Heroin in Two US Cities. *Journal of Psychoactive Drugs*, 48(4), 270–278. https://doi.org/10.1080/02791072.2016.1207826

225 NIDA. (2022, December 19). What are the short- and long-term effects of inhalant use? Retrieved from https://nida.nih.gov/publications/research-reports/inhalants/what-are-short-long-term-effects-inhalant-use

226 Powers, A. R., 3rd, Gancsos, M. G., Finn, E. S., Morgan, P. T., & Corlett, P. R. (2015). Ketamine-Induced Hallucinations. *Psychopathology*, 48(6), 376–385. https://doi.org/10.1159/000438675

227 Glasner-Edwards, S., & Mooney, L. J. (2014). Methamphetamine psychosis: Epidemiology and management. *CNS Drugs*, 28(12), 1115–1126. https://doi.org/10.1007/s40263-014-0209-8

228 American Addiction Centers Editorial Staff. (2023, September 6). The Effects of Meth on Your Body. *DrugAbuse*. https://drugabuse.com/featured/the-effects-of-meth-on-your-body/

229 Hakim, R. C., BCCCP, & Hannemann, K. (January 8, 2024). Acetaminophen / Dextromethorphan / Doxylamine. *GoodRx*. Retrieved from https://www.goodrx.com/nyquil/what-is

230 Gateway Foundation. (2022). Most Commonly Abused Prescription Drugs. https://www.gatewayfoundation.org/addiction-blog/most-commonly-abused-prescription-drugs/

231 Miller, L. (2024). How to Stop Drinking: Benefits of Quitting Alcohol. *American Addiction Centers*. https://americanaddictioncenters.org/alcohol/quitting-benefits

232 White, A. M. (2003). What happened? Alcohol, memory blackouts, and the brain. Alcohol Research & Health: *The Journal of the National Institute on Alcohol Abuse and Alcoholism*, 27(2), 186–196.

233 NIAAA Spectrum. (2023, May 22). Alcohol and other substance use to cope with social anxiety. *NIAAA Spectrum*, 15(2). https://www.niaaa.nih.gov/news-events/research-update/alcohol-and-other-substance-use-cope-social-anxiety

234 Mayo Clinic Staff. (2023, December 21). Obsessive-compulsive disorder (OCD). *Mayo Clinic.* https://www.mayoclinic.org/diseases-conditions/obsessive-compulsive-disorder/symptoms-causes/syc-20354432

235 NIAAA. (2021). The cycle of alcohol addiction. https://www.niaaa.nih.gov/publications/cycle-alcohol-addiction

236 Hagman, B. T., Falk, D., Litten, R., & Koob, G. F. (2022). Defining recovery from alcohol use disorder: Development of an NIAAA research definition. *The American Journal of Psychiatry.* Advance online publication. https://doi.org/10.1176/appi.ajp.21090963

237 Diana, M. (2011). The dopamine hypothesis of drug addiction and its potential therapeutic value. *Frontiers in Psychiatry*, 2, 64. https://doi.org/10.3389/fpsyt.2011.00064

238 Schrader, J.(2016, May 12). Adrenaline addiction. *Psychology Today.* https://www.psychologytoday.com/us/blog/how-do-life/201605/adrenaline-addiction

239 Bapat, M. (2022, May 20). How does OCD affect addiction risk and treatment? *GoodRx.* https://www.goodrx.com/conditions/obsessive-compulsive-disorder/ocd-and-addiction

240 Toohey, S. (2021, August 4). Delirium tremens (DTs). *Medscape.* https://emedicine.medscape.com/article/166032-overview?form=fpf

241 Cleveland Clinic. (2023, March 16). Addiction. *Cleveland Clinic.* https://my.clevelandclinic.org/health/diseases/6407-addiction

242 The Recovery Village. (2023, July 12). How to tell the difference between dependence vs. addiction. https://www.therecoveryvillage.com/drug-addiction/dependence-vs-addiction/

243 Grant, J. E., Potenza, M. N., Weinstein, A., & Gorelick, D. A. (2010). Introduction to behavioral addictions. *The American Journal of Drug and Alcohol Abuse*, 36(5), 233–241. https://doi.org/10.3109/00952990.2010.491884

244 Fox, T. P., Oliver, G., & Ellis, S. M. (2013). The destructive capacity of drug abuse: An overview exploring the harmful potential of drug abuse both to the individual and to society. *ISRN Addiction*, 2013, 450348. https://doi.org/10.1155/2013/450348

245 Pozza, A., Albert, U., & Dèttore, D. (2019). Perfectionism and Intolerance of Uncertainty are Predictors of OCD Symptoms in Children and Early Adolescents: A Prospective, Cohort, One-Year, Follow-Up Study. *Clinical Neuropsychiatry*, 16(1), 53–61.

246 Mayo Clinic Staff. (2022). Drug addiction (substance use disorder). *Mayo Clinic.* https://www.mayoclinic.org/diseases-conditions/drug-addiction/symptoms-causes/syc-20365112

247 Mishra, M. (Reviewed by). (2023, February 14). John Bonham | Alcohol poisoning death. *Ark Behavioral Health.* https://www.arkbh.com/celebrity-deaths/musicians/john-bonham/

248 Osna, N. A., & Kharbanda, K. K. (2016). Multi-Organ Alcohol-Related Damage: Mechanisms and Treatment. *Biomolecules*, 6(2), 20. https://doi.org/10.3390/biom6020020

249 NIDA. (2022, September 27). Part 1: The Connection Between Substance Use Disorders and Mental Illness. Retrieved from https://nida.nih.gov/publications/research-reports/common-comorbidities-substance-use-disorders/part-1-connection-between-substance-use-disorders-mental-illness

250 Sharp, A. (2024, February 21). The legal consequences of alcohol misuse. *American Addiction Centers.* https://americanaddictioncenters.org/alcohol/legal-consequences

251 Mayo Clinic Staff. (2022, August 5). Allergies. *Mayo Clinic.* Retrieved from https://www.mayoclinic.org/diseases-conditions/allergies/symptoms-causes/syc-20351497

252 eMedicineHealth. (2022, August 5). Allergic Reaction. Retrieved from https://www.emedicinehealth.com/allergic_reaction/article_em.htm

253 Bhattacharya, S. (2010). The facts about penicillin allergy: a review. *Journal of Advanced Pharmaceutical Technology & Research*, 1(1), 11-17. PMID: 22247826; PMCID: PMC3255391.

254 Andrade, J. (2013). Sensory Imagery in Craving. In Principles of Addiction. *Comprehensive Addictive Behaviors and Disorders*, Volume 1. https://doi.org/10.1016/C2011-0-07778-5

255 Anderson, K. (2022, December 2). The History of the "Allergy" Myth of Alcohol Addiction. *Filter Magazine.* Retrieved from https://filtermag.org/the-history-of-the-allergy-myth-of-alcohol-addiction/

256 Kelly, J. F. (2019, March). E. M. Jellinek's Disease Concept of Alcoholism. *Addiction*, 114(3), 555-559. https://doi.org/10.1111/add.14400

257 National Institute on Drug Abuse (NIDA). (2022, March 22). Drugs and the Brain. Retrieved from https://nida.nih.gov/publications/drugs-brains-behavio r-science-addiction/drugs-brain

258 Choice House. (2020, September 30). I Don't Understand the First Step – What is Unmanageability? Recovery. Retrieved from https://choicehousecolorado.co m/i-dont-understand-the-first-step-what-is-unmanageability/

259 U.S. Department of Health and Human Services, National Institutes of Health. (2023). Obsessive-Compulsive Disorder: When Unwanted Thoughts or Repetitive Behaviors Take Over (NIH Publication No. 23-MH-4676, Revised 2023).

260 Enoch, M. A. (2012). The influence of gene-environment interactions on the development of alcoholism and drug dependence. *Current Psychiatry Reports*, 14(2), 150–158. https://doi.org/10.1007/s11920-011-0252-9

261 Keng, S. L., Smoski, M. J., & Robins, C. J. (2011). Effects of mindfulness on psychological health: A review of empirical studies. *Clinical Psychology Review*, 31(6), 1041–1056. https://doi.org/10.1016/j.cpr.2011.04.006

262 Sissons, B. (November 28, 2023). Everything you need to know about nicotine. *Medical News Today*. Retrieved from https://www.medicalnewstoday.com/ articles/240820

263 NIDA. (2021). What are the treatments for heroin use disorder?. Retrieved from https://nida.nih.gov/publications/research-reports/heroin/what-are-treatment s-heroin-use-disorder

264 Alonso, F. (2019). Driving Under the Influence (DUI). In *Encyclopedia of Victimology and Crime Prevention* (pp. 392-394). doi:10.4135/9781483392240.n130

265 Sloan, F. A. (2020, February). Drinking and Driving. *NBER Working Paper Series*. Paper No. 26779. Retrieved from https://www.nber.org/system/files/ working_papers/w26779/w26779.pdf

266 Erasmus, M. S. (2016). The Object Relations of individuals who misuse alcohol and have co-morbid Depressive or Bipolar Disorders and/or Personality Disorders. Retrieved from https://www.academia.edu/64342117/The_object_re lations_of_individuals_who_misuse_alcohol_and_have_co_morbid_depres sive_or_bipolar_disorders_and_or_personality_disorders

267 Box-Steffensmeier, J. M., Burgess, J., Corbetta, M., Crawford, K., Duflo, E., Fogarty, L., Gopnik, A., Hanafi, S., Herrero, M., Hong, Y.-y., Kameyama, Y., Lee, T. M. C., Leung, G. M., Nagin, D. S., Nobre, A. C., Nordentoft, M., Okbay, A., Perfors, A., Rival, L. M., Sugimoto, C. R., Tungodden, B., & Wagner, C.

(2022). The future of human behaviour research. *Nature Human Behaviour*, 6(1), 15–24. https://doi.org/10.1038/s41562-021-01275-6

268 Dick, D. M., Smith, G., Olausson, P., Mitchell, S. H., Leeman, R. F., O'Malley, S. S., & Sher, K. (2010). Understanding the construct of impulsivity and its relationship to alcohol use disorders. *Addictive Biology*, 15(2), 217–226. https://doi.org/10.1111/j.1369-1600.2009.00190.x

269 Rausch, A. (2023, December 29). The Angry Drunk: How Alcohol, Rage, & Aggression Are Connected. Retrieved from https://www.choosingtherapy.com/angry-drunk/

270 Loy, J. K., Seitz, N. N., Bye, E. K., Dietze, P., Kilian, C., Manthey, J., Raitasalo, K., Soellner, R., Trolldal, B., Törrönen, J., & Kraus, L. (2021, October 18). Changes in Alcoholic Beverage Choice and Risky Drinking among Adolescents in Europe 1999-2019. *International Journal of Environmental Research and Public Health*, 18(20), 10933. https://doi.org/10.3390/ijerph182010933

271 Jacob, D. (2021). Health Risks of Chronic Heavy Drinking. Retrieved from https://www.medicinenet.com/alcohol_abuse_health_risks_pictures_slide-show/article.htm

272 National Academies of Sciences, Engineering, and Medicine; Health and Medicine Division; Food and Nutrition Board; Committee to Review the Process to Update the Dietary Guidelines for Americans. (2017). Redesigning the Process for Establishing the Dietary Guidelines for Americans. Washington, DC: *National Academies Press*. Retrieved from https://www.ncbi.nlm.nih.gov/books/NBK469839/

273 NIAAA. (2023). Drinking Levels Defined. Alcohol's Effects on Health. Retrieved from https://www.niaaa.nih.gov/alcohol-health/overview-alcohol-consumption/moderate-binge-drinking

274 Rehm, J. (2011). The risks associated with alcohol use and alcoholism. *Alcohol Research & Health*, 34(2), 135–143. PMID: 22330211; PMCID: PMC3307043.

275 Bienvenu, M. (2023, April 30). Is Anyone Really a 'High-Functioning Alcoholic'? *WebMD*. https://www.webmd.com/mental-health/addiction/features/high-functioning-alcoholic

276 DiClemente, C. C., Bellino, L. E., & Neavins, T. M. (1999). Motivation for change and alcoholism treatment. *Alcohol Research & Health*, 23(2), 86–92.

277 Witkiewitz, K., & Tucker, J. A. (2020). Abstinence Not Required: Expanding the Definition of Recovery from Alcohol Use Disorder. *Alcoholism: Clinical and Experimental Research*, 44(1), 36–40. https://doi.org/10.1111/acer.14235

278 Chappel, J. N., & DuPont, R. L. (1999). Twelve-step and mutual-help programs for addictive disorders. *Psychiatric Clinics of North America*, 22(2), 425–446. https://doi.org/10.1016/s0193-953x(05)70085-x

279 Donovan, D. M., Ingalsbe, M. H., Benbow, J., & Daley, D. C. (2013). 12-step interventions and mutual support programs for substance use disorders: An overview. *Social Work in Public Health*, 28(3-4), 313–332. https://doi.org/10.10 80/19371918.2013.774663

280 Professor Buzzkill. (2017, May 29). Albert Einstein: The definition of insanity is doing the same thing over and over and expecting different results. Retrieved from https://professorbuzzkill.com/2017/05/29/einstein-insanity-qnq/

281 Fordyce, K. (2023, May 28). Addiction: What Is Denial? *WebMD*. Retrieved from https://www.webmd.com/mental-health/addiction/addiction-what-is-denial

282 The Recovery Village. (2023, November 21). How to Wean Off Alcohol Safely. Retrieved from https://www.therecoveryvillage.com/alcohol-abuse/alcohol-taper/

283 Fitzpatrick, A. P., & Cooper, P. (2006). Diagnosis and management of patients with blackouts. *Heart*, 92(4), 559-568. https://doi.org/10.1136/hrt.2005.068650

284 National Institute on Alcohol Abuse and Alcoholism. (2023, February). Interrupted Memories: Alcohol-Induced Blackouts. *Alcohol's Effects on Health*. https://www.niaaa.nih.gov/publications/brochures-and-fact-sheets/interrupte d-memories-alcohol-induced-blackouts

285 Medicover Hospitals. (2021, March 11). What is Blackout? Retrieved from https://www.medicoverhospitals.in/symptoms/blackouts

286 Lee, H., Roh, S., & Kim, D. J. (2009). Alcohol-induced blackout. *International Journal of Environmental Research and Public Health*, 6(11), 2783–2792. https://doi.org/10.3390/ijerph6112783

287 Traylor, J., Overstreet, L., & Lang, D. (2022). Psychodynamic Theory: Freud. Retrieved from https://iastate.pressbooks.pub/individualfamilydevelopment/chapter/freuds-psychodynamic-theory/

288 Hosseinbor, M., Yassini Ardekani, S. M., Bakhshani, S., & Bakhshani, S. (2014). Emotional and social loneliness in individuals with and without substance dependence disorder. *International Journal of High Risk Behaviors and Addiction*, 3(3), e22688. https://doi.org/10.5812/ijhrba.22688

289 Cleveland Clinic medical professional. (2022, April 28). Paranoid Personality Disorder. Retrieved from https://my.clevelandclinic.org/health/diseases/9784 -paranoid-personality-disorder

290 Cleveland Clinic medical professional. (2023, September 28). Avoidant Personality Disorder. Retrieved from https://my.clevelandclinic.org/health/diseases/9761-avoidant-personality-disorder

291 Gupta, S. (2022, August 19). What Are the 12 Steps of Narcotics Anonymous (NA)? Retrieved from https://www.verywellmind.com/what-are-the-12-steps-of-na-narcotics-anonymous-5525334

292 Dąbrowska, K., Moskalewicz, J., & Wieczorek, Ł. (2017). Barriers in Access to the Treatment for People with Gambling Disorders. Are They Different from Those Experienced by People with Alcohol and/or Drug Dependence? *Journal of Gambling Studies*, 33(2), 487–503. https://doi.org/10.1007/s10899-016-9655-1

293 Mann, K., Hermann, D., & Heinz, A. (2000). One hundred years of alcoholism: The twentieth century. *Alcohol and Alcoholism*, 35(1), 10–15. https://doi.org/10.1093/alcalc/35.1.10

294 Topkaya, N., Şahin, E., Krettmann, A. K., & Essau, C. A. (2021). Stigmatization of people with alcohol and drug addiction among Turkish undergraduate students. *Addictive Behaviors Reports*, 14, 100386. https://doi.org/10.1016/j.abrep.2021.100386

295 Lampe, L., & Malhi, G. S. (2018). Avoidant personality disorder: Current insights. *Psychology Research and Behavior Management*, 11, 55–66. https://doi.org/10.2147/PRBM.S121073

296 BBC News. (2021, December 6). 'Stop saying junkie' plea to end addiction stigma. https://www.bbc.com/news/uk-scotland-59542090

297 Long, T., & Cooke, F. L. (2023). Advancing the field of employee assistance programs research and practice: A systematic review of quantitative studies and future research agenda. *Human Resource Management Review*, 33(2), 100941. https://doi.org/10.1016/j.hrmr.2022.100941

298 Addiction Center. (2024, January 3). Drug And Alcohol Detox. Retrieved from https://www.addictioncenter.com/treatment/drug-and-alcohol-detox/

299 Diaper, A. M., Law, F. D., & Melichar, J. K. (2014). Pharmacological strategies for detoxification. *British Journal of Clinical Pharmacology*, 77(2), 302–314. https://doi.org/10.1111/bcp.12245

300 Hayashida, M. (1998). An overview of outpatient and inpatient detoxification. *Alcohol Health and Research World*, 22(1), 44–46.

301 Ziaaddini, H., Qahestani, A., & Moin Vaziri, M. (2009). Comparing Symptoms of Withdrawal, Rapid Detoxification, and Detoxification with Clonidine in Drug Dependent Patients. *Addiction Health*, 1(2), 63–68.

302 Pantiel, T. (2023, October 26). Holistic Therapy. Retrieved from https://www.addictioncenter.com/treatment/holistic-therapy/

303 Zaidi, U. (2020, July 24). Role of Social Support in Relapse Prevention for Drug Addicts.

304 World Health Organization. (2009). Clinical Guidelines for Withdrawal Management and Treatment of Drug Dependence in Closed Settings. Methadone maintenance treatment (pp. 6). *Geneva.* Available from: https://www.ncbi.nlm.nih.gov/books/NBK310658/

305 Kleber, H. D. (2007). Pharmacologic treatments for opioid dependence: detoxification and maintenance options. *Dialogues in Clinical Neuroscience*, 9(4), 455–470. https://doi.org/10.31887/DCNS.2007.9.2/hkleber

306 Substance Abuse and Mental Health Services Administration (US). (2006). Detoxification and Substance Abuse Treatment. *Treatment Improvement Protocol (TIP) Series*, No. 45. Rockville, MD. Retrieved from https://www.ncbi.nlm.nih.gov/books/NBK64116/

307 De Leon, G. (2013). Therapeutic Communities. In Interventions for Addiction. ISBN: 978-0-12-384885-7.

308 Hoffman, M. (2024, February 12). Counseling and Substance Use Disorders. *WebMD.* https://www.webmd.com/mental-health/addiction/counseling-and-addiction-how-therapy-can-help

309 Davis, C. (2018). Home detox - supporting patients to overcome alcohol addiction. *Australian Prescriber*, 41(6), 180–182. https://doi.org/10.18773/austprescr.2018.059

310 Belote, A. (2024, February 22). Physical Dependence On Alcohol. *Addiction Center.* Retrieved from https://www.addictioncenter.com/alcohol/physical-dependence/

311 Saitz, R. (1998). Introduction to alcohol withdrawal. *Alcohol Health and Research World*, 22(1), 5–12. PMID: 15706727; PMCID: PMC6761824.

312 Trevisan, L. A., Boutros, N., Petrakis, I. L., & Krystal, J. H. (1998). Complications of alcohol withdrawal: pathophysiological insights. *Alcohol Health and Research World*, 22(1), 61–66. PMID: 15706735; PMCID: PMC6761825.

313 Enoch, M.-A., & Goldman, D. (2002). Problem drinking and alcoholism: Diagnosis and treatment. *American Family Physician*, 65, 441–448.

314 American Psychological Association. (2012). What you need to know about willpower: The psychological science of self-control. Retrieved from https://www.apa.org/topics/personality/willpower

315 Cherry, K. (2022, November 14). What Was the Milgram Experiment? *Verywell Mind.* https://www.verywellmind.com/the-milgram-obedience-experiment-2795243

316 Smith, M., Robinson, L., & Segal, J. (2024, February 5). Overcoming Alcohol Addiction. *HelpGuide.* https://www.helpguide.org/articles/addictions/overcoming-alcohol-addiction.htm

317 Padovano, H. T., Levak, S., Vadhan, N. P., Kuerbis, A., & Morgenstern, J. (2022, March). The Role of Daily Goal Setting Among Individuals with Alcohol Use Disorder. *Drug and Alcohol Dependence Reports*, 2, 100036. https://doi.org/10.1016/j.dadr.2022.100036

318 Melemis, S. M. (2015). Relapse Prevention and the Five Rules of Recovery. *Yale Journal of Biology and Medicine*, 88(3), 325–332. PMID: 26339217; PMCID: PMC4553654.

319 Greene, D. (2021). Revisiting 12-Step Approaches: An Evidence-Based Perspective. DOI: 10.5772/intechopen.95985.

320 Smarmore Rehab Clinic. (2024, January 23). The Importance of Boundaries in Addiction Recovery. Retrieved from https://www.smarmore-rehab-clinic.com/addiction-resources/boundaries-in-addiction-recovery/

321 Cherry, K. (2023, December 01). Step 7 of the AA 12-Step Program. *Verywell Mind.* Retrieved from https://www.verywellmind.com/step-7-of-the-aa-12-step-program-5271444

322 Guenzel, N., & McChargue, D. (2023, July 21). Addiction Relapse Prevention. In StatPearls [Internet]. Treasure Island (FL): *StatPearls Publishing.* Retrieved from https://www.ncbi.nlm.nih.gov/books/NBK551500/

323 NIDA. (2023, September 25). Treatment and Recovery. Retrieved from https://nida.nih.gov/publications/drugs-brains-behavior-science-addiction/treatment-recovery

324 Davis, J. (2023, May 28). Alcohol Use Disorder: What to Know About Relapse. *WebMD.* https://www.webmd.com/mental-health/addiction/alcohol-use-disorder-relapse

325 Scholten, W., Ten Have, M., van Geel, C., van Balkom, A., de Graaf, R., & Batelaan, N. (2023). Recurrence of anxiety disorders and its predictors in the general population. *Psychological Medicine*, 53(4), 1334–1342. https://doi.org/10.1017/S0033291721002877

326 The Recovery Village. (2023, June 20). Euphoric Recall. https://www.therecoveryvillage.com/recovery/relapse/euphoric-recall/#:~:text=Euphoric%20recall%20can%20lead%20to,people%20more%20likely%20to%20relapse.

327 Integrative Life Center. (2021, March 8). Euphoric Recall: What It Is, and How To Deal With It. https://integrativelifecenter.com/treatment-programs/euphoric-recall-what-it-is-and-how-to-deal-with-it/

328 Palmer, C. (2021, September 15). How Drug and Alcohol Addiction Impacts Your Mind, Body, and Health. *GoodRx.* https://www.goodrx.com/conditions/substance-use-disorder/physical-neurological-effects-of-addiction

329 Sadava, S. W., Thistle, R., & Forsyth, R. (1978). Stress, escapism and patterns of alcohol and drug use. *Journal of Studies on Alcohol,* 39(5), 725-736. https://doi.org/10.15288/jsa.1978.39.725

330 Patterson, E. (2024, February 9). Penalties and Sentencing for Drug Abuse, Selling, and Smuggling in the USA. *DrugAbuse.com.* https://drugabuse.com/addiction/drug-abuse/penalties/

331 Minnesota Department of Health. (2022, August 11). New study shows economic and social impact of excessive drinking in Minnesota. Retrieved from https://www.health.state.mn.us/news/pressrel/2022/alcohol081122.html

332 Peirce, R. S., Frone, M. R., Russell, M., & Cooper, M. L. (1994). Relationship of Financial Strain and Psychosocial Resources to Alcohol Use and Abuse: The Mediating Role of Negative Affect and Drinking Motives. *Journal of Health and Social Behavior,* 35(4), 291–308. https://doi.org/10.2307/2137211

333 Mosel, S. (2024, March 4). Mental Effects of Alcohol: Effects of Alcohol on the Brain. *American Addiction Centers.* Retrieved from https://americanaddictioncenters.org/alcohol/risks-effects-dangers/mental

334 WebMD Editorial Contributors. (2023, July 7). What Is Abstinence? *WebMD.* Retrieved from https://www.webmd.com/sex/what-is-abstinence

335 Manwarren Generes, W. (Ed.). (2024, March 1). How to Get Sober: A Guide to Sobriety. *American Addiction Centers.* Retrieved from https://americanaddictioncenters.org/sobriety-guide

336 WebMD Editorial Contributors. (2023, July 8). What to Know About Dry Drunk Syndrome. *WebMD.* Retrieved from https://www.webmd.com/mental-health/addiction/what-to-know-dry-drunk-syndrome

337 Hinders, D. (2019, September 13). What Is Emotional Sobriety? *Waypoint Recovery Center.* Retrieved from https://waypointrecoverycenter.com/blog/what-is-emotional-sobriety/

338 Thurga. (2022, November 23). 11 Signs You Have Emotional Sobriety. *Recoverlution.* Retrieved from https://www.recoverlution.com/knowledge/emotional-sobriety-development

339 Wood, T. (2020, August 11). How To Handle Negative Emotions Without Drugs or Alcohol. *Rehab 4 Alcoholism.* Retrieved from https://www.rehab4alcoholism.com/guides/handle-negative-emotions-without-drugs-alcohol

340 Nash, J. (2022, August 1). What Is Behavior Therapy? Your Ultimate Practitioner's Guide. *Positive Psychology.* Retrieved from https://positivepsychology.com/behavior-therapy/

341 Webster, A. (2024, January 3). Cognitive-Behavioral Therapy (CBT) for Addiction and Substance Abuse. *American Addiction Centers.* Retrieved from https://americanaddictioncenters.org/therapy-treatment/cognitive-behavioral-therapy

342 Kessler, T. (2017, September 10). Untreated Alcoholism or the 'Dry Drunk' Syndrome. Retrieved from https://www.thomkesslertherapist.com/blog--articles/untreated-alcoholism-or-the-dry-drunk-syndrome

343 Smith Haghighi, A. (2022, May 24). What is 'dry drunk syndrome,' and whom does it affect? *Medical News Today.* Retrieved from https://www.medicalnewstoday.com/articles/dry-drunk-syndrome

344 White, W. (2007, November 1). Addiction recovery: Its definition and conceptual boundaries. *Journal of Substance Abuse Treatment*, 33(3), 229-241. https://doi.org/10.1016/j.jsat.2007.04.015

345 Roberts, G., & Wolfson, P. (2004, January 1). The rediscovery of recovery: Open to all. *Advances in Psychiatric Treatment*, 10(1), 37-48. https://doi.org/10.1192/apt.10.1.37

346 Dermatis, H., & Galanter, M. (2016, April). The Role of Twelve-Step-Related Spirituality in Addiction Recovery. *Journal of Relig Health*, 55(2), 510-521. https://doi.org/10.1007/s10943-015-0019-4

347 Weinandy, J. T. G., & Grubbs, J. B. (2021). Religious and spiritual beliefs and attitudes towards addiction and addiction treatment: A scoping review. *Addictive Behaviors Reports*, 14, 100393. https://doi.org/10.1016/j.abrep.2021.100393

348 Pongsavee, K., Payakkakom, A., Phukao, D., & Guadamuz, T. E. (2023). Natural recovery from alcohol: A systematic review of the literature 2006–2019. *Journal of Substance Use*, 28(2), 166-171. https://doi.org/10.1080/14659891.2021.2020348

349 Webster, A. (2024, February 22). Support Groups For Alcohol Addiction. *Addiction Center.* Retrieved from https://www.addictioncenter.com/alcohol/support-groups/

350 Jason, L. A., Majer, J. M., Bobak, T. J., & O'Brien, J. (2022). Medication assisted therapy and recovery homes. *Journal of Prevention & Intervention in the Community*, 50(2), 178–190. https://doi.org/10.1080/10852352.2021.1934940

351 National Cancer Institute. (2023). Complementary and Alternative Medicine. Retrieved from https://www.cancer.gov/about-cancer/treatment/cam

352 Pantiel, T. (2024, January 9). Inpatient Vs. Outpatient Rehab. *Addiction Center*. Retrieved from https://www.addictioncenter.com/treatment/inpatient-outpatient-rehab/

353 Mayo Clinic Staff. (2021, June 19). Social anxiety disorder (social phobia). *Mayo Clinic*. Retrieved from https://www.mayoclinic.org/diseases-conditions/social-anxiety-disorder/symptoms-causes/syc-20353561

354 Andy. (2022, October 26). The alcoholic – An egomaniac with an inferiority complex. *AA for Agnostics*. Retrieved from https://aaforagnostics.com/blog/the-alcoholic-an-egomaniac-with-an-inferiority-complex/

355 Cherry, K. (2022, November 8). What Are Psychological Theories? *Verywell Mind*. Retrieved from https://www.verywellmind.com/what-is-a-theory-2795970

356 Heyes, C. (2012). New thinking: The evolution of human cognition. *Philosophical Transactions of the Royal Society of London. Series B, Biological Sciences*, 367(1599), 2091–2096. https://doi.org/10.1098/rstb.2012.0111

357 Murray, K. (2023, August 16). Achieving Transformation Through Rehab. *RehabSpot*. Retrieved from https://www.rehabspot.com/treatment/spiritual/transformation/

358 Griffiths, M. D. (2016, May 11). The Myth of the Addictive Personality. *Psychology Today*. Retrieved from https://www.psychologytoday.com/us/blog/in-excess/201605/the-myth-the-addictive-personality

359 VandeZande, J. (2020, April 6). The Toughest Human Character Trait: Humility. *West Bend Community Church Blog*. Retrieved from https://west-bendchurch.org/community-church-blog/the-toughest-human-character-trait-humility/

360 Bockius, C. (2017, August 18). Life Lessons on Humility. Retrieved from https://byrslf.co/life-lessons-on-humility-6a01a352e4a5

361 Yang, H. (2022, June 3). Humility vs Humble: What's the Difference? *ProWritingAid*. Retrieved from https://prowritingaid.com/humilty-vs-humble

362 Contreras, A. (2020, July 22). Your Emotional Brain on Resentment, Part 1. *Psych Central*. Retrieved from https://psychcentral.com/pro/your-emotional-brain-on-resentment-part-1#1

363 Melemis, S. M. (2015). Relapse Prevention and the Five Rules of Recovery. *The Yale Journal of Biology and Medicine*, 88(3), 325–332.

364 Hodgman-Korth, M. (2024, January 5). Making Amends in Recovery. *American Addiction Centers*. Retrieved from https://americanaddictioncenters.org/addiction-recovery/making-amends

365 Fair Oaks Recovery Center. (2017, April 3). What are "Living Amends?" *Fair Oaks Recovery Center Blog*. Retrieved from https://fairoaksrecoverycenter.com/blog/living-amends/

366 Smiddy, C. (2020, October 8). How to Make Amends in Addiction Recovery. *Hired Power*. Retrieved from https://www.hiredpower.com/blog/how-to-make-amends-in-addiction-recovery/

367 McDonough, B. (2020, October 7). Higher Power: Can Faith Really Help You Get Through Rehab? *Holdfast Recovery Blog*. Retrieved from https://www.holdfastrecovery.com/blog/2020/october/higher-power-can-faith-really-help-you-get-throu/

368 Niemiec, R. (2020, April 20). What Does Spirituality Mean To You? *Via Character Blog*. Retrieved from https://www.viacharacter.org/topics/articles/what-does-spirituality-mean-to-you

369 Tonigan, J. S., Rynes, K. N., & McCrady, B. S. (2013). Spirituality as a change mechanism in 12-step programs: A replication, extension, and refinement. *Substance Use & Misuse*, 48(12), 1161–1173. https://doi.org/10.3109/10826084.2013.808540

370 Spero Recovery. (2024, January 22). The Power in the First Step: Accepting Powerlessness. Retrieved from https://www.sperorecovery.org/the-power-in-the-first-step-accepting-powerlessness/

371 Gershon, L. (2022, October 19). The Story Behind "This is Your Brain on Drugs." *JSTOR Daily*. Retrieved from https://daily.jstor.org/the-story-behind-this-is-your-brain-on-drugs/

372 Jones, A. (2022, October 14). Self-care: What is it? Why is it so important for your health? *UAB News*. Retrieved from https://www.uab.edu/news/youcanuse/item/13176-self-care-what-is-it-why-is-it-so-important-for-your-health

373 Evidation. (2023, July 26). Self-care activities for mental health: nurturing your mental well-being. https://evidation.com/blog/self-care-activities-for-mental-health-nurturing-your-mental-well-being

374 Deering, S., & Blumberg, P. O. (2024, February 1). 50 self-care ideas for when you need a mood boost. *Today*. Retrieved from https://www.today.com/life/inspiration/self-care-ideas-rcna65285

ADDICTION ABC'S (DEFINITIONS)

A.

<u>Abstain:</u> To restrain from doing or enjoying something.

<u>Abstinent:</u> Absence of something.

<u>ADHD (Attention-Deficit / Hyperactivity Disorder):</u> People with ADHD may have trouble paying attention, controlling impulsive behaviors (may act without thinking about what the result will be), or be overly active.

<u>Addictive Personality:</u> Contrary to what you may have heard, we don't have addictive personalities. We may have certain traits about us (in our brains) that we have addictions towards, but not everything about us makes us addictive people. (Ex.): we may be addicted to drugs or alcohol, or sex, or gambling … even working out at the gym or collecting things, but there is still no definition as a person having an addictive personality.

<u>Ad-nauseum:</u> referring to something that has been done or repeated so often that it has become annoying or tiresome.

Agnostic: a person who believes that nothing is known or can be known of the existence or nature of God or of anything beyond material phenomena; a person who claims neither faith nor disbelief in God.

Altruism/Altruistic: Doing the right thing without expecting anything in return.

Amends, making an: Reaching out and being able to mend harms we caused whereas we are granted forgiveness.

Anonymity: Nameless in secrecy

Auditory learning: In my case, I learn or understand better when it is verbally taught to me as opposed to reading it. However, I learn faster and easier if it is shown to me.

AW (Alcohol Withdrawal): Withdrawal effects from alcohol in the bloodstream.

B.

BDD (Body Dysmorphic Disorder): Excessive dislike of a part of one's body

Blackout: Blackout drunk describes memory loss from heavy alcohol intake. Blackouts happen if you drink too much, too quickly.

C.

Chronic: A problem that continues over an extended period of time.

Compulsive: Irresistible urges. Going against mindful/ conscious behaviors.

Compulsion: An irrational need or irresistible urge to perform some action, often despite negative consequences.

D.

DBT (dialectical behavior therapy): is a type of cognitive-behavioral treatment that aims to find

and change negative thought patterns while also encouraging people to change their behavior for the better.

Debilitating Illness: A health condition that causes a loss of energy or strength.

DOC (Drug of choice): Your personal drug of choice.

Dopamine: A type of neurotransmitter. Your body makes it, and your nervous system uses it to send messages between nerve cells. That's why it's sometimes called a chemical messenger. Dopamine plays a role in how we feel pleasure. It's a big part of our unique human ability to think and plan. It helps us strive, focus, and find things interesting.

Dry drunk: Untreated alcoholism. Remaining abstinent from drinking or doing drugs, but not following all the other important aspects of living a "true" sober life. While still not actually drinking of using, yet always thinking negatively about things and not being happy. E.g.: "I am not drinking anymore, so how can I have a meaningful relationship without alcohol in my life?" Or, "Now that I am straight, it's probably too late to be successful again, or even experience failure that would make me wiser!"

E.

Emotional Sobriety: Clean and sober, and living mentally fit

Endorphins, Dopamine, Serotonin: Chemicals in your brain that facilitate memory and emotional functions.

Euphoric Recall: Only remembering the good times and generally overlooking the bad ones. Opposite of morbid reflection.

F.

FOMO (fear of missing out): Having a fear of missing out on something—usually something good.

Free Will: God has given me the ability to choose my own path.

G.

Gateway Drug: Gateway drugs are those that may lead to the use of other types of high-risk addictive drugs.

Genetic Predisposition: An increased chance that a person will develop a disease based on their genetic makeup.

H.

Higher power: A higher power is a chosen person, object, or force greater than ourselves that we look to for guidance each day. It can even be a mystical feeling of belief. For most people, this is God. In my case, I simply call it MY Higher power—my Creator. The creator of me and everything around me.

Holistic: Natural

Homo Sapiens: Humans

I.

<u>Illicit:</u> Illegal

<u>Impulse Addiction:</u> Includes pathological tendencies like gambling, kleptomania (stealing), trichotillomania (hair pulling), shopping, pyromania (starting fires)

<u>Inebriated:</u> Behaving as though affected by alcohol including exhilaration, and a dumbed or stupefied manner.

L.

<u>Living Amends:</u> Living a completely new, sober lifestyle, and being committed to that lifestyle for both you and those you've harmed in the past.

M.

<u>Metabolize:</u> To change food into a form that can be used by your body.

<u>Metaphor:</u> The use of a word or phrase to refer to something that it is not, invoking a direct similarity between the word or phrase used and the thing described. Depicting a meaning for something using an example.

<u>Morbid Reflection:</u> Looking back on a bad moment in time.

N.

<u>Narcissistic:</u> Having an inflated idea of one's own importance. Obsessed with one's own self-image and ego.

<u>Neurotic:</u> Overly anxious.

P.

Paradox: When a bad situation has to occur, that seems so negative, but needs to happen so that the end result turns into a good outcome.

Pathological: Caused by a physical or mental disorder.

Profit Motive: What's in it for me money-wise?

Psychosis: A severe mental disorder, sometimes with physical damage to the brain, marked by a deranged personality and a distorted view of reality.

PTSD (Post Traumatic Stress Disorder): A mental disorder that is triggered by a traumatic experience. This comes in the form of nightmares, flashbacks, or anxiety disorders, etc. It can be caused by the involvement or the witness of a traumatic instance. It can be related to a sexual experience, a terrifying situation like an accident, but is also very common with military acts as in war.

R.

Resentment: A feeling of anger or displeasure stemming from belief that one has been wronged by others or betrayed; indignation.

Restitution: The act of making good or compensating for loss or injury.

S.

Spiritual Awakening: A spiritual awakening is a call to higher consciousness and deeper mental awareness. The process of spiritual awakening brings about personal transformation and a shift in one's worldview.

<u>Spiritual Experience:</u> An incident that goes beyond human understanding in how this experience could have happened in the first place.

U.

<u>Untreated Alcoholism:</u> also Dry Drunk Syndrome. Only living clean and sober, but not emotionally fit

V.

<u>Virtuous:</u> Having excellent moral character.

** These words or phrases are ones I compiled as being the most important and useful to me in restoring my mental health and well-being. At some point, all of them have been explained to me while living life and along my journey in Recovery. However, their mentioned meanings are completely derived from my own observations and thought processes. None of said meanings were taken directly from any printed materials.*

BIBLIOGRAPHY

1   Addelabu, O. (2015). Social Media, Advertising Messages and the Youth: Any Influence? *New Media and Mass Communication*, 39, ISSN 2224-3267.

2   Adrenaline addiction 101: How, what, who? (2020). Retrieved from https://rosglasrecovery.com/adrenaline-addiction-101/

3   Ahmad, A. (2011). A Short Description of Social Networking Websites And Its Uses. *International Journal of Advanced Computer Sciences and Applications*, 2. https://doi.org/10.14569/IJACSA.2011.020220

4   Alavi, S. S., Ferdosi, M., Jannatifard, F., Eslami, M., Alaghemandan, H., & Setare, M. (2012). Behavioral addiction versus substance addiction: Correspondence of psychiatric and psychological views. *International Journal of Preventive Medicine*, 3(4), 290–294.

5   Al-Ghanim, D. A., Al-Salat, G. M., & Al-Shaikh, R. S. (2018). The role of cosmetic dentistry in restoring a youthful appearance in Saudi population: An overview. *World Journal of Pharmaceutical Research*, 7(10), 249-258. https://doi.org/10.20959/wjpr201810-12312

6   Alonso, F. (2019). Driving Under the Influence (DUI). In *Encyclopedia of Victimology and Crime Prevention* (pp. 392-394). doi:10.4135/9781483392240.n130

7   "Am I an Adrenaline Junkie? Read This if You Are!" (2023). Retrieved from https://kentuckycounselingcenter.com/adrenaline-junkie/

8   American Addiction Centers [Editorial Staff]. (2024, March 1). Signs & Symptoms of Addiction (Physical & Mental). Retrieved from https://american-addictioncenters.org/adult-addiction-treatment-programs/signs

9   American Addiction Centers. (2024, March 1). Alcohol moderation management: Programs and steps to control drinking. Edited by A. Sharp. Retrieved from https://americanaddictioncenters.org/blog/alcohol-moderation-management

10   American Addiction Centers Editorial Staff. (2023, December 1). Stimulant detox, withdrawal symptoms, and addiction treatment. Retrieved from https://drugabuse.com/stimulants/detox-withdrawal/

11   American Addiction Centers Editorial Staff. (2023, September 6). The Effects of Meth on Your Body. *DrugAbuse.* https://drugabuse.com/featured/the-effects-of-meth-on-your-body/

12   American Psychological Association. (2011, October 1). The danger of stimulants. *Monitor on Psychology*, 42(9). Retrieved from https://www.apa.org/monitor/2011/10/stimulants

13   American Psychological Association. (2012). What you need to know about willpower: The psychological science of self-control. Retrieved from https://www.apa.org/topics/personality/willpower

14   Anderson, K. (2022, December 2). The History of the "Allergy" Myth of Alcohol Addiction. Retrieved from https://filtermag.org/the-history-of-the-allergy-myth-of-alcohol-addiction/

15   Anderson, K. (2022, December 2). The History of the "Allergy" Myth of Alcohol Addiction. *Filter Magazine.* Retrieved from https://filtermag.org/the-history-of-the-allergy-myth-of-alcohol-addiction/

16   Andy. (2022, October 26). The alcoholic – An egomaniac with an inferiority complex. *AA for Agnostics.* Retrieved from https://aaforagnostics.com/blog/the-alcoholic-an-egomaniac-with-an-inferiority-complex/

17   Andrade, J. (2013). Sensory Imagery in Craving. In Principles of Addiction. *Comprehensive Addictive Behaviors and Disorders*, Volume 1. https://doi.org/10.1016/C2011-0-07778-5

18   Arora, S., & Gulhima, A. (2014). Laser hair removal. Retrieved from https://doi.org/10.13140/2.1.2589.0887

19   Ballara, N. B. (2023). The Power of Social Validation: A Literature Review on How Likes, Comments, and Shares Shape User Behavior on Social Media. *International Journal of Research Publication and Reviews*, 4(7), 3355-3367. https://doi.org/10.55248/gengpi.4.723.51227

20   Bapat, M. (2022, May 20). How does OCD affect addiction risk and treatment? *GoodRx.* https://www.goodrx.com/conditions/obsessive-compulsive-disorder/ocd-and-addiction

21 BBC News. (2021, December 6). 'Stop saying junkie' plea to end addiction stigma. https://www.bbc.com/news/uk-scotland-59542090

22 Beckhusen, B. (2016). Mobile Apps and the ultimate addiction to the Smartphone. Retrieved from https://www.diva-portal.org/smash/get/diva2:950846/FULLTEXT01.pdf

23 Belote, A. (2024, February 22). Physical Dependence On Alcohol. *Addiction Center*. Retrieved from https://www.addictioncenter.com/alcohol/physical-dependence/

24 Bezinović, P., & Malatestinić, D. (2009). Perceived exposure to substance use and risk-taking behavior in early adolescence: cross-sectional study. *Croatian Medical Journal*, 50(2), 157–164. https://doi.org/10.3325/cmj.2009.50.157

25 Bhattacharya, S. (2010). The facts about penicillin allergy: a review. *Journal of Advanced Pharmaceutical Technology & Research*, 1(1), 11-17. PMID: 22247826; PMCID: PMC3255391.

26 Bickel, J. (2020, December 28). Tea bringing people together (just less literally lately). *T Ching*. Retrieved from https://tching.com/2020/12/tea-bringing-peopl e-together-less-literally/

27 Bienvenu, M. (2023, April 30). Is Anyone Really a 'High-Functioning Alcoholic'? *WebMD*. https://www.webmd.com/mental-health/addiction/features/high-functioning-alcoholic

28 Bjornsson, A. S., Didie, E. R., & Phillips, K. A. (2010). Body dysmorphic disorder. *Dialogues in Clinical Neuroscience*, 12(2), 221–232. https://doi.org/10.31887/DCNS.2010.12.2/abjornsson

29 Bockius, C. (2017, August 18). Life Lessons on Humility. Retrieved from https://byrslf.co/life-lessons-on-humility-6a01a352e4a5

30 Box-Steffensmeier, J. M., Burgess, J., Corbetta, M., Crawford, K., Duflo, E., Fogarty, L., Gopnik, A., Hanafi, S., Herrero, M., Hong, Y.-y., Kameyama, Y., Lee, T. M. C., Leung, G. M., Nagin, D. S., Nobre, A. C., Nordentoft, M., Okbay, A., Perfors, A., Rival, L. M., Sugimoto, C. R., Tungodden, B., & Wagner, C. (2022). The future of human behaviour research. *Nature Human Behaviour*, 6(1), 15–24. https://doi.org/10.1038/s41562-021-01275-6

31 Brewer, A. (2023, November 6). Opioid vs. Opiate: What's the Difference? *GoodRx*. Retrieved from https://www.goodrx.com/classes/opioids

32 Brewer, J. A., & Potenza, M. N. (2008). The neurobiology and genetics of impulse control disorders: relationships to drug addictions. *Biochemical Pharmacology*, 75(1), 63–75. https://doi.org/10.1016/j.bcp.2007.06.043

33   Bruce, D. F. (2022, March 17). Prescription drug abuse: Addiction, types, and treatment. *WebMD*. Reviewed by S. Bhandari, MD. Retrieved from https://www.webmd.com/mental-health/addiction/abuse-of-prescription-drugs

34   Bruinsma, K., & Taren, D. L. (1999). Chocolate: Food or Drug? *Journal of the American Dietetic Association*, 99(10), 1249–1256. https://doi.org/10.1016/S0002-8223(99)00307-7

35   Buckland, P. R. (2020). The Biological Guises and Allures of Addiction: Late Lessons from a Rapidly Expanding Research Front. In Pemanloe, A., Pal, R., & Jaya, R. (Eds.), *Recent Advancements in Neurology & Neurological Disorders*, pp. 72-92. Elsevier.

36   Budney, A. J., & Emond, J. A. (2014). Caffeine addiction? Caffeine for youth? Time to act! *Addiction*, 109(7), 1085-1086. https://doi.org/10.1111/add.12594

37   Bulik, C. M. (2005). Exploring the gene-environment nexus in eating disorders. *Journal of Psychiatry & Neuroscience*: JPN, 30(5), 335–339.

38   Burd, E. M. (2003). Human papillomavirus and cervical cancer. *Clinical Microbiology Reviews*, 16(1), 1–17. https://doi.org/10.1128/CMR.16.1.1-17.2003

39   Burhan, R., & Moradzadeh, J. (2020). Neurotransmitter Dopamine (DA) and its Role in the Development of Social Media Addiction. *Journal of Neurology & Neurophysiology*, 11(7), 507.

40   Butler Center for Research. (2015, September 1). Drug Abuse, Dopamine and the Brain's Reward System. *Hazelden Betty Ford Foundation*. Retrieved from https://www.hazeldenbettyford.org/research-studies/addiction-research/drug-abuse-brain

41   Camilleri, C., Perry, J. T., & Sammut, S. (2021). Compulsive internet pornography use and mental health: A cross-sectional study in a sample of university students in the United States. *Frontiers in Psychology*, 11, 613244. https://doi.org/10.3389/fpsyg.2020.613244

42   Carmen, R. A., Guitar, A. E., & Dillon, H. M. (2012). Ultimate answers to proximate questions: The evolutionary motivations behind tattoos and body piercings in popular culture. *Review of General Psychology*, 16(2), 134–143. https://doi.org/10.1037/a0027908

43   Casperson, S. L., Lanza, L., Albajri, E., & Nasser, J. A. (2019). Increasing Chocolate's Sugar Content Enhances Its Psychoactive Effects and Intake. *Nutrients*, 11(3), 596. https://doi.org/10.3390/nu11030596

44   Castle, D. J., Phillips, K. A., & Dufresne, R. G., Jr (2004). Body dysmorphic disorder and cosmetic dermatology: More than skin deep. *Journal of Cosmetic Dermatology*, 3(2), 99–103. https://doi.org/10.1111/j.1473-2130.2004.00105.x

45   Chappel, J. N., & DuPont, R. L. (1999). Twelve-step and mutual-help programs for addictive disorders. *Psychiatric Clinics of North America*, 22(2), 425–446. https://doi.org/10.1016/s0193-953x(05)70085-x

46   Chaudhary, S., Singh, A. P., & Varshney, A. (2022). Psychodynamic perspective of sexual obsessions in obsessive-compulsive disorder. *Annals of Neurosciences*, 29(2-3), 159–165. https://doi.org/10.1177/09727531221115305

47   Chen, T., Samaranayake, P., Cen, X., Qi, M., & Lan, Y. (2022). The Impact of Online Reviews on Consumers' Purchasing Decisions: Evidence From an Eye-Tracking Study. *Frontiers in Psychology*, 13. https://doi.org/10.3389/fpsyg.2022.865702

48   Chen, Z., Xing, Y., & Zhang, Z. (2021). The Review of Antisocial Personality Disorder. Advances in Social Science, *Education and Humanities Research*, Volume 586. https://doi.org/10.2991/assehr.k.211020.192

49   Cherry, K. (2022, November 8). What Are Psychological Theories? *Verywell Mind*. Retrieved from https://www.verywellmind.com/what-is-a-theory-2795970

50   Cherry, K. (2022, November 14). What Was the Milgram Experiment? *Verywell Mind*. https://www.verywellmind.com/the-milgram-obedience-experiment-2795243

51   Cherry, K. (2023, December 01). Step 7 of the AA 12-Step Program. *Verywell Mind*. Retrieved from https://www.verywellmind.com/step-7-of-the-aa-12-step-program-5271444

52   Choi, J., & Kim, K. (2021). The relationship between impulsiveness, self-esteem, irrational gambling belief and problem gambling: Moderating effects of gender. *International Journal of Environmental Research and Public Health*, 18(10), 5180. https://doi.org/10.3390/ijerph18105180

53   Choice House. (2020, September 30). I Don't Understand the First Step – What is Unmanageability? *Recovery*. Retrieved from https://choicehousecolorado.com/i-dont-understand-the-first-step-what-is-unmanageability/

54   Chu, B., Marwaha, K., Sanvictores, T., & Ayers, D. (2022). Physiology, stress reaction. In StatPearls. Treasure Island, FL: *StatPearls Publishing*. Available from: https://www.ncbi.nlm.nih.gov/books/NBK541120/

55   Cipriano, A., Cella, S., & Cotrufo, P. (2017). Nonsuicidal self-injury: A systematic review. *Frontiers in Psychology*, 8. https://doi.org/10.3389/fpsyg.2017.01946

56   Cleveland Clinic. (2023, March 16). Addiction. *Cleveland Clinic*. https://my.clevelandclinic.org/health/diseases/6407-addiction

57   Cleveland Clinic. (2023, October 23). Cocaine (Crack). *Cleveland Clinic*. Retrieved from https://my.clevelandclinic.org/health/articles/4038-cocaine-crack

58 Cleveland Clinic medical professional. (2022, April 28). Paranoid Personality Disorder. Retrieved from https://my.clevelandclinic.org/health/diseases/9784 -paranoid-personality-disorder

59 Cleveland Clinic medical professional. (2023, April 18). Hallucinogens. Retrieved from https://my.clevelandclinic.org/health/articles/6734-hallucinogens-lsd-pe yote-psilocybin-and-pcp

60 Cleveland Clinic medical professional. (2023, September 28). Avoidant Personality Disorder. Retrieved from https://my.clevelandclinic.org/health/ diseases/9761-avoidant-personality-disorder

61 Coe, S. D. (2023). The True History of Chocolate [Summary]. Retrieved from https://www.bookey.app/book/the-true-history-of-chocolate#freePdf

62 Contreras, A. (2020, July 22). Your Emotional Brain on Resentment, Part 1. *Psych Central*. Retrieved from https://psychcentral.com/pro/your-emotional-brai n-on-resentment-part-1#1

63 Czarniecka-Skubina, E., Pielak, M., Sałek, P., Korzeniowska-Ginter, R., & Owczarek, T. (2021). Consumer choices and habits related to coffee consumption by Poles. *International Journal of Environmental Research and Public Health*, 18(8), 3948. https://doi.org/10.3390/ijerph18083948

64 DąBrowska, K., Moskalewicz, J., & Wieczorek, Ł. (2017). Barriers in Access to the Treatment for People with Gambling Disorders. Are They Different from Those Experienced by People with Alcohol and/or Drug Dependence? *Journal of Gambling Studies*, 33(2), 487–503. https://doi.org/10.1007/s10899-016-9655-1

65 Daniell, M. (2021, December 30). Gene Simmons uncensored: KISS icon talks vodka, anti-vaxxers and final tour. *Toronto Sun*. Retrieved from https://toron- tosun.com/entertainment/celebrity/gene-simmons-uncensored-kiss-icon-talk s-vodka-anti-vaxxers-and-final-tour

66 Davies, G., Elison, S., Ward, J., & et al. (2015). The role of lifestyle in perpetuating substance use disorder: the Lifestyle Balance Model. *Substance Abuse Treatment, Prevention, and Policy*, 10(1), 2. https://doi.org/10.1186/1747-597X-10-2

67 Davis, C. (2018). Home detox - supporting patients to overcome alcohol addiction. *Australian Prescriber*, 41(6), 180–182. https://doi.org/10.18773/ austprescr.2018.059

68 Davis, J. (2023, May 28). Alcohol Use Disorder: What to Know About Relapse. *WebMD*. https://www.webmd.com/mental-health/addiction/ alcohol-use-disorder-relapse

69 De Leon, G. (2013). Therapeutic Communities. In *Interventions for Addiction*. ISBN: 978-0-12-384885-7.

70 Deering, S., & Blumberg, P. O. (2024, February 1). 50 self-care ideas for when you need a mood boost. *Today.* Retrieved from https://www.today.com/life/inspiration/self-care-ideas-rcna65285

71 Dennis, M., & Scott, C. K. (2007). Managing addiction as a chronic condition. *Addiction Science & Clinical Practice*, 4(1), 45–55. https://doi.org/10.1151/ascp074145

72 Dermatis, H., & Galanter, M. (2016, April). The Role of Twelve-Step-Related Spirituality in Addiction Recovery. *Journal of Relig Health*, 55(2), 510-521. https://doi.org/10.1007/s10943-015-0019-4

73 De Luca, V. (2022, December 27). Understanding how plants produce cocaine. *Proceedings of the National Academy of Sciences*, 119(52), e2218838120. https://doi.org/10.1073/pnas.2218838120

74 DeCamp, W., & Bakken, N. W. (2016). Self-injury, suicide ideation, and sexual orientation: Differences in causes and correlates among high school students. *Journal of Injury & Violence Research*, 8(1), 15–24. https://doi.org/10.5249/jivr.v8i1.545

75 Dhingra, M., & Mudgal, R. (2019). Historical Evolution of Social Media: An Overview. *SSRN Electronic Journal.* https://doi.org/10.2139/ssrn.3395665

76 Diaper, A. M., Law, F. D., & Melichar, J. K. (2014). Pharmacological strategies for detoxification. *British Journal of Clinical Pharmacology*, 77(2), 302–314. https://doi.org/10.1111/bcp.12245

77 Diana, M. (2011). The dopamine hypothesis of drug addiction and its potential therapeutic value. *Frontiers in Psychiatry*, 2, 64. https://doi.org/10.3389/fpsyt.2011.00064

78 Dick, D. M., Smith, G., Olausson, P., Mitchell, S. H., Leeman, R. F., O'Malley, S. S., & Sher, K. (2010). Understanding the construct of impulsivity and its relationship to alcohol use disorders. *Addictive Biology*, 15(2), 217–226. https://doi.org/10.1111/j.1369-1600.2009.00190.x

79 DiClemente, C. C., Bellino, L. E., & Neavins, T. M. (1999). Motivation for change and alcoholism treatment. *Alcohol Research & Health*, 23(2), 86–92.

80 DiFeliceantonio, A. G., Mabrouk, O. S., Kennedy, R. T., & Berridge, K. C. (2012). Enkephalin surges in dorsal neostriatum as a signal to eat. *Current Biology*, 22(20), 1918–1924. https://doi.org/10.1016/j.cub.2012.08.014

81 Dima, R., Tieppo Francio, V., Towery, C., & Davani, S. (2018). Review of literature on low-level laser therapy benefits for nonpharmacological pain control in chronic pain and osteoarthritis. *Alternative Therapies in Health and Medicine*, 24(5), 8-10. PMID: 28987080.

82 Donovan, D. M., Ingalsbe, M. H., Benbow, J., & Daley, D. C. (2013). 12-step interventions and mutual support programs for substance use disorders: An overview. *Social Work in Public Health*, 28(3-4), 313–332. https://doi.org/10.1080/19371918.2013.774663

83 Drewnowski, A., Mennella, J., Johnson, S., & Bellisle, F. (2012). Sweetness and food preference. *The Journal of Nutrition*, 142, 1142S-1148S. https://doi.org/10.3945/jn.111.149575

84 Drug Enforcement Administration. (2023, January). Fentanyl (Trade Names: Actiq®, FentoraTM, Duragesic®). Drug & Chemical Evaluation Section. *Diversion Control Division*. Retrieved from https://www.deadiversion.usdoj.gov/drug_chem_info/fentanyl.pdf

85 Ducci, F., & Goldman, D. (2012). The genetic basis of addictive disorders. *The Psychiatric Clinics of North America*, 35(2), 495–519. https://doi.org/10.1016/j.psc.2012.03.010

86 Duffy, A., Dawson, D. L., & das Nair, R. (2016). Pornography addiction in adults: A systematic review of definitions and reported impact. *Journal of Sexual Medicine*, 13(5), 760-777. https://doi.org/10.1016/j.jsxm.2016.03.002

87 Dwyer, K. (2020, August 18). What is tea culture? Lessons from around the world. *Pique Life*. Retrieved from https://blog.piquelife.com/tea-culture/

88 Editorial Staff. (2023, July 19). Salvia vs. DMT: Effects & Differences. Retrieved from https://oxfordtreatment.com/substance-abuse/hallucinogens/salvia-vs-dmt/

89 Edwards, S., & Koob, G. F. (2013). Escalation of drug self-administration as a hallmark of persistent addiction liability. *Behavioural pharmacology*, 24(5-6), 356–362. https://doi.org/10.1097/FBP.0b013e3283644d15

90 eMedicineHealth. (2022, August 5). Allergic Reaction. Retrieved from https://www.emedicinehealth.com/allergic_reaction/article_em.htm

91 Emini, N. N., & Bond, M. J. (2014). Motivational and psychological correlates of bodybuilding dependence. *Journal of Behavioral Addictions*, 3(3), 182–188. https://doi.org/10.1556/JBA.3.2014.3.6

92 Enoch, M. A. (2012). The influence of gene-environment interactions on the development of alcoholism and drug dependence. *Current Psychiatry Reports*, 14(2), 150–158. https://doi.org/10.1007/s11920-011-0252-9

93 Enoch, M.-A., & Goldman, D. (2002). Problem drinking and alcoholism: Diagnosis and treatment. *American Family Physician*, 65, 441–448.

94 Erasmus, M. S. (2016). The Object Relations of individuals who misuse alcohol and have co-morbid Depressive or Bipolar Disorders and/or Personality

Disorders. Retrieved from https://www.academia.edu/64342117/The_object_relations_of_individuals_who_misuse_alcohol_and_have_co_morbid_depressive_or_bipolar_disorders_and_or_personality_disorders

95 Evidation. (2023, July 26). Self-care activities for mental health: nurturing your mental well-being. https://evidation.com/blog/self-care-activities-for-mental-h ealth-nurturing-your-mental-well-being

96 Fair Oaks Recovery Center. (2017, April 3). What are "Living Amends?" *Fair Oaks Recovery Center Blog*. Retrieved from https://fairoaksrecoverycenter.com/ blog/living-amends/

97 Fariba KA, Gokarakonda SB. (2023, August 14). Impulse Control Disorders. In: StatPearls. Treasure Island (FL): *StatPearls Publishing*. Available from: https:// www.ncbi.nlm.nih.gov/books/NBK562279/

98 Felman, A. (2023, May 31). What is addiction? *Medical News Today*. Retrieved from https://www.medicalnewstoday.com/articles/323465

99 Fitzpatrick, A. P., & Cooper, P. (2006). Diagnosis and management of patients with blackouts. *Heart*, 92(4), 559-568. https://doi.org/10.1136/hrt.2005.068650

100 Fletcher, J. (2022). What to know about hypersexuality. *Medical News Today*. Retrieved from https://www.medicalnewstoday.com/articles/hypersexuality

101 Fong, T. W. (2005). The biopsychosocial consequences of pathological gambling. *Psychiatry (Edgmont (Pa. : Township))*, 2(3), 22–30.

102 Fong, T. W. (2006). Understanding and managing compulsive sexual behaviors. *Psychiatry (Edgmont (Pa. : Township))*, 3(11), 51–58.

103 Fordyce, K. (2023, May 28). Addiction: What Is Denial? *WebMD*. Retrieved from https://www.webmd.com/mental-health/addiction/addiction-what-is-denial

104 Forsström, D., Lindner, P., Månsson, K. N. T., Ojala, O., Hedman-Lagerlöf, M., El Alaoui, S., Rozental, A., Lundin, J., Jangard, S., Shahnavaz, S., Sörman, K., Lundgren, T., & Jayaram-Lindström, N. (2022). Isolation and worry in relation to gambling and onset of gambling among psychiatry patients during the COVID-19 pandemic: A mediation study. *Frontiers in Psychology*, 13, 1045709. https://doi.org/10.3389/fpsyg.2022.1045709

105 Fox, T. P., Oliver, G., & Ellis, S. M. (2013). The destructive capacity of drug abuse: An overview exploring the harmful potential of drug abuse both to the individual and to society. *ISRN Addiction*, 2013, 450348. https://doi. org/10.1155/2013/450348

106 Gateway Foundation. (2021). Gambling and Depression [Mental Health Treatment]. Retrieved from https://www.gatewayfoundation.org/addiction-blog/ problem-gambling/

107 Gateway Foundation. (2022). Most Commonly Abused Prescription Drugs. https://www.gatewayfoundation.org/addiction-blog/most-commonly-abused-prescription-drugs/

108 Gatkine, T., Shete, V., Mahajan, N., & Mahajan, U. (2019). Potential of phyto-constituents as skin tanning agents. *Research Journal of Topical and Cosmetic Sciences*, 10, 34. doi:10.5958/2321-5844.2019.00008.6

109 Gershon, L. (2022, October 19). The Story Behind "This is Your Brain on Drugs." *JSTOR Daily*. Retrieved from https://daily.jstor.org/the-story-behind-this-is-your-brain-on-drugs/

110 Gilliland, R., South, M., Carpenter, B., & Hardy, S. (2011, March 8). The roles of shame and guilt in hypersexual behavior. *Sexual Addiction and Compulsivity*, 18. https://doi.org/10.1080/10720162.2011.551182

111 Glasner-Edwards, S., & Mooney, L. J. (2014). Methamphetamine psychosis: Epidemiology and management. *CNS Drugs*, 28(12), 1115–1126. https://doi.org/10.1007/s40263-014-0209-8

112 Goerling, E., & Wolfe, E. (2022). Introduction to human sexuality: Chapter 16 - Variations in sexual behavior. *Open Oregon Educational Resources*. Retrieved from https://open.umn.edu/opentextbooks/textbooks/1273

113 Goh, C. M. J., Asharani, P. V., Abdin, E., Shahwan, S., Zhang, Y., Sambasivam, R., Vaingankar, J. A., Ma, S., Chong, S. A., & Subramaniam, M. (2022). Gender Differences in Alcohol Use: a Nationwide Study in a Multiethnic Population. *International Journal of Mental Health and Addiction*. https://doi.org/10.1007/s11469-022-00921-y

114 Grant, J. E., & Chamberlain, S. R. (2016). Expanding the definition of addiction: DSM-5 vs. ICD-11. *CNS Spectrums*, 21(4), 300–303. https://doi.org/10.1017/S1092852916000183

115 Grant, J. E., Potenza, M. N., Weinstein, A., & Gorelick, D. A. (2010). Introduction to behavioral addictions. *The American Journal of Drug and Alcohol Abuse*, 36(5), 233–241. https://doi.org/10.3109/00952990.2010.491884

116 Greene, D. (2021). Revisiting 12-Step Approaches: An Evidence-Based Perspective. DOI: 10.5772/intechopen.95985.

117 Griffin, J. B. Jr.. (1990). Loss of Control. In H. K. Walker, W. D. Hall, & J. W. Hurst (Eds.), Clinical Methods: The History, Physical, and Laboratory Examinations (3rd ed., Chapter 204). *Boston: Butterworths*. Retrieved from https://www.ncbi.nlm.nih.gov/books/NBK317/

118 Griffiths, M. D. (2016, May 11). The Myth of the Addictive Personality. *Psychology Today*. Retrieved from https://www.psychologytoday.com/us/blog/in-excess/201605/the-myth-the-addictive-personality

119 Griffiths, M. D., Demetrovics, Z., & Atroszko, P. A. (2018). Ten myths about work addiction. *Journal of Behavioral Addictions*, 7(4), 845–857. https://doi.org/10.1556/2006.7.2018.05

120 Griffiths, M., Kuss, D., & King, D. (2013). Video game addiction: Past, present and future (Vol. 8). *Current Psychiatry Review*.

121 Guenzel, N., & McChargue, D. (2023, July 21). Addiction Relapse Prevention. In StatPearls. Treasure Island (FL): *StatPearls Publishing*. Retrieved from https://www.ncbi.nlm.nih.gov/books/NBK551500/

122 Gupta, M., & Sharma, A. (2021). Fear of missing out: A brief overview of origin, theoretical underpinnings and relationship with mental health. *World Journal of Clinical Cases*, 9(19), 4881–4889. https://doi.org/10.12998/wjcc.v9.i19.4881

123 Gupta, S. (2022, August 19). What Are the 12 Steps of Narcotics Anonymous (NA)? Retrieved from https://www.verywellmind.com/what-are-the-12-steps-of-na-narcotics-anonymous-5525334

124 Gupta, S. (2022, September 30). Substance use vs. substance abuse: What are the differences? *Verywell Mind*. Retrieved from https://www.verywellmind.com/substance-use-vs-substance-use-disorder-whats-the-difference-6385961#citation-2

125 Hagan, E. (2021). Four reasons why individuals engage in self-harm. *Psychology Today*. Retrieved from https://www.psychologytoday.com/us/blog/happiness-is-state-mind/202103/four-reasons-why-individuals-engage-in-self-harm

126 Hagen, A. E. F., Nogueira-Arjona, R., Sherry, S. B., Rodriguez, L. M., Yakovenko, I., & Stewart, S. H. (2023). What explains the link between romantic conflict with gambling problems? Testing a serial mediational model. *Frontiers in Psychology*, 14, 1018098. https://doi.org/10.3389/fpsyg.2023.1018098

127 Hagman, B. T., Falk, D., Litten, R., & Koob, G. F. (2022). Defining recovery from alcohol use disorder: Development of an NIAAA research definition. *The American Journal of Psychiatry*. Advance online publication. https://doi.org/10.1176/appi.ajp.21090963

128 Hakim, R. C., BCCCP, & Hannemann, K. (January 8, 2024). Acetaminophen / Dextromethorphan / Doxylamine. *GoodRx*. Retrieved from https://www.goodrx.com/nyquil/what-is

129 Hanson, D. M. (2007, November). The Meth Lab Menace. *HMP Global Learning Network*. Retrieved from https://www.hmpgloballearningnetwork. com/site/emsworld/article/10321509/meth-lab-menace

130 Hardi, M. (2020). Chocolate and Endorphins. Retrieved from https://remix-snacks.ca/blogs/remix-blog/chocolate-and-endorphin

131 Hartney, E. (2023, August 16). Caffeine addiction symptoms and withdrawal. *Verywell Mind*. Retrieved from https://www.verywellmind.com/caffeine-addiction-4157287

132 Hasanović, M., Kuldija, A., Pajević, I., Jakovljević, M., & Hasanović, M. (2021). Gambling disorder as an addictive disorder and creative psychopharmacotherapy. *Psychiatria Danubina*, 33(Suppl 4), 1118-1129. PMID: 35354178.

133 Hayashida, M. (1998). An overview of outpatient and inpatient detoxification. *Alcohol Health and Research World*, 22(1), 44–46.

134 Heirene, R. M., Shearer, D., Roderique-Davies, G., & Mellalieu, S. D. (2016). Addiction in extreme sports: An exploration of withdrawal states in rock climbers. *Journal of Behavioral Addictions*, 5(2), 332–341. https://doi.org/10.1556/2006.5.2016.039

135 Henden, E., Melberg, H. O., & Røgeberg, O. J. (2013). Addiction: choice or compulsion? *Frontiers in psychiatry*, 4, 77. https://doi.org/10.3389/fpsyt.2013.00077

136 Heyes, C. (2012). New thinking: The evolution of human cognition. Philosophical Transactions of the Royal Society of London. Series B, *Biological Sciences*, 367(1599), 2091–2096. https://doi.org/10.1098/rstb.2012.0111

137 Hinders, D. (2019, September 13). What Is Emotional Sobriety? *Waypoint Recovery Center*. Retrieved from https://waypointrecoverycenter.com/blog/what-is-emotional-sobriety/

138 Hodgman-Korth, M. (2024, January 5). Making Amends in Recovery. *American Addiction Centers*. Retrieved from https://americanaddictioncenters.org/addiction-recovery/making-amends

139 Hoffman, M. (2024, February 12). Counseling and Substance Use Disorders. *WebMD*. https://www.webmd.com/mental-health/addiction/counseling-and-addiction-how-therapy-can-help

140 Hosseinbor, M., Yassini Ardekani, S. M., Bakhshani, S., & Bakhshani, S. (2014). Emotional and social loneliness in individuals with and without substance dependence disorder. *International Journal of High Risk Behaviors and Addiction*, 3(3), e22688. https://doi.org/10.5812/ijhrba.22688

141 Hua, K., Zulkefli, Z., & Lim, C. (2022). Voice of Academia: The Langkawi Island Market Potential for Extreme Outdoor Sports Tourism.

142 Institute of Medicine (US) Committee on Military Nutrition Research; Marriott, B. M. (Editor). (1994). Food components to enhance performance: An evaluation of potential performance-enhancing food components for operational rations. *National Academies Press (US)*. Retrieved from https://www.ncbi.nlm.nih.gov/books/NBK209050/

143 Integrative Life Center. (2021, March 8). Euphoric Recall: What It Is, and How To Deal With It. https://integrativelifecenter.com/treatment-programs/euphoric-recall-what-it-is-and-how-to-deal-with-it/

144 Izul A., Hidayah N., & Lasan B. (2020). Fear of Missing Out (FoMO) in Analysis of Cognitive Behavior Therapy (CBT). https://doi.org/10.2991/assehr.k.201204.040

145 Jacob, D. (2021). Health Risks of Chronic Heavy Drinking. Retrieved from https://www.medicinenet.com/alcohol_abuse_health_risks_pictures_slideshow/article.htm

146 Jain, A., & Yilanli, M. (2023). Bulimia Nervosa. In StatPearls [Internet]. Treasure Island (FL): *StatPearls Publishing*; 2024 Jan-. Available from: https://www.ncbi.nlm.nih.gov/books/NBK562178/

147 Jacques, A., Chaaya, N., Beecher, K., Ali, S. A., Belmer, A., & Bartlett, S. (2019). The impact of sugar consumption on stress-driven, emotional and addictive behaviors. *Neuroscience & Biobehavioral Reviews*, 103. https://doi.org/10.1016/j.neubiorev.2019.05.021

148 Jason, L. A., Majer, J. M., Bobak, T. J., & O'Brien, J. (2022). Medication assisted therapy and recovery homes. *Journal of Prevention & Intervention in the Community*, 50(2), 178–190. https://doi.org/10.1080/10852352.2021.1934940

149 Jaworska, D., & Iwanicka, K. (2024). Exploring the role of fear of missing out in coping and risk-taking among alcohol use disorder and general young adult populations. *Addictive Behaviors Reports*, 19, 100532. https://doi.org/10.1016/j.abrep.2024.100532

150 Jazaeri, S. A., & Habil, M. H. (2012). Reviewing two types of addiction - pathological gambling and substance use. *Indian Journal of Psychological Medicine*, 34(1), 5–11. https://doi.org/10.4103/0253-7176.96147

151 Ji, Y., Liu, S., Xu, H., & Zhang, B. (2023, February 7). The Causes, Effects, and Interventions of Social Media Addiction. *Journal of Education, Humanities and Social Sciences*, 8, 897-903. https://doi.org/10.54097/ehss.v8i.4378

152 Jniene, A., Errguig, L., El Hangouche, A. J., Rkain, H., Aboudrar, S., Ftouh, M., & Dakka, T. (2019). Perception of sleep disturbances due to bedtime use of blue light-emitting devices and its impact on habits and sleep quality

among young medical students. *BioMed Research International*, 2019, 1-8. doi:10.1155/2019/7012350

153 Jones, A. (2022, October 14). Self-care: What is it? Why is it so important for your health? *UAB News*. Retrieved from https://www.uab.edu/news/youcanuse/item/13176-self-care-what-is-it-why-is-it-so-important-for-your-health

154 Judd, D., King, C. R., & Galke, C. (2023). The opioid epidemic: A review of the contributing factors, negative consequences, and best practices. *Cureus*, 15(7), e41621. https://doi.org/10.7759/cureus.41621

155 Kampman, K. M. (2008). The search for medications to treat stimulant dependence. *Addiction Science & Clinical Practice*, 4(2), 28–35. https://doi.org/10.1151/ascp084228

156 Kasia. (2020). 18 Adrenaline Adventures: Activities For The Ultimate Rush. Retrieved from https://kasiawrites.com/adrenaline-adventures-activities-for-bucket-list/

157 Kelly, J. F. (2019, March). E. M. Jellinek's Disease Concept of Alcoholism. *Addiction*, 114(3), 555-559. https://doi.org/10.1111/add.14400

158 Keng, S. L., Smoski, M. J., & Robins, C. J. (2011). Effects of mindfulness on psychological health: A review of empirical studies. *Clinical Psychology Review*, 31(6), 1041–1056. https://doi.org/10.1016/j.cpr.2011.04.006

159 Kessler, T. (2017, September 10). Untreated Alcoholism or the 'Dry Drunk' Syndrome. Retrieved from https://www.thomkesslertherapist.com/blog--articles/untreated-alcoholism-or-the-dry-drunk-syndrome

160 Katz, D. L., Doughty, K., & Ali, A. (2011). Cocoa and chocolate in human health and disease. Antioxidants & Redox Signaling, 15(10), 2779–2811. https://doi.org/10.1089/ars.2010.3697

161 Kazemi, F., & Esmaeili, M. (2010). The role of media on consumer brand choice: A case study of chocolate industry. *International Journal of Business and Management*, 5. https://doi.org/10.5539/ijbm.v5n9p147

162 KidsHealth Medical Experts. (2023). What Is MDMA (Ecstasy)? Retrieved from https://kidshealth.org/en/parents/drugs-ecstasy.html

163 King, D., & Delfabbro, P. (2020). Video game addiction. In *Clinical Psychology of Internet Addiction* (pp. 185-213). 10.1016/B978-0-12-818626-8.00007-4

164 Kleber, H. D. (2007). Pharmacologic treatments for opioid dependence: detoxification and maintenance options. *Dialogues in Clinical Neuroscience*, 9(4), 455–470. https://doi.org/10.31887/DCNS.2007.9.2/hkleber

165 Klonsky, E. D., Victor, S. E., & Saffer, B. Y. (2014). Nonsuicidal self-injury: What we know, and what we need to know. *Canadian Journal*

of Psychiatry. Revue Canadienne de Psychiatrie, 59(11), 565–568. https://doi. org/10.1177/070674371405901101

166 Knoedler, L., Ruppel, F., Kauke-Navarro, M., Obed, D., Wu, M., Prantl, L., Broer, P. N., Panayi, A. C., & Knoedler, S. (2023). Hair transplantation in the United States: A population-based survey of female and male pattern baldness. Plastic and Reconstructive Surgery. *Global Open*, 11(11), e5386. https://doi. org/10.1097/GOX.0000000000005386

167 Koomson, I., Churchill, S. A., & Munyanyi, M. E. (2022). Gambling and financial stress. *Social Indicators Research*, 163, 473–503. https://doi.org/10.1007/ s11205-022-02898-6

168 Kosut, M. (2015). Tattoos and body modification. *International Encyclopedia of the Social & Behavioral Sciences*, 2nd edition, 24, 32–38. https://doi.org/10.1016/ B978-0-08-097086-8.64027-8

169 Kuldip Singh, M., & Samah, N. (2018). Impact of Smartphone: A Review on Positive and Negative Effects on Students. *Asian Social Science*, 14, 83. doi:10.5539/ass.v14n11p83

170 Kumar, H., & Aagrwal, M. (2023). Filtering the reality: Exploring the dark and bright sides of augmented reality–based filters on social media. *Australian Journal of Management*. Advance online publication. https://doi. org/10.1177/03128962231199356

171 Kyle, D., & Mahler, H. I. M. (1996). The effects of hair color and cosmetics use on perceptions of a female's ability. *Psychology of Women Quarterly*, 20(3), 447-455.

172 Lampe, L., & Malhi, G. S. (2018). Avoidant personality disorder: Current insights. *Psychology Research and Behavior Management*, 11, 55–66. https://doi. org/10.2147/PRBM.S121073

173 Laurence, E. (2023). The psychology behind the fear of missing out (FOMO). *Forbes*. Retrieved from https://www.forbes.com/health/mind/ the-psychology-behind-fomo/

174 Latvala, T., Lintonen, T., & Konu, A. (2019). Public health effects of gambling – debate on a conceptual model. *BMC Public Health*, 19, 1077. https://doi. org/10.1186/s12889-019-7391-z

175 Latvala, T. A., Lintonen, T. P., Browne, M., Rockloff, M., & Salonen, A. H. (2021). Social disadvantage and gambling severity: A population-based study with register-linkage. *European Journal of Public Health*, 31(6), 1217–1223. https://doi.org/10.1093/eurpub/ckab162

176 Lee, H., Roh, S., & Kim, D. J. (2009). Alcohol-induced blackout. *International Journal of Environmental Research and Public Health*, 6(11), 2783–2792. https://doi.org/10.3390/ijerph6112783

177 Lelonek-Kuleta, B., & Bartczuk, R. P. (2021). Coping Strategies and Motivation to Play Determinants of Behavioral Patterns of Playing Pay-to-Win Games. https://doi.org/10.31234/osf.io/t86er

178 Liappis, E., Papadeli, C., Tselekidou, E., Chaidemenos, I., Korsavvidis, D., & General Dentist. (2024). FOMO Social Phenomenon: How and to What Extent Does It Affect Dental Students? A 2022 Research. *Global Journal of Clinical Medicine and Medical Research (GJCMMR)*. ISSN: 2583-987X

179 Ling, R. (2004). The Mobile Connection: The Cell Phone's Impact on Society. ISBN: 1558609369.

180 Locke, A., & Arnocky, S. (2020). Eating disorders. In *Encyclopedia of Evolutionary Psychological Science* (pp. 1-8). https://doi.org/10.1007/978-3-319-16999-6_696-1

181 Lockett, E. (2023, June 16). What research says about the long-term effects of MDMA use. *Healthline*. Retrieved from https://www.healthline.com/health/substance-use/mdma-long-term-effects

182 Long, T., & Cooke, F. L. (2023). Advancing the field of employee assistance programs research and practice: A systematic review of quantitative studies and future research agenda. *Human Resource Management Review*, 33(2), 100941. https://doi.org/10.1016/j.hrmr.2022.100941

183 Loy, J. K., Seitz, N. N., Bye, E. K., Dietze, P., Kilian, C., Manthey, J., Raitasalo, K., Soellner, R., Trolldal, B., Törrönen, J., & Kraus, L. (2021, October 18). Changes in Alcoholic Beverage Choice and Risky Drinking among Adolescents in Europe 1999-2019. *International Journal of Environmental Research and Public Health*, 18(20), 10933. https://doi.org/10.3390/ijerph182010933

184 Lu, X., Watanabe, J., Liu, Q., Uji, M., Shono, M., & Kitamura, T. (2011). Internet and mobile phone text-messaging dependency: Factor structure and correlation with dysphoric mood among Japanese adults. *Computers in Human Behavior*, 27, 1702-1709. Retrieved from https://api.semanticscholar.org/CorpusID:19610431

185 Lüscher, C., Robbins, T. W., & Everitt, B. J. (2020). The transition to compulsion in addiction. Nature reviews. *Neuroscience*, 21(5), 247–263. https://doi.org/10.1038/s41583-020-0289-z

186 Ma, X., Nan, F., Liang, H., Shu, P., Fan, X., Song, X., Hou, Y., & Zhang, D. (2022). Excessive intake of sugar: An accomplice of inflammation. *Frontiers in Immunology*, 13, 988481. https://doi.org/10.3389/fimmu.2022.988481

187 Ma, Z., Liu, Y., Wan, C., & et al. (2022). Health-related quality of life and influencing factors in drug addicts based on the scale QLICD-DA: a cross-sectional study. *Health and Quality of Life Outcomes*, 20(1), 109. https://doi.org/10.1186/s12955-022-02012-x

188 MacKey, B. (2020, October 29). The Addiction Cycle. *Rehab 4 Addiction*. Retrieved from https://www.rehab4addiction.co.uk/resources/addiction-cycle

189 Maffetone, P. B., & Laursen, P. B. (2017). The prevalence of overfat adults and children in the US. *Frontiers in Public Health*, 5, 290. https://doi.org/10.3389/fpubh.2017.00290

190 Maguire, L. C. (1922). Nymphomania. *The Veterinary Journal*, 78(8), 272-283. https://doi.org/10.1016/S0372-5545(17)53017-5.

191 Mann, K., Hermann, D., & Heinz, A. (2000). One hundred years of alcoholism: The twentieth century. *Alcohol and Alcoholism*, 35(1), 10–15. https://doi.org/10.1093/alcalc/35.1.10

192 Marcucci, M. C., Ferreira da Silva, A. G., Gonçalves, C. P., Sawaya, A. C. H. F., Alonso, R. C. B., Oliveira, M. M. de, & Barbin, D. F. (2021). Quality parameters, caffeine and theobromine contents and antioxidant activity of artisan and commercial chocolate from Brazil. *Open Access Library Journal*, 8(5). https://doi.org/10.4236/oalib.1107377

193 Marionneau, V., & Nikkinen, J. (2022). Gambling-related suicides and suicidality: A systematic review of qualitative evidence. *Frontiers in Psychiatry*, 13, 980303. https://doi.org/10.3389/fpsyt.2022.980303

194 Marwah, M., Kerure, A., & Marwah, G. (2021). Microblading and the science behind it. *Indian Dermatology Online Journal*, 12(1), 6-11. https://doi.org/10.4103/idoj.IDOJ_230_20

195 Mars, S. G., Bourgois, P., Karandinos, G., Montero, F., & Ciccarone, D. (2016). The Textures of Heroin: User Perspectives on "Black Tar" and Powder Heroin in Two US Cities. *Journal of Psychoactive Drugs*, 48(4), 270–278. https://doi.org/10.1080/02791072.2016.1207826

196 Mayo Clinic. (2024). Cold sore. Retrieved from https://www.mayoclinic.org/diseases-conditions/cold-sore/multimedia/cold-sore-/img-20005981

197 Mayo Clinic Staff. (2021, June 19). Social anxiety disorder (social phobia). *Mayo Clinic*. Retrieved from https://www.mayoclinic.org/diseases-conditions/social-anxiety-disorder/symptoms-causes/syc-20353561

198 Mayo Clinic Staff. (2022). Cosmetic surgery. *Mayo Clinic*. Retrieved from https://www.mayoclinic.org/tests-procedures/cosmetic-surgery/about/pac-20385138

199 Mayo Clinic Staff. (2022). Drug addiction (substance use disorder). *Mayo Clinic*. https://www.mayoclinic.org/diseases-conditions/drug-addiction/symptoms-causes/syc-20365112

200 Mayo Clinic Staff. (2022, August 5). Allergies. *Mayo Clinic*. Retrieved from https://www.mayoclinic.org/diseases-conditions/allergies/symptoms-causes/syc-20351497

201 Mayo Clinic Staff. (2023, December 21). Obsessive-compulsive disorder (OCD). *Mayo Clinic*. https://www.mayoclinic.org/diseases-conditions/obsessive-compulsive-disorder/symptoms-causes/syc-20354432

202 McDonough, B. (2020, October 7). Higher Power: Can Faith Really Help You Get Through Rehab? *Holdfast Recovery Blog*. Retrieved from https://www.holdfastrecovery.com/blog/2020/october/higher-power-can-faith-really-help-you-get-throu/

203 Melmer, A., Kempf, P., & Laimer, M. (2018). The role of physical exercise in obesity and diabetes. *Praxis*, 107, 971-976. https://doi.org/10.1024/1661-8157/a003065

204 Melemis, S. M. (2015). Relapse Prevention and the Five Rules of Recovery. *The Yale Journal of Biology and Medicine*, 88(3), 325–332.

205 Meredith, S. E., Juliano, L. M., Hughes, J. R., & Griffiths, R. R. (2013). Caffeine use disorder: A comprehensive review and research agenda. *Journal of Caffeine Research*, 3(3), 114–130. https://doi.org/10.1089/jcr.2013.0016

206 Mestre-Bach, G., Steward, T., Granero, R., Fernández-Aranda, F., Talón-Navarro, M. T., Cuquerella, À., Baño, M., Moragas, L., Del Pino-Gutiérrez, A., Aymamí, N., Gómez-Peña, M., Mallorquí-Bagué, N., Vintró-Alcaraz, C., Magaña, P., Menchón, J. M., & Jiménez-Murcia, S. (2018). Gambling and impulsivity traits: A recipe for criminal behavior? *Frontiers in Psychiatry*, 9, 6. https://doi.org/10.3389/fpsyt.2018.00006

207 Miller, L. (2024). How to Stop Drinking: Benefits of Quitting Alcohol. *American Addiction Centers*. https://americanaddictioncenters.org/alcohol/quitting-benefits

208 Minowa, Y., & Belk, R. W. (Eds.). (2018). Gifts, Romance, and Consumer Culture (1st ed.). *Routledge*. https://doi.org/10.4324/9781315144658

209 Mishra, M. (Reviewed by). (2023, February 14). John Bonham | Alcohol poisoning death. *Ark Behavioral Health*. https://www.arkbh.com/celebrity-deaths/musicians/john-bonham/

210 Misra, V., Shrivastava, A., Shukla, S., & Ansari, M. I. (2016). Effect of sugar intake towards human health. *Journal of Medical Sciences and Health*. doi:10.21276/sjm.2016.1.2.2

211 Minnesota Department of Health. (2022, August 11). New study shows economic and social impact of excessive drinking in Minnesota. Retrieved from https://www.health.state.mn.us/news/pressrel/2022/alcohol081122.html

212 Mongkonkansai, J., Madardam, A. P. U., & Veerasakul, S. (2020). Smartphone Usage Posture (Sitting and Lying Down) and Musculoskeletal Symptoms among school-aged children (6-12 years old) in Nakhon Si Thammarat, Thailand. doi:10.21203/rs.3.rs-51245/v1

213 Mosel, S. (2024, March 4). Mental Effects of Alcohol: Effects of Alcohol on the Brain. *American Addiction Centers*. Retrieved from https://americanaddictioncenters.org/alcohol/risks-effects-dangers/mental

214 Moutier, C. (2023). Nonsuicidal self-injury (NSSI). *American Foundation for Suicide Prevention*. Retrieved from https://www.merckmanuals.com/professional/psychiatric-disorders/suicidal-behavior-and-self-injury/nonsuicidal-self-injury-nssi

215 Muratovic, N. (2023). Porn addiction and productivity: Understanding the link. Retrieved from https://americanaddictioncentersreviews.com/porn-addiction-and-productivity/

216 Mundada, P., Kohler, R., Boudabbous, S., Toutous Trellu, L., Platon, A., & Becker, M. (2017). Injectable facial fillers: Imaging features, complications, and diagnostic pitfalls at MRI and PET CT. *Insights into Imaging*, 8(6), 557–572. https://doi.org/10.1007/s13244-017-0575-0

217 Manwarren Generes, W. (Ed.). (2024, March 1). How to Get Sober: A Guide to Sobriety. *American Addiction Centers*. Retrieved from https://americanaddictioncenters.org/sobriety-guide

218 Milosevic, T. (2011). Workaholism in America: A European's Perspective. *HuffPost*. Retrieved from https://www.huffpost.com/entry/workaholism-america-europe_b_805975

219 Murray, K. (2023, August 16). Achieving Transformation Through Rehab. *RehabSpot*. Retrieved from https://www.rehabspot.com/treatment/spiritual/transformation/

220 National Academies of Sciences, Engineering, and Medicine; Health and Medicine Division; Food and Nutrition Board; Committee to Review the Process to Update the Dietary Guidelines for Americans. (2017). Redesigning the Process for Establishing the Dietary Guidelines for Americans. Washington,

DC: *National Academies Press*. Retrieved from https://www.ncbi.nlm.nih.gov/books/NBK469839/

221 National Cancer Institute. (2023). Complementary and Alternative Medicine. Retrieved from https://www.cancer.gov/about-cancer/treatment/cam

222 National Institute on Alcohol Abuse and Alcoholism. (2023, February). Interrupted Memories: Alcohol-Induced Blackouts. Alcohol's Effects on Health.

223 National Institute on Drug Abuse. (2011). Prescription drug abuse (NIH Publication No. 11-4881). Retrieved from https://nida.nih.gov/sites/default/files/rxreportfinalprint.pdf

224 National Institute on Drug Abuse. (2021, April 12). Is nicotine addictive? Retrieved from https://nida.nih.gov/publications/research-reports/tobacco-nicotine-e-cigarettes/nicotine-addictive

225 National Institute on Drug Abuse. (2021, April 13). What are the effects of MDMA? Retrieved from https://nida.nih.gov/publications/research-reports/mdma-ecstasy-abuse/what-are-effects-mdma

226 National Institute on Drug Abuse. (2023, May 30). Preface. Retrieved from https://nida.nih.gov/research-topics/addiction-science/drugs-brain-behavior-science-of-addiction (Accessed 7 Mar. 2024).

227 Nasser, J., Bradley, L., Leitzsch, J., Chohan, O., Fasulo, K., Haller, J., Jaeger, K., Szulanczyk, B., & Parigi, A. (2011). Psychoactive effects of tasting chocolate and desire for more chocolate. *Physiology & Behavior*, 104, 117–121. https://doi.org/10.1016/j.physbeh.2011.04.040

228 Nash, J. (2022, August 1). What Is Behavior Therapy? Your Ultimate Practitioner's Guide. *Positive Psychology*. Retrieved from https://positivepsychology.com/behavior-therapy/

229 NIAAA. (2021). The cycle of alcohol addiction. https://www.niaaa.nih.gov/publications/cycle-alcohol-addiction

230 NIAAA Spectrum. (2023, May 22). Alcohol and other substance use to cope with social anxiety. *NIAAA Spectrum*, 15(2). https://www.niaaa.nih.gov/news-events/research-update/alcohol-and-other-substance-use-cope-social-anxiety

231 NIDA. (2018, June 6). Understanding Drug Use and Addiction DrugFacts. *National Institute on Drug Abuse*. Retrieved from https://nida.nih.gov/publications/drugfacts/understanding-drug-use-addiction

232 NIDA. (2021). Is marijuana addictive?. Retrieved from https://nida.nih.gov/publications/research-reports/marijuana/marijuana-addictive on 2024, March 21

233 NIDA. (2021, April 13). Why is there comorbidity between substance use disorders and mental illnesses? *National Institute on Drug Abuse*. Retrieved

from https://nida.nih.gov/publications/research-reports/common-comorbiditie
s-substance-use-disorders/why-there-comorbidity-between-substance-us
e-disorders-mental-illnesses

234 NIDA. (2022, December 19). What are the short- and long-term effects of inhalant use? Retrieved from https://nida.nih.gov/publications/research-reports/
inhalants/what-are-short-long-term-effects-inhalant-use

235 NIDA. (2022, September 27). Part 1: The Connection Between Substance
Use Disorders and Mental Illness. Retrieved from https://nida.nih.gov/publi-
cations/research-reports/common-comorbidities-substance-use-disorders/part-
1-connection-between-substance-use-disorders-mental-illness

236 NIDA. (2023). Is marijuana a gateway drug?. Retrieved from https://nida.nih.
gov/publications/research-reports/marijuana/marijuana-gateway-drug on 2024,
March 21

237 NIDA. (2023, September 25). Treatment and Recovery. Retrieved from
https://nida.nih.gov/publications/drugs-brains-behavior-science-addiction/
treatment-recovery

238 NIDA. (2024, January 5). Drug Misuse and Addiction. *National Institute
on Drug Abuse*. Retrieved from https://nida.nih.gov/publications/drugs-brain
s-behavior-science-addiction/drug-misuse-addiction

239 Niemiec, R. (2020, April 20). What Does Spirituality Mean To You? Via
Character Blog. Retrieved from https://www.viacharacter.org/topics/articles/
what-does-spirituality-mean-to-you

240 Nikolic, A., Bukurov, B., Kocic, I., Vukovic, M., Ladjevic, N., Vrhovac, M.,
Pavlović, Z., Grujicic, J., Kisic, D., & Sipetic, S. (2023). Smartphone addiction,
sleep quality, depression, anxiety, and stress among medical students. *Frontiers
in public health*, 11, 1252371. https://doi.org/10.3389/fpubh.2023.1252371

241 National Institute on Drug Abuse (NIDA). (2022, March 22). Drugs and the
Brain. Retrieved from https://nida.nih.gov/publications/drugs-brains-behavio
r-science-addiction/drugs-brain

242 NIDA. (2021). What are the treatments for heroin use disorder?. Retrieved from
https://nida.nih.gov/publications/research-reports/heroin/what-are-treatment
s-heroin-use-disorder

243 NIAAA. (2023). Drinking Levels Defined. Alcohol's Effects on Health. Retrieved
from https://www.niaaa.nih.gov/alcohol-health/overview-alcohol-consumption/
moderate-binge-drinking

244 National Research Council (US) Committee on the Social and Economic
Impact of Pathological Gambling. (1999). Pathological Gambling: A Critical

Review. Washington (DC): *National Academies Press (US)*. Available from: https://www.ncbi.nlm.nih.gov/books/NBK230628/

245 Nyrhinen, J., Lonka, K., Sirola, A., Ranta, M., & Wilska, T. A. (2023). Young adults' online shopping addiction: The role of self-regulation and smartphone use. *International Journal of Consumer Studies*. https://doi.org/10.1111/ijcs.12961

246 Office of National Drug Control Policy. (2024). Congressional Budget Submission FY 2024. Retrieved from https://www.whitehouse.gov/wp-content/uploads/2023/03/FY-2024-ONDCP-CONGRESSIONAL-BUDGET-SUBMISSION-FINAL.pdf

247 Okechukwu, C. E. (2021). Does frequent pornography use adversely affect men's sexual health? A call for clinical investigation. https://doi.org/10.4103/MTSM.MTSM_20_20

248 Onifade, T. (2022, January 5). Effects of Social Media Validation. *Journal of Social Media Studies*, 1.

249 Osborn, C. O. (2023). How do muscle and fat affect weight? [Reviewed by Jake Tipane, CPT]. *Healthline*. Retrieved from https://www.healthline.com/health/does-muscle-weigh-more-than-fat

250 Osna, N. A., & Kharbanda, K. K. (2016). Multi-Organ Alcohol-Related Damage: Mechanisms and Treatment. *Biomolecules*, 6(2), 20. https://doi.org/10.3390/biom6020020

251 Oxford Treatment Center. (2023). Common Drug Withdrawal Symptoms. Edited by L. Close & Reviewed by R. Kelley, *NREMT*. Retrieved from https://oxfordtreatment.com/addiction-treatment/detox/withdrawal-symptoms/

252 Padovano, H. T., Levak, S., Vadhan, N. P., Kuerbis, A., & Morgenstern, J. (2022, March). The Role of Daily Goal Setting Among Individuals with Alcohol Use Disorder. *Drug and Alcohol Dependence Reports*, 2, 100036. https://doi.org/10.1016/j.dadr.2022.100036

253 Palmer, C. (2021, September 15). How Drug and Alcohol Addiction Impacts Your Mind, Body, and Health. *GoodRx*. https://www.goodrx.com/conditions/substance-use-disorder/physical-neurological-effects-of-addiction

254 Pantiel, T. (2024, January 9). Inpatient Vs. Outpatient Rehab. *Addiction Center*. Retrieved from https://www.addictioncenter.com/treatment/inpatient-outpatient-rehab/

255 Pantiel, T. (2023, October 26). Holistic Therapy. Retrieved from https://www.addictioncenter.com/treatment/holistic-therapy/

256 Parhami, I., Siani, A., Rosenthal, R. J., Lin, S., Collard, M., & Fong, T. W. (2012). Sleep and gambling severity in a community sample of gamblers.

Journal of Addictive Diseases, 31(1), 67–79. https://doi.org/10.1080/10550887.2011.642754

257 Parhami, I., Siani, A., Rosenthal, R. J., & Fong, T. W. (2013). Pathological gambling, problem gambling and sleep complaints: An analysis of the National Comorbidity Survey: Replication (NCS-R). *Journal of Gambling Studies*, 29(2), 241–253. https://doi.org/10.1007/s10899-012-9299-8

258 Parker, G. (2006). Mood state effects of chocolate. *Journal of Affective Disorders*. https://doi.org/10.1016/j.jad.2006.02.007

259 Paton, A. (2005). Alcohol in the body. BMJ (Clinical Research Ed.), 330(7482), 85–87. https://doi.org/10.1136/bmj.330.7482.85

260 Patterson, E. (2024, February 9). Penalties and Sentencing for Drug Abuse, Selling, and Smuggling in the USA. *DrugAbuse.com*. https://drugabuse.com/addiction/drug-abuse/penalties/

261 Pedersen, T. (2023, December 1). What is a controlled substance? *Healthline.* Retrieved from https://www.healthline.com/health/what-is-a-controlled-substance

262 Peirce, R. S., Frone, M. R., Russell, M., & Cooper, M. L. (1994). Relationship of Financial Strain and Psychosocial Resources to Alcohol Use and Abuse: The Mediating Role of Negative Affect and Drinking Motives. *Journal of Health and Social Behavior*, 35(4), 291–308. https://doi.org/10.2307/2137211

263 Perry, E. (2022). How to use fear as a motivator. *BetterUp*. Retrieved from https://www.betterup.com/blog/fear-as-a-motivator

264 Petry, N. M., Zajac, K., & Ginley, M. K. (2018). Behavioral Addictions as Mental Disorders: To Be or Not To Be?. *Annual Review of Clinical Psychology*, 14, 399–423. https://doi.org/10.1146/annurev-clinpsy-032816-045120

265 Picard, G. (2023). 50 Best Adrenaline Activities for Thrillseekers. Retrieved from https://tourscanner.com/blog/best-adrenaline-activities/

266 Pierce, J. P. (2022). Quitting smoking by age 35 years—A goal for reducing mortality. *JAMA Network Open*, 5(10), e2231487. doi:10.1001/jamanetworkopen.2022.31487

267 Pilver, C. E., & Potenza, M. N. (2013). Increased incidence of cardiovascular conditions among older adults with pathological gambling features in a prospective study. *Journal of Addiction Medicine*, 7(6), 387–393. https://doi.org/10.1097/ADM.0b013e31829e9b36

268 Pittman, G. (2010, September 29). Can lasers help you stop smoking? Check the data. *Reuters*. Retrieved from https://www.reuters.com/article/idUSTRE68S3TM/

269 Polk, S. E., Schulte, E. M., Furman, C. R., & Gearhardt, A. N. (2017). Wanting and liking: Separable components in problematic eating behavior? *Appetite*, 115, 45–53. https://doi.org/10.1016/j.appet.2016.11.015

270 Poison & Drug Information Service, Alberta Health Services. (2023, June 1). Substance use: Common drugs. *Alberta Health Services*. Retrieved from https://myhealth.alberta.ca/Alberta/Pages/Substance-use-caffeine.aspx

271 Pongsavee, K., Payakkakom, A., Phukao, D., & Guadamuz, T. E. (2023). Natural recovery from alcohol: A systematic review of the literature 2006–2019. *Journal of Substance Use*, 28(2), 166-171. https://doi.org/10.1080/14659891.2021.2020348

272 Popescu, A., Marian, M., Drăgoi, A. M., & Costea, R. V. (2021). Understanding the genetics and neurobiological pathways behind addiction (Review). *Experimental and Therapeutic Medicine*, 21(5), 544. https://doi.org/10.3892/etm.2021.9976

273 Power of Positivity. (2017). 10 Behaviors Of An Egomaniac (And How To Avoid Having Them). Retrieved from https://www.powerofpositivity.com/egomaniac-behaviors/

274 Powers, A. R., 3rd, Gancsos, M. G., Finn, E. S., Morgan, P. T., & Corlett, P. R. (2015). Ketamine-Induced Hallucinations. *Psychopathology*, 48(6), 376–385. https://doi.org/10.1159/000438675

275 Pozza, A., Albert, U., & Dèttore, D. (2019). Perfectionism and Intolerance of Uncertainty are Predictors of OCD Symptoms in Children and Early Adolescents: A Prospective, Cohort, One-Year, Follow-Up Study. *Clinical Neuropsychiatry*, 16(1), 53–61.

276 Pozza, A., Coluccia, A., Gualtieri, G., Carabellese, F., Masti, A., & Ferretti, F. (2020). Post-traumatic stress disorder secondary to manic episodes with hypersexuality in bipolar disorder: A case study of forensic psychotherapy. *Clinical Neuropsychiatry*, 17(3), 181–188. https://doi.org/10.36131/cnfioritieditore20200306

277 Privara, M., & Bob, P. (2023). Pornography consumption and cognitive-affective distress. *The Journal of Nervous and Mental Disease*, 211(8), 641–646. https://doi.org/10.1097/NMD.0000000000001669

278 Professor Buzzkill. (2017, May 29). Albert Einstein: The definition of insanity is doing the same thing over and over and expecting different results. Retrieved from https://professorbuzzkill.com/2017/05/29/einstein-insanity-qnq/

279 Ramos-Matos, C. F., Bistas, K. G., & Lopez-Ojeda, W. (2023, May 29). Fentanyl. In StatPearls. Treasure Island (FL): *StatPearls Publishing.* Retrieved from https://www.ncbi.nlm.nih.gov/books/NBK459275/

280 Rausch, A. (2023, December 29). The Angry Drunk: How Alcohol, Rage, & Aggression Are Connected. Retrieved from https://www.choosingtherapy.com/angry-drunk/

281 Raypole, C. (2019). How to Tell if You're an Adrenaline Junkie. *Healthline.* Retrieved from https://www.healthline.com/health/adrenaline-junkie

282 Rehm, J. (2011). The risks associated with alcohol use and alcoholism. *Alcohol Research & Health,* 34(2), 135–143. PMID: 22330211; PMCID: PMC3307043.

283 Roberts, G., & Wolfson, P. (2004, January 1). The rediscovery of recovery: Open to all. *Advances in Psychiatric Treatment,* 10(1), 37-48. https://doi.org/10.1192/apt.10.1.37

284 Rosenfield, M. (2016). Computer vision syndrome (a.k.a. digital eye strain). *Optometry in Practice,* 17, 1-10.

285 Rowden, A. (2021). What is an adrenaline junkie? *Medical News Today.* Retrieved from https://www.medicalnewstoday.com/articles/adrenaline-junkie

286 Russell, K. R., & Hartung, S. Q. (2016). Identifying the signs of self-harm in students. *NASN School Nurse,* 31(2), 121–124. https://doi.org/10.1177/1942602X15574776

287 Rutgers Researchers Delve Deep Into the Genetics of Addiction. (2022, November 9). Retrieved from https://ritms.rutgers.edu/news/rutgers-researchers-delve-deep-into-the-genetics-of-addiction/

288 Sadava, S. W., Thistle, R., & Forsyth, R. (1978). Stress, escapism and patterns of alcohol and drug use. *Journal of Studies on Alcohol,* 39(5), 725-736. https://doi.org/10.15288/jsa.1978.39.725

289 Saitz, R. (1998). Introduction to alcohol withdrawal. *Alcohol Health and Research World,* 22(1), 5–12. PMID: 15706727; PMCID: PMC6761824.

290 Salma, H. (2014). Online Shopping Addiction: The Case of Malaysian Youth Consumers. Retrieved from https://www.academia.edu/9954154/Online_Shopping_Addiction_The_Case_of_Malaysian_Youth_Consumers_2014

291 Santos-Longhurst, A. (2022, February 17). Opiate vs. Opioid: What's the Difference? *Healthline.* Retrieved from https://www.healthline.com/health/opiate-vs-opioid

292 Sarwer, D. B., & Crerand, C. E. (2008). Body dysmorphic disorder and appearance enhancing medical treatments. *Body Image,* 5(1), 50-58. https://doi.org/10.1016/j.bodyim.2007.08.003

293 Scholten, W., Ten Have, M., van Geel, C., van Balkom, A., de Graaf, R., & Batelaan, N. (2023). Recurrence of anxiety disorders and its predictors in the general population. *Psychological Medicine*, 53(4), 1334–1342. https://doi.org/10.1017/S0033291721002877

294 Schrader, J. (2016, May 12). Adrenaline addiction. *Psychology Today*. https://www.psychologytoday.com/us/blog/how-do-life/201605/adrenaline-addiction

295 Schuckit, M. A. (1996). Alcohol, Anxiety, and Depressive Disorders. *Alcohol Health and Research World*, 20(2), 81–85.

296 Seçuk, B., & Seçim, Y. (2024). Concept of artisan chocolate from the perspective of chocolatiers. *International Journal of Food Design*, 9, 27-52. https://doi.org/10.1386/ijfd_00064_1

297 Shafi, A., Berry, A. J., Sumnall, H., Wood, D. M., & Tracy, D. K. (2022). Synthetic opioids: A review and clinical update. *Therapeutic Advances in Psychopharmacology*, 12, 20451253221139616. https://doi.org/10.1177/20451253221139616

298 Sharma, R., Tyagi, P., Singh, U., Khatter, A., Sharma, A., & Kumar, K. (2020). Exploring shopaholics' attitudes and behaviors: A dose, defense, or disorder? *Indian Journal of Health Social Work*.

299 Sharp, A. (2024, February 21). The legal consequences of alcohol misuse. *American Addiction Centers*. https://americanaddictioncenters.org/alcohol/legal-consequences

300 Sharpe, M., & Mead, D. (2021). Problematic pornography use: Legal and health policy considerations. *Current Addiction Reports*, 8(4), 556–567. https://doi.org/10.1007/s40429-021-00390-8

301 Shoukat, S. (2019). Cell phone addiction and psychological and physiological health in adolescents. *EXCLI Journal*, 18, 47–50.

302 Sheehy, K., Noureen, A., Khaliq, A., Dhingra, K., Husain, N., Pontin, E. E., Cawley, R., & Taylor, P. J. (2019). An examination of the relationship between shame, guilt and self-harm: A systematic review and meta-analysis. *Clinical Psychology Review*, 73, 101779. https://doi.org/10.1016/j.cpr.2019.101779

303 Siegel, A. (2024). Role of adrenaline in addiction: Definition, function, production, release, and its connection to addiction. *Olympic Behavioral Health*. Retrieved from https://olympicbehavioralhealth.com/rehab-blog/adrenaline-in-addiction/

304 Sindi, S. A., Alghamdi, M. K., Sindi, E. E., Bondagji, M. F., Baashar, D. S., Malibary, J. A., & Alkot, M. M. (2023). The prevalence and characteristics of body dysmorphic disorder among adults in Makkah City, Saudi

Arabia: A cross-sectional study. *Cureus*, 15(2), e35316. https://doi.org/10.7759/cureus.35316

305 Sissons, B. (November 28, 2023). Everything you need to know about nicotine. *Medical News Today*. Retrieved from https://www.medicalnewstoday.com/articles/240820

306 Sloan, E. (2021). How To Differentiate Between a Pathological and Compulsive Liar—And Navigate a Relationship With Either One. *Well+Good*. Retrieved from https://www.wellandgood.com/difference-between-compulsive-pathological-liar/

307 Sloan, F. A. (2020, February). Drinking and Driving. *NBER Working Paper Series*. Paper No. 26779. Retrieved from https://www.nber.org/system/files/working_papers/w26779/w26779.pdf

308 Smith, M., Robinson, L., & Segal, J. (2024, February 5). Overcoming Alcohol Addiction. *HelpGuide*. https://www.helpguide.org/articles/addictions/overcoming-alcohol-addiction.htm

309 Smarmore Rehab Clinic. (2024, January 23). The Importance of Boundaries in Addiction Recovery. Retrieved from https://www.smarmore-rehab-clinic.com/addiction-resources/boundaries-in-addiction-recovery/

310 Smiddy, C. (2020, October 8). How to Make Amends in Addiction Recovery. *Hired Power*. Retrieved from https://www.hiredpower.com/blog/how-to-make-amends-in-addiction-recovery/

311 Smit, H., Gaffan, E., & Rogers, P. (2004). Methylxanthines are the psycho-pharmacologically active constituents of chocolate. *Psychopharmacology*, 176(3-4), 412-419. https://doi.org/10.1007/s00213-004-1898-3

312 Smith Haghighi, A. (2022, May 24). What is 'dry drunk syndrome,' and whom does it affect? *Medical News Today*. Retrieved from https://www.medicalnewstoday.com/articles/dry-drunk-syndrome

313 Spero Recovery. (2024, January 22). The Power in the First Step: Accepting Powerlessness. Retrieved from https://www.sperorecovery.org/the-power-in-the-first-step-accepting-powerlessness/

314 Striley, C. L., Griffiths, R. R., & Cottler, L. B. (2011). Evaluating dependence criteria for caffeine. *Journal of Caffeine Research*, 1(4), 219–225. https://doi.org/10.1089/jcr.2011.0029

315 Stuart, A., & Booth, S. (2023, September 28). Caffeine myths and facts. *WebMD*. Retrieved from https://www.webmd.com/diet/caffeine-myths-and-facts

316 Substance Abuse and Mental Health Services Administration (US). (2006). Detoxification and Substance Abuse Treatment. *Treatment Improvement Protocol*

(TIP) Series, No. 45. Rockville, MD. Retrieved from https://www.ncbi.nlm.nih.gov/books/NBK64116/

317 Suescun, L. (2021, April 1). *International Tables for Crystallography*, Volume H, Powder Diffraction. First edition. Edited by C. J. Gilmore, J. A. Kaduk, & H. Schenk. *Wiley.* https://doi.org/10.1107/S1600576720015666

318 Sun, M., & Wang, L. (2022). Effect of bodybuilding and fitness exercise on physical fitness based on deep learning. *Emergency Medicine International*, 2022, 3891109. https://doi.org/10.1155/2022/3891109

319 Sussman, S. (2012). Workaholism: A Review. *Journal of Addiction Research & Therapy, Suppl* 6(1), 4120. https://doi.org/10.4172/2155-6105.S6-001

320 Sussman, S., & Sussman, A. N. (2011). Considering the definition of addiction. *International Journal of Environmental Research and Public Health*, 8(10), 4025–4038. https://doi.org/10.3390/ijerph8104025

321 Syvertsen, A., Leino, T., Pallesen, S., Smith, O. R. F., Sivertsen, B., Griffiths, M. D., & Mentzoni, R. A. (2023). Marital status and gambling disorder: A longitudinal study based on national registry data. *BMC Psychiatry*, 23(1), 199. https://doi.org/10.1186/s12888-023-04697-w

322 Taqui, A. M., Shaikh, M., Gowani, S. A., et al. (2008). Body dysmorphic disorder: Gender differences and prevalence in a Pakistani medical student population. *BMC Psychiatry*, 8, 20. https://doi.org/10.1186/1471-244X-8-20

323 Terenius, L. (2011). From Opiate Pharmacology to Opioid Peptide Physiology. *Upsala Journal of Medical Sciences*, 105(1), 1-16. https://doi.org/10.1517/03009734000000043

324 Thappa, D. M. (2022). Body contouring (sculpting) – Why are non-invasive techniques preferred? *Journal of Clinical and Scientific Dermatology*, 2, 86. https://doi.org/10.25259/CSDM_99_2022

325 Theoharis, M. (2022). What is illegal gambling? Criminal Defense Lawyer. Retrieved from https://www.criminaldefenselawyer.com/crime-penalties/federal/Illegal-Gambling.htm

326 The Recovery Village. (2023, June 20). Euphoric Recall. https://www.therecoveryvillage.com/recovery/relapse/euphoric-recall/#:~:text=Euphoric%20recall%20can%20lead%20to,people%20more%20likely%20to%20relapse.

327 The Recovery Village. (2023, July 12). How to tell the difference between dependence vs. addiction. https://www.therecoveryvillage.com/drug-addiction/dependence-vs-addiction/

328 The Recovery Village. (2023, November 21). How to Wean Off Alcohol Safely. Retrieved from https://www.therecoveryvillage.com/alcohol-abuse/alcohol-taper/

329 The Social and Health Research Center. (2016, October). Fat versus muscle? Retrieved from https://sahrc.org/2016/10/fat-versus-muscle/

330 Thompson, K., & Tieperman, J. (2024). How to Get an Adrenaline Rush: At-Home Ideas. Retrieved from https://www.wikihow.com/Get-an-Adrenaline-Rush

331 Thurga. (2022, November 23). 11 Signs You Have Emotional Sobriety. *Recoverlution.* Retrieved from https://www.recoverlution.com/knowledge/emotional-sobriety-development

332 Timeline of State Marijuana Legalization Laws. (2016, May 2). *Third Way.* Retrieved from https://www.thirdway.org/infographic/timeline-of-state-marijuana-legalization-laws

333 Tonigan, J. S., Rynes, K. N., & McCrady, B. S. (2013). Spirituality as a change mechanism in 12-step programs: A replication, extension, and refinement. Substance Use & Misuse, 48(12), 1161–1173. https://doi.org/10.3109/10826084.2013.808540

334 Toohey, S. (2021, August 4). Delirium tremens (DTs). *Medscape.* https://emedicine.medscape.com/article/166032-overview?form=fpf

335 Topkaya, N., Şahin, E., Krettmann, A. K., & Essau, C. A. (2021). Stigmatization of people with alcohol and drug addiction among Turkish undergraduate students. *Addictive Behaviors Reports*, 14, 100386. https://doi.org/10.1016/j.abrep.2021.100386

336 Traylor, J., Overstreet, L., & Lang, D. (2022). Psychodynamic Theory: *Freud.* Retrieved from https://iastate.pressbooks.pub/individualfamilydevelopment/chapter/freuds-psychodynamic-theory/

337 Treadwell, S. D., & Robinson, T. G. (2007). Cocaine use and stroke. *Postgraduate Medical Journal*, 83(980), 389–394. https://doi.org/10.1136/pgmj.2006.055970

338 Trevisan, L. A., Boutros, N., Petrakis, I. L., & Krystal, J. H. (1998). Complications of alcohol withdrawal: pathophysiological insights. *Alcohol Health and Research World*, 22(1), 61–66. PMID: 15706735; PMCID: PMC6761825.

339 United States Public Health Service Office of the Surgeon General; National Center for Chronic Disease Prevention and Health Promotion (US) Office on Smoking and Health. (2020). Smoking Cessation: *A Report of the Surgeon General.* Available from: https://www.ncbi.nlm.nih.gov/books/NBK555596/

340 U.S. Department of Health and Human Services, National Institutes of Health. (2023). Obsessive-Compulsive Disorder: When Unwanted Thoughts

or Repetitive Behaviors Take Over (NIH Publication No. 23-MH-4676, Revised 2023).

341 van Tuijl, P., Tamminga, A., Meerkerk, G. J., Verboon, P., Leontjevas, R., & van Lankveld, J. (2020). Three diagnoses for problematic hypersexuality; Which criteria predict help-seeking behavior? *International Journal of Environmental Research and Public Health*, 17(18), 6907. https://doi.org/10.3390/ijerph17186907

342 VandeZande, J. (2020, April 6). The Toughest Human Character Trait: Humility. *West Bend Community Church Blog*. Retrieved from https://westbendchurch.org/community-church-blog/the-toughest-human-character-trait-humility/

343 Verma, H. V. (2013). Coffee and tea: Socio-cultural meaning, context and branding. *Asia-Pacific Journal of Management Research and Innovation*, 9(2), 157–170. https://doi.org/10.1177/2319510X13504283

344 Vidyasankar, G., Souza, C., Lai, C., & Mulpuru, S. (2015). A severe complication of crack cocaine use. *Canadian Respiratory Journal*, 22(2), 77–79. https://doi.org/10.1155/2015/263969

345 Villena, A., & Actis, C. (2019). Consequence of pornography use: Brief report. *Cuadernos de Medicina Psicosomática y Psiquiatría de Enlace*.

346 Waals, L., Baetens, I., Rober, P., et al. (2018). The NSSI Family Distress Cascade Theory. *Child and Adolescent Psychiatry and Mental Health*, 12, 52. https://doi.org/10.1186/s13034-018-0259-7

347 Wagenaar, W. A. (1988). Paradoxes of Gambling Behaviour (1st ed.). *Routledge*.

348 Walker, J. M. (2018). Anxiety, stress, depression, and addiction of the US celebrities at the light of the Creative Economy Era. Retrieved from https://www.academia.edu/35986276/Anxiety_Stress_Depression_and_Addiction_of_the_US_Celebrities_at_the_light_of_the_Creative_Economy_Era

349 WebMD Editorial Contributors. (2023, July 7). What Is Abstinence? *WebMD*. Retrieved from https://www.webmd.com/sex/what-is-abstinence

350 WebMD Editorial Contributors. (2023, July 8). What to Know About Dry Drunk Syndrome. *WebMD*. Retrieved from https://www.webmd.com/mental-health/addiction/what-to-know-dry-drunk-syndrome

351 WebMD Editorial Contributor. (2023). What to Know About an Adrenaline Rush. Retrieved from https://www.webmd.com/a-to-z-guides/what-to-know-adrenaline-rush

352 Webster, A. (2024, January 3). Cognitive-Behavioral Therapy (CBT) for Addiction and Substance Abuse. *American Addiction Centers*. Retrieved from https://americanaddictioncenters.org/therapy-treatment/cognitive-behavioral-therapy

353 Webster, A. (2024, February 22). Support Groups For Alcohol Addiction. *Addiction Center*. Retrieved from https://www.addictioncenter.com/alcohol/support-groups/

354 Westover, A., & Marangell, L. (2002). A cross-national relationship between sugar consumption and major depression? *Depression and Anxiety*, 16, 118-120. https://doi.org/10.1002/da.10054

355 Westwater, M. L., Fletcher, P. C., & Ziauddeen, H. (2016). Sugar addiction: The state of the science. *European Journal of Nutrition*, 55(Suppl 2), 55–69. https://doi.org/10.1007/s00394-016-1229-6

356 Weinandy, J. T. G., & Grubbs, J. B. (2021). Religious and spiritual beliefs and attitudes towards addiction and addiction treatment: A scoping review. *Addictive Behaviors Reports*, 14, 100393. https://doi.org/10.1016/j.abrep.2021.100393

357 White, A. M. (2003). What happened? Alcohol, memory blackouts, and the brain. Alcohol Research & Health: *The Journal of the National Institute on Alcohol Abuse and Alcoholism*, 27(2), 186–196.

358 White, W. (2007, November 1). Addiction recovery: Its definition and conceptual boundaries. *Journal of Substance Abuse Treatment*, 33(3), 229-241. https://doi.org/10.1016/j.jsat.2007.04.015

359 Witkiewitz, K., & Tucker, J. A. (2020). Abstinence Not Required: Expanding the Definition of Recovery from Alcohol Use Disorder. Alcoholism: *Clinical and Experimental Research*, 44(1), 36–40. https://doi.org/10.1111/acer.14235

360 Wolz, I., Sauvaget, A., Granero, R., et al. (2017). Subjective craving and event-related brain response to olfactory and visual chocolate cues in binge-eating and healthy individuals. *Scientific Reports*, 7, 41736. https://doi.org/10.1038/srep41736

361 Wood, T. (2020, August 11). How To Handle Negative Emotions Without Drugs or Alcohol. *Rehab 4 Alcoholism*. Retrieved from https://www.rehab4alcoholism.com/guides/handle-negative-emotions-without-drugs-alcohol

362 World Health Organization. (2023, August 29). Opioid overdose. *World Health Organization*. Retrieved from https://www.who.int/news-room/fact-sheets/detail/opioid-overdose

363 World Health Organization. (2009). Clinical Guidelines for Withdrawal Management and Treatment of Drug Dependence in Closed Settings.

Methadone maintenance treatment (pp. 6). *Geneva*. Available from: https://www.ncbi.nlm.nih.gov/books/NBK310658/

364 Wu, X. (2023). Research on the Ways to Overcome Social Media Addiction. *SHS Web of Conferences*, 155, 02023. https://doi.org/10.1051/shsconf/202315502023

365 Yang, H. (2022, June 3). Humility vs Humble: What's the Difference? *ProWritingAid*. Retrieved from https://prowritingaid.com/humilty-vs-humble

366 Yoder, V., Virden, T., & Amin, K. (2005). Internet pornography and loneliness: An association? *Sexual Addiction & Compulsivity*, 12, 19-44. https://doi.org/10.1080/10720160590933653

367 Yoshimura, H. (2023, November 17). Sugar cravings: Unraveling the mystery of our sweet addiction. *Rupa Health*. Retrieved from https://rupahealth.com/post/sugar-cravings-unraveling-the-mystery-of-our-sweet-addiction

368 "Your Brain on Chocolate." (2012). Genetic Engineering & Biotechnology News. Retrieved from https://www.genengnews.com/news/your-brain-on-chocolate/

369 Zaidi, U. (2020, July 24). Role of Social Support in Relapse Prevention for Drug Addicts.

370 Zayed, A. (2023). Compulsive buying disorder (CBD): Is it really an addiction? Retrieved from https://diamondrehabthailand.com/what-is-compulsive-buying-disorder/

371 zhao, J., Jia, T., Wang, X., Xiao, Y., & Wu, X. (2022). Risk Factors Associated With Social Media Addiction: An Exploratory Study. *Frontiers in Psychology*, 13, 837766. https://doi.org/10.3389/fpsyg.2022.837766

372 Ziaaddini, H., Qahestani, A., & Moin Vaziri, M. (2009). Comparing Symptoms of Withdrawal, Rapid Detoxification, and Detoxification with Clonidine in Drug Dependent Patients. *Addiction Health*, 1(2), 63–68.s

373 Zou, Z., Wang, H., d'Oleire Uquillas, F., Wang, X., Ding, J., & Chen, H. (2017). Definition of Substance and Non-substance Addiction. *Advances in Experimental Medicine and Biology*, 1010, 21-41. doi:10.1007/978-981-10-5562-1_2